Between the Lines

Between the Lines

You, Me and Sicily

ANNE REINTJES KROUSE
and
SUE GARNER HALL

Between the Lines: You, Me and Sicily

Printed in the United States of America

Luminare Press
442 Charnelton St.
Eugene, OR 97401
www.luminarepress.com

LCCN: 2021925548
ISBN: 978-1-64388-914-6

Life is nothing without friendship.

Cicero (106-43 BC)

Once upon a time two twenty-something year old graduate students started talking...and never stopped. It was the beginning of a beautiful friendship. And here's their story...

Returning a flannel shirt borrowed by her sister from Sue's husband during a sailing outing, Anne knocked on Sue's apartment door in Greenville, North Carolina, one fall day. They weren't exactly strangers, although they had never spoken to each other. Anne and Sue had graduated from the same high school one year apart, Anne in 1969 and Sue in 1970. In the returning of this old flannel shirt, a friendship was born.

Fast forward fifteen years, one divorce, two marriages, and six children later, to the spring of 1989. Sue, Maurice, Hillary, Matthew, and Drew are heading to Sicily, leaving behind Anne, Charles, Hailey, Laura, and Stephen. A civilian job aboard the US Navy base in Sicily awaits Maurice. Italy and all its wonders await Sue.

In the spring of 1989, the best way to communicate across the Atlantic Ocean was writing letters. Transatlantic telephone calls were prohibitively expensive, poor quality, and required one party to leave home to find a telephone. Email was nonexistent. So, they wrote letters, lots of letters. Letters that were heartfelt, revealing, therapeutic, and cathartic. Now thirty years later, they realize these letters tell the story of two families, two continents, and two friends, a story of divergence, convergence, and how friendship can be a lifeline.

Mother of All Junkets

June 13, 1989

Dear Anne,

Well, here we are. I cannot begin to describe the past two days that have finally gotten us here, but I'll try. Leaving at the New Bern airport was exciting. Ray and Lib were there so the children had one set of grandparents to see them off. Carol was there and Brad from work and his family were there as well. There were a few tears but not from us as we felt very positive and left on that note. The commuter flight to Charlotte was uneventful but we had to run across the airport to make our flight to Philadelphia. When we boarded, our seats were not together but we managed to change seats with a few people so we could at least see each other. The lady sitting next to me told me the rock band Poison was on the flight. I tried not to see that as a bad omen.

We had a two-hour layover in Philadelphia before boarding the L1011 jumbo jet. The plane was packed, about 350 people. The children sat in the three seats near the window and our seats were on the same row but in the midsection. I white-knuckled it all the way as I don't like flying and especially don't like doing it with the children. After about 500 recitations of the Lord's Prayer, we landed in the Azores to refuel around 11:30PM. From there we flew to Aviano, Italy, and got off the plane for about an hour and a half. Flying over the Alps was really beautiful and the mountains surrounding Aviano were quite picturesque. Then we re-boarded and finished the last leg on to Sicily.

We arrived around noon and were transported over to our hotel. On the ride over, I took one look and decided I hated this place, could never adjust to it, and understood what a giant mistake this was, probably the biggest one of my entire life. I tried to be neutral about it but it was impossible to imagine living in such unfamiliar surroundings. I guess it was fatigue, exhaustion, or a mental breakdown but I came close to losing it.

At first glimpse, the countryside appeared so desolate I was sure we were in some third-world country. It sure did not look like any travel brochure of Italy that I've ever seen! No fountains, no art, no monuments, just dry scrub brush and some mangy-looking sheep in the distance. I was thinking aloud, "Oh Lord, what have we done?" I was so shocked by this first impression that I told the kids not to open their suitcases as we were not staying here, not in this Italy. I did see an Italian flag, so I guess I will have to take their word for it and now I am feeling a bit curious to check out the surroundings, even if it appears to be the outer reaches of Mongolia.

I finally collapsed, slept for nineteen hours straight, and woke up feeling much better. All the reasons we came were in the forefront of my mind and I felt like I could face whatever. We didn't lose any of the children or luggage, but that doesn't mean I feel, in any conceivable way, in my right mind. I sure hope we can acclimate to our new lives here, especially after those flights. I might be ready to board another plane in about two years, but at this point, I'm not sure. Right now, I am still in a bit of shock, and can't believe we actually did it! Moved to Sicily with three children, five bicycles, and an upright piano. What mother in her right mind does that?

There are two NATO bases here. One is right across the street from our hotel but we are not allowed to go there until we get ID cards, which should be soon. The other one is where most of the military personnel work and is about fifteen minutes away. It also has the airport. With all the luggage and children, it took three vehicles to get us over to the hotel. The children rode with me in a car driven by a military person who was racing the other cars to test out which road was the quickest. Judging by that ride, I am assuming there are no speed limits here. I was just glad to be on solid ground after the flight, even though riding with a Mario Andretti at the wheel was not my idea of relief. I used to wonder what my nerves were being tested for with three small children. I think I know now.

Actually, the hotel is very nice. We have two adjoining rooms both with two queen-sized beds, a large bathroom, mini-fridge, and a TV. They are spacious and clean. Both rooms have a balcony with sliding glass doors facing Mt. Etna. Last night you could see the lava at the top flare up and several little villages on the mountainside were shooting off beautiful fireworks. We watched all this from our rooms and it was quite a sight to see.

Right now, the kids are watching *Crocodile Dundee* in Italian. Strange, to say the least, and if they would just move that huge volcano that I can see from my window a little farther away, I might be able to stay here for a while... maybe. Only time will tell now what is in store for us, good or bad.

It was a big decision to pick up everything and move across the ocean to a foreign country and I am now feeling the full weight of embarking on this course for the family. The kids seem fine so far, no one has cried, they like the pizza, and they didn't strangle me in my sleep, so I live to fight another day. I'll write more once I get the lay of the land. I am still recovering from the trauma of it all and it is going to take me a few more days to fully regain my dauntless nature and get my bearings. I have let the children open their suitcases, so I guess we are staying…awhile.

Much love,
Sue

PS I am anxious to hear from you, especially how the job is going. It's incredible how that worked out. I was so was proud of myself for snagging the "At-Risk Counselor" job and I really did have high hopes for it. So much for Sue Hall, Career Woman! I was so looking forward to finally being back in the work world after years as a stay-at-home mom. Wasn't it ironic that I got the phone call announcing that we got the job in Sicily within the first ten minutes of starting that first day on the job? I was tempted to pick up my pocketbook and just go home then and there. I did hold it together for a few weeks before I exited stage left, as gracefully as I could. So much for well-thought-out plans. I'm so glad you were able to walk in as my replacement. That took some of the guilt away for giving them the shaft. Humm. Nice job in my hometown versus live in Italy and see the world…it wasn't that hard a decision for me. But this better work out because my name probably is mud now in the school system back home. So let me know how it is going with you on that front. I am sure you will do a bang-up job and, hopefully, this move will prove to be the right choice for me. We shall see.

Hillary, Drew, and Matthew at the Sigonella Inn, June 13, 1989

Scouting the Foreign Prairie

June 15, 1989

Dear Anne,

Well, yesterday armed with my shiny new ID card issued by the base, I ventured out to see what I could on foot. I can't get a driver's license until I complete a course which will start next week. This hotel is located right across from the base, but there is not much else within walking distance. There are a few restaurants and businesses nearby, but the main attraction, for now, is the NATO base, known locally as NAS I. It has all the civilian facilities, like the school, library, commissary, pools, gym, bowling alley, movie theatre, stores, and restaurants. A little slice of *Americano,* it even has a Baskin Robbins. It appears I can have as much of the motherland as I should ever want or need. However, you know that is not what I came for, exactly the opposite; but I must admit it is reassuring to know it is there and, of course, the kids are thrilled.

The flora and fauna are surprisingly tropical, with date palms, bougainvillea in all colors, and lots of olive trees. The weather is beautiful and I am itching to get out and explore beyond the base. There is a very medieval-looking town up on a high ridge that I can see from my hotel window, and

I am anxious to ferret out all its wonders. There is even a castle at the top, and I am beginning to think there is more to this place than just the sheep.

One funny thing is a little old man who parks in front of our hotel every day selling peanuts out of the trunk of his car. He sings out all day long, "*Nocia*...Peanuts." *Nocia* is the Italian word for nuts, but when he calls the words out it sounds exactly like "Not Yo Penis." Trust me, the kids have gotten a kick out of that and they have not tired of saying it over and over every five minutes. I suppose I should be glad they are learning Italian, but really!

Enough for now, I will write more soon. Thank God, I have you to share all this with, otherwise, I think I would burst with all the new and different aspects of life I am experiencing. Love you,

Susannah, *Baronessa di*
New Horizons

Bye Bye Birdie
June 17, 1989

Dear Anne,

Have you noticed that I am gone yet? I have vanished, but I'm not vanquished, at least not yet. Leaving home was decidedly traumatic for us all. The jolt hit us pretty hard on arrival but we are coming around to the idea of it and are enjoying ourselves. I am hoping beyond hope that it was hardest on me alone. I'm sure you know as a mother, I feel responsible, not just for my own welfare, but for everyone else's too. At least when they left, the children had love and good wishes from their friends and family, even tinged with a bit of envy, I think. I sure did not feel any good wishes from my side of the family.

The morning we left, we stopped by my mother's house to say goodbye. That was a big mistake. The children all gave her big hugs and told her they would write. She said very little, as she was choking back tears. The only thing she said to me, in her most sarcastic voice, was "This is a real thrill, isn't it?" I will not soon forget the look of utter contempt on her face. No bon voyage…no good wishes… no safe travels. I wasn't surprised. She had told me she wanted to get the sheriff to arrest me at the airport since I had no right to take her grandchildren out of the country. I had hoped that when we actually did leave, she would break down and show a bit of love towards me, but that did not happen. It was all bitterness and spite. So, I had better get used to being a motherless child, as she is like a snapping turtle when she has a grudge. She doesn't back down. I am hoping this turns out well or I will have some crow to eat and groveling to do. She won't ever see it as a good thing, but we might. Trying to make her happy was always a lost cause, and I was never really able to do that even living near her and letting her call all the shots. Our relationship was shaky at best, and coming here, I have really thrown down the gauntlet. I genuinely hope that this adventure does turn out well, even if our triumph hurts her feelings. It is a big gamble, but isn't everything in life? Right now, I just hope we all survive it as these Sicilians drive like maniacs. Aggressive driving is the Italian blood sport, I think. I have heard that Sicily is in the *Guinness Book of World Records* for the most spectacular wrecks. I believe it, too. So, say a prayer for us. I would hate for my mother to have that satisfaction…

Much love,
Susannah, *Baronessa di*
Lost Causes

Charms of the Foreign Life

June 18, 1989 | Sunday 9:30 PM

Dear Anne,

By now, you are probably getting tired of reading all these letters from me…I can't help it, it's therapy for me. I need to talk to you and this is my only method. Just please don't tell other people how many times I have written because I can't possibly write everyone equally. We have continued to spread our wings and check out our new surroundings.

Last night we were invited to a cookout at the home of a co-worker from the office named Tony. He is an African American military guy who is married to a Sicilian named Anna. Their home was way up on the mountain and it seemed that we drove forever to get there. Actually, we didn't drive but rode with our sponsor Captain Abrams, who is a Native American. Without a car, we are at the mercy of others for the time being. There was a Mexican couple there, also.

Don Matthews who is the boss of the office was there and he is the quintessential parody of a southern gentleman. Talks nonstop about how rich, smart, and well-bred he is. Overbearing to say the least. He dresses in white suits and a fedora (for real). All that was missing was a gold-tipped cane. Ha! Talk about culture shock, I am being immersed up to my eyeballs. I never really appreciated how diverse the US military is and never really understood how sheltered my life has been up until now. I am happy to broaden my views and experiences, but I must admit I feel gob-smacked with diversity.

The villa was beautiful, lots of tile, with many levels and terraces, but it all felt so strange. It was full of antiques and seemed dark and foreign and this little Southern Baptist knew immediately that I have a way to go before I am used to this cosmopolitan lifestyle.

We started our indoctrination class on Friday. It will last a week and is supposed to teach us everything we will need to know to survive in Sicily. On Friday, they covered security and said it is pretty safe overall. The main thing is that the Italians think all Americans are rich and easy prey. They said not to leave anything in your car, try to not dress like an American, (ha) but that Italians love children. The only thing safer in Italy than a woman with children is a pregnant woman with children. They said not to be alarmed if Italians come up and want to touch your children. Showing kindness to a child or even touching them can impart a special blessing passed from God. Seems Italians are way more touchy-feely than Americans on the whole. The official greeting for everyone is a kiss on each cheek along with the handshake.

The culmination of the class will be getting our driver's licenses and we have started looking for a car. There are many for sale as people are rotating in and out of this base every few years. We have looked at a BMW, but everyone advises to get a Fiat since they always have parts and are easy to repair. It will be really nice to have some wheels. Our Volvo from home won't arrive for another two months.

Today the hotel had a huge Sunday buffet brunch with about fifty items, all served beautifully out by the pool. We ate and swam in the pool all afternoon. Later we had dinner by candlelight *al fresco* with a live band in the most romantic setting. The landscaping here is breathtaking, palm trees, bougainvillea, geraniums and I am still having to pinch myself at times to realize this is my life. The hotel really is first class and the pool is to die for. It has an elevated kiddie pool that spills over as a waterfall into the huge pool which has a swim-up bar at the end where you can order drinks and sandwiches. All the waiters are dressed in white jackets and black ties and it is quite swanky. Don't feel sorry for me in this primitive place! The manager looks exactly like you would picture a Mafia boss and all the staff are Sicilian...really beautiful people.

Yesterday we bought a step-down transformer so we could use some American appliances. I have a hair dryer and, of course, a coffee pot. When I turned on the hairdryer all the lights went out and I thought I had blacked out the entire hotel. Luckily, every room has its own breaker box but the power grid won't let you operate two things at once.

I shopped at the Exchange yesterday and don't feel sorry for me there either. There were all kinds of great name brands and so cheap. I bought Drew a pair of Converse All-Star high top tennis shoes for $4.49 and no tax. Got Matt some nice swim trunks for $3.50. They have Krups coffee makers, name brand clothing, and really everything you could ever want. I won't want for anything.

We have seen two Sicilian wedding receptions here at the hotel. Large parties and the bridal gowns are amazing. They dress their children like little dolls, long evening dresses for the girls and darling suits for the boys.

We took all three children yesterday for haircuts and the

Sicilian man who cut their hair spoke some broken English. Matt, of course, was horsing around in the chair and touching his hair and the stylist said, "Why toucha now? Toucha later." Matthew was highly offended but I thought it was hilarious.

We have talked to a few people who have been here awhile and they all seem to like it. They say if we want a stand-alone villa, we will probably have to move up north or down south at the beach. Some people live an hour away from the base all along the coast or up on the mountain. One lady we met said she is taking a villa with a view of the Cyclops rocks. It has three floors each with a balcony and also a garage. A dentist is leaving and she is moving in. She advised us to ask everyone as people are coming and going from here all the time. Because of the children, we will be allotted rent for a four-bedroom house and she said for that money we could get a very nice place. I knew those kids would pay off someday!

I just finished *My Antonia* and liked it. A story of immigrants who carve out a life in a strange, harsh, and fertile new world. I could relate in some respects. I am so glad they have a well-stocked library here and I plan to make good use of it soon. Well, I had better close for now and get some sleep. I don't expect you to write as often as I do. I have lots of time on my hands that I know you don't have. I do want to hear all the news about everything, especially the job, and all the news from home. You know my curiosity level. I can't wait to get my first letter from you. So far, things here have been great and we have talked about how close we came to not coming. What an experience it has been already. So glad we didn't miss it.

Love you,
Susannah, *Baronessa di* Good Life

Monday, June 19, 1989

Dear Sue,

Here's what we picture you doing…lounging by the pool, snorkeling in the Med, eating fresh fruits and Italian pastries, dining on pasta at midnight, humming "*O Bella Mia*" as you stroll among the shepherds, and writing wish-you-were-here cards to all the poor schmucks you left behind. Here's how to picture us...moping around hot, humid, mosquito-infested Carteret county looking so down and out that people say, "Ya'll look like you have lost your best friend," to which we all answer, "We have!" We miss you guys and are ready to come for a visit!

Not much news here. I finished my first week of work taking over this at-risk counselor job you left behind and it was a doozy. Kids not knowing whether they passed or failed, Dick telling me to let them come to the community college to make up credit hours whenever they wanted, the community college staff telling me I have to be there when the students come, and me, running around trying to figure out what the hell is going on. Hopefully, it's going to be better this week. I watched the video of the rap session you did with the students before you left. I thought it was very good. You looked great on camera, Sue. I felt like I had a little visit from you, seeing you and hearing your voice. Dick is going to edit it and take it on the road. Just think, famous on multiple continents.

Charles, Stephen, and I see the ENT tomorrow about possibly putting in tubes. Stephen is basically over the ear infection but, according to the pediatrician, it's been one of the most antibiotic resistant cases he has seen. It is hard to think of going through this with a nine-month-old but maybe at this age, it will be easier to keep the water out of his ears.

Can't think of much else going on. The girls start swimming lessons today. I'll put this in the mail tomorrow. Miss you all. Take care of each other.

Love, Anne

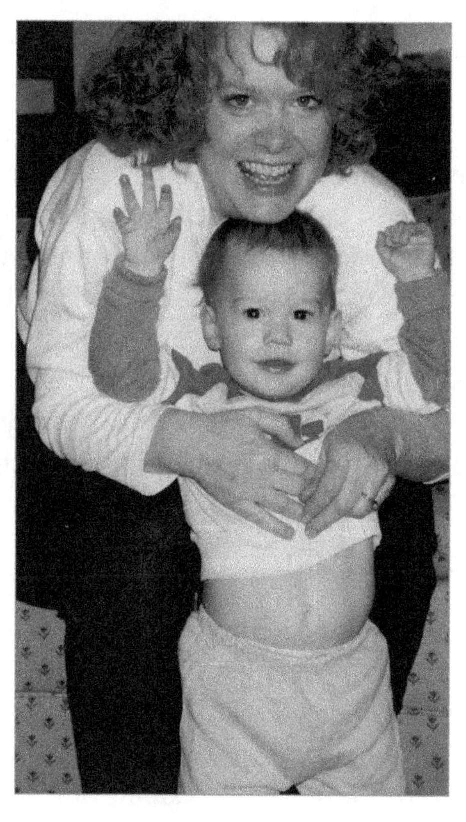

Anne with Stephen, Summer, 1989

Living Well is the Best Revenge
June 20, 1989

Dear Anne,

I think I can get used to this lifestyle. Pinch me...this peachy life is agreeing with me. The hotel is great...maids to do the beds and provide fresh linens...buffet breakfast served daily... poolside restaurant downstairs with live entertainment...a swim-up bar in the pool that provides espresso, drinks, ice cream, and sandwiches (the kids are running up quite a tab there) and I am a lady of leisure. I feel like I am living the life of the rich and famous, sunning poolside, writing long letters, exhaling deeply. What a difference and what a gift. Not sure I will rush out and find a house anytime soon if it means giving up this cushy lifestyle. Our household goods won't arrive for 60 to 90 days, so I intend to enjoy this relaxing existence to the fullest. I'm becoming so spoiled rotten; I may never be the same.

Just think, a week ago I was struggling to work a full-time job, get meals on the table, sheets changed, housework done, bills paid, running in place in the never-ending cycle of working motherhood, and now my biggest concern is getting an even tan. Am I daydreaming or is all this really happening? I must remember to thank my Fairy Godmother and Uncle Sam. I am not sure I can readjust to any sort of normal existence after this. There is so much to look forward to, like exploring this island, learning the language, finding a home, shopping the markets… I am like the proverbial kid in the candy store who must remember to close her mouth to keep from drooling. It is somewhat hard for me to absorb this embarrassment of riches, but I intend to give it my best shot. Be happy for me as I surrender to luxury. It's a new experience and I am drenched in pool water and bliss.

Much love,
Susannah, *Baronessa di* Lucky Stars

The Sigonella Inn pool

Friday, June 23, 1989

Dear Sue,

I was so glad to get your letters! They were the high point of my week. I've gotten two letters and one postcard. The mail service seems good, especially when you consider these letters are going from the tip of North Carolina to the tip of Italy. If you guys were coming home in two months, I might be able to stand it. Two years is another story. Oh well, I'll do my best.

Sicily sounds wonderful! After reading your letter about the trip, I doubted if I would ever get up enough courage to make the trek but now, after reading your second letter, I can hardly wait! It all sounds amazing. It seems like the bases can handle all your needs. I'll be asking you to buy stuff for me, rather than vice versa. I think we should come in the middle of next summer. Meanwhile, keep those letters coming!

I said the high point was getting your letter this week. Well, the low point was getting tubes put in Stephen's ears. We saw Dr. Grady Tuesday morning and he scheduled the procedure for Wednesday. Stephen was over the ear infection, but still had fluid in his ears and was congested again. After enduring a week of taking him in for daily antibiotic injections, we were ready to try something else! Poor little fellow would start crying when our car pulled in the pediatrician's parking lot. So, to make an excruciatingly long story short, we arrived at the outpatient surgery center in New Bern at 6:30 Wednesday morning. Stephen was taken back at 7:30 and was finished by 8:00. He was only *under* for four minutes, but the wait seemed an eternity for Charles and me. Everything went fine. He's still on antibiotics for a couple days and we have to put drops in his ears, but he does seem to feel much better. We're praying this makes a difference. I asked the pediatrician if there was a higher prevalence of this problem in boys, but he poo-pooed that idea. I just seem to hear about more boys needing tubes. Another weakness of that sex?

The job is going fine. I went yesterday to finally discuss my salary and do the paperwork for payroll. I will get paid on my AG certificate and, according to DPI, I have ten years of experience. Apparently, they added up everything and gave me credit for all the bits-and-pieces of part-time work that I had managed to juggle when the girls were little. The ten years qualify me to start receiving additional longevity pay. Things are looking up. I may not have a best friend to pal around with, but at least I'm feeling rich!

Everyone has been very nice helping me adjust to your old job. After the first week of learning the ropes, I've been spending all my time at the community college. I'm supposed to function strictly as a teacher with *no* counseling, according to Dick. (It's hard to call him Mr. Rogers. In my book there is only one Mr. Rogers!) He's a funny guy, very gung-ho, and idealistic about the program. His first plan was to let the students pick any time slot from 8:00 a.m. to 9:30 p.m. to come to the Guided Studies Lab at the community college and I had to be available to help them. That certainly wasn't workable! It's more under control now. When I make contact,

I tell the students when I'll be there and that's when they can come. Since the Guided Studies Lab is closed the week of July 4th, I'll be taking that week off and working a week in August instead. That was Dick's idea. It sounded okay to me until I realized that I was giving up a paid holiday, which I would not be getting in August. He agreed to let me work a four-day week in August, but then proceeded to reprimand me for sounding as if I was only concerned about the money. He went on to lecture me about this being a *service-oriented* job. It was a relatively mild reprimand, but it made me so angry! I said something to the effect that I had learned to look out for myself and that I was very invested in doing a good job but, clearly, my family and I came first. Well, actually, what I said didn't sound quite that self-assured. In reality, I kind of hung my head and mumbled something about attempting to keep it fair. He went on to say that if I had pointed out that discrepancy in front of the assistant superintendent, it would have reflected poorly on me because the assistant superintendent would have felt that I was just in it for the money. Hmm... So this morning I was on the job before 8:00, the first one here, in case Dick dropped by on his way to work. He hasn't been by, so here I sit writing a letter to you.

At lunchtime, I am going to see Carolyn's sister, Beth, and buy some hand-me-downs from her two girls. I've gotten things from her before and they are always really cute and in pristine condition. I looked last night for some clothes my girls had outgrown that I could offer Carolyn's other niece. I had to look hard to find clothes that didn't have someone else's name in them, Emily, Julie, etc. It's hard to put a price on clothes which I bought used or was given. I think some were from Beth in the first place. I managed to scrape together a little pile.

Hailey went today to play with Maria. Janice offered to pick her up and bring her home. I had to bribe Hailey with $4.00 to go. She, Laura, and Melissa have been thick-as-thieves and Hailey couldn't stand the idea of Laura and Melissa playing together without her.

Can't think of much else to report and I need to start making phone calls. By the way, what is the *wildlife* like in Sicily?

Take care of yourself and please keep those letters coming. I want to hear every detail. I am so glad it's turning out so wonderfully. You made the right decision. I just hope you eventually come back to Morehead.

I really miss you and send lots of love, Anne

Magical Mystery Tour

June 25, 1989

Dear Anne,

Got your letter and was so happy to hear from you…you might not know how much mail can mean. It was like Christmas. Leaving the known to step off into the unknown is hard and a bit scary, but hearing from home sure helps. I read your letter three times. I do feel a sense of freedom to be striking out on our own, but it is bittersweet to think of the distance between us now, so your letter was just the balm I needed. We are all fine…Hillary has written several letters home to grandparents stating she wants to go home and live with them. Needless to say, they never got mailed, but overall, the kids seem happy. The important thing seems to be to channel their focus forward and not look back. If we do that, we seem to be fine. Our daily routine is to swim in the pool, eat out somewhere for lunch, go to the library, shop a little, or go to the movies. Not a bad summer routine. We need to start house hunting soon.

It's pretty overwhelming to have to choose where to live. There are too many choices…the seaside, the coastal region, the mountains, close to base or far away. Each has positives and negatives. Most Italians live in apartments without yards. That will be hard for us if we have to settle for that. The really great places are farther out which would mean a lot more driving and that could be dangerous and would also limit the children having access to all the things provided by the base. I don't really care just as long as we are in a town with a bar...not for the liquor, but for the cappuccino and the pastries. I'm hooked on the espresso, cappuccino, and all the *dolce* (sweets). These Italians are serious about their coffee and food. I read that the very first cookbook in the Western world was written in Sicily. When walking the streets, you can smell the aroma of the bars before you even see them.

We went to the Catania market earlier this week. Catania is one of the largest cities in Sicily, second only to Palermo. Via Etnea is the main shopping street and leads both to the fish and meat market and further down to the larger street market. The street market is miles of open-air stalls with everything from bras to baby goats. It is noisy, bustling and, at times, like a street opera with vendors calling out "*DEICI MILLE, DEICE MILLE*!" Some are singing, some are clapping, some standing on chairs above the crowds...It is quite a show at times. Vegetables, cheese, fish, household items, clothes, linens, shoes, toys, hats...you name it... it is there. It is worth the trip just to see this market. It is smelly in places but infinitely interesting. It is crowded and everyone is bumping into each other or at least rubbing shoulders. We were repeatedly warned that it is the perfect environment for pickpockets and robbery. I did not even take a purse, just buttoned my money in my shirt pocket. One is expected to bargain and as they recognize us immediately as Americans, all prices are naturally inflated. The bargaining is fun and it is a bit of drama. It's good to have a poker face and even sometimes walk away or pretend to do so. We spent about five hours there and didn't see it all. My favorite stall was the one with the tables of old used linens and clothes to dig through. I found pillowcases with five-inch handmade lace on them and some used spreads with elaborate handwork. There were Moroccan men selling leather items and umbrellas on the sidewalk and I bought a large leather belt from one of them. The market is open each day, except Sunday, from 7:00 in the morning until 1:00, and then they pack it all up and it disappears like magic. This place is enchanted and I am totally bewitched.

Love you,
Susannah, *Baronessa di* Wonders

PS I hope Stephen's tubes solve the problem. Thank God for the postal system and twenty-two cent stamps.

Beating the Bushes

June 26, 1989

Dear Anne,

Well, I'm happy to report that outside this marvelous hotel lies wonderful Italy after all. We rented a car, loaded up the kids, and hit the road this weekend in both directions. On Saturday we cautiously drove south to a tiny town called Brucoli, a seaside village. It has just a few shops and restaurants but a nice sandy beach on a bay which was great for snorkeling. The water was very clear and that beautiful Mediterranean blue. Cows were grazing on the shoreline. The countryside is unspoiled and we drove through orange, lemon, and olive groves in bloom. It was all charming and natural and just our speed as we understand that we better stick to the countryside for starters. After swimming, we ate at the seaside restaurant. I had spaghetti with crab sauce which was out of this world. The food is spectacular everywhere and we have been told not to worry about the possibility of food poisoning as the Italians are incredibly fastidious, not to mention they use all fresh ingredients. I have heard that Italians actually think Americans are the slovenly ones, whatever, I plan to eat everywhere and taste everything.

On Sunday we ventured north to Taormina, an area that is spectacularly gorgeous. Really, it is magnificent. So much so that Hubby commented that it looked like it was built by Walt Disney, mythical and like a movie set. High cliffs, crystal blue water, rugged islands just offshore, serene bays, and beautiful beaches. Too enchanting. The town of Taormina sits high above the sea and is known as an international resort, a hot spot for the rich and famous. We stayed by the seaside and swam. The beach is all smooth, large pebbles that soak up the heat, which is good because the water is like iced tea.

We covered lots of territory for our first weekend foray. The driving is difficult, maniacal if you ask me. For one thing, they drive at horrendous speeds, no limit, very aggressively, and the way cars pass is either ingenious or pure lunacy, I can't decide. The car being passed and any oncoming cars have to move to the side, and the passer shoots through the middle. It is by law the responsibility of the non-passing cars to see that the passing car makes it. It is so strange to see a car pull out to pass with an oncoming car heading straight towards them. There is room on a two-lane road, if done properly, but not a lot of margin for error. We went through Catania on the way home and driving in the city is quite the challenge. Catania is the largest city near us, with about 300,000 inhabitants. At each stoplight on a two-lane street, they make about four or five rows, inching as close together and all trying to get ahead of one another. Every car shows the dents and scars of previous chariot races, mirrors hanging, fenders bent. No wonder. Truly like playing actual bumper cars. When the light turns green, they all take off to the races like they are going to a fire. Marvelous and insane. I hope

I can adjust, but most of all I hope I live through this and get brave enough to drive everywhere. Yikes!

Much love,
Susannah, *Baronessa di* Speedways

Tuesday, June 27, 1989

Dear Sue,

The girls received your card and the bookplates yesterday and were thrilled. Thank you for thinking of them. We talk about all of you often, like you'll be back soon. I don't let on to them that your taste of the good life and discovery of your Italian soul means that we will have to head to Sicily to ever see you guys again.

I thought about you this weekend during a spectacular thunderstorm, which I typically love and you typically hate. It was one of those powerful natural wonders that comes up suddenly without warning and offers an amazing light show and full orchestra. However, this particular day it just so happened that Charles and the guy helping him finish this house were up on the roof where they had just cut a hole running the length of the ridge. It all ended okay, but not without picturing myself as a widow with three children and a flooded house.

For the most part, our summer is going fairly well. The job is certainly interesting and I am enjoying most of the students. They are so typically adolescent! In other words, sometimes very hard to like. One of your former students, who has been in to discuss his hours, has such a terrible attitude. However, during our last session, I kept my cool and he left feeling that he had won. Honestly, I can't believe

Dick insists that I *only teach* and not do any counseling. How in the hell does he think teachers dealing daily with teenagers manage *that* challenge without constant and very skilled *counseling*? When Dick says things like that, I keep my cool and he leaves thinking he has won...

I am anxious to see some pictures. I received your letter yesterday describing the villa of M's coworker. I know you are excited about what you'll find to rent. I bought a *Home* magazine the other day because it featured an article about making your home look European. Quite a stretch for me, I'm afraid. One can only wish.

Hailey and Laura spent practically the whole weekend with friends and we were down to only Stephen. I couldn't believe how easy life is with just one! We ended up taking him to the Krouses and going to a movie. Saw Robin Williams in *Dead Poets Society.*

Gale and I took turns going over to the cosmetology department. She got a facial and I got a manicure. It was wonderful and cost me only $1.50 since college staff pays half price. I've decided to make a habit of going over there. Dick is on vacation next week, so I won't have to worry about his dropping by to check on me. Please keep those letters coming. We miss you all.

Love, Anne

Sex Happens

June 29, 1989

Dear Anne,

I had no idea I would cry today on the phone. I hadn't planned on that. I was so excited to hear from you; I was counting the days to our call, but when I heard your dear sweet voice, it really choked me up. Luckily, my fiscal sense kicked in and I was able to pull it together. I know I woke you up, but I was determined to be the first person to say "Happy Birthday" to you. This six-hour time difference is a challenge. The only possible place to make an international call from this hotel is the AT&T phone booth located in the lobby and the charges are about $10.00 per minute. Crazy expensive. Unfortunately, our calls will be few and far between and it's not going to get any better I'm afraid, because we won't be getting a phone installed once we get a house. There is a six-month waiting list to get one, a $600 installation fee, and as I have no one local to call here, I guess I will just drive to the hotel if I have to make a state-side call. Clearly not the best situation that our communications will have to rely on our letters, but it's the best I can do. Thank goodness the mail is cheap and seems reliable. I can afford to be liberal with my epistles. Get ready to read…

I love sharing with you… it is the next best thing to you being here. Hearing your voice on the phone made my day which had been not so great up to that point. I had walked about six blocks carrying a heavy package to return only to find the place closed, then took some great photos and proceeded to open the camera in broad daylight without rewinding the film, spilled a chili-dog all down the front of me after having just given Matthew a long lecture about it being too hot for messy ice cream and he needed to learn to be neater. Sometimes I fail miserably at this motherhood thing and karma strikes deep! Ouch.

The children have gone bowling with new friends we met in the hotel. They are a military family and, as a matter of fact, we were on the same flight together from Philadelphia. The mom Jackie is about my age and has a daughter, Candice, who is eleven and an only child. Jackie invited them as Candice wanted company. I hope this keeps up as I am thoroughly enjoying my few moments of freedom. The kids have adjusted remarkably well to being here, although Matthew did wake up the other morning and said he was dreaming of his classmates at St. Andrews and missed them all… even the girls! That's pretty severe.

I got your letter about Dick and I know what you mean about him, can't believe what he said to you about the salary. Last time I checked Carteret County Board of Education was not a volunteer organization. I hope you like the job. I was only there for two months, but I did like it. Not enough to stay evidently, so here I am and there you are. Ha!

We have enjoyed the library here. We go almost every other day. One day this week I was deep in the stacks and realized I hadn't heard a peep from the children for a while…when I found them, they were pouring over a children's sex education book. I stopped and listened for a minute to their comments, "See I told you so" and "That's sick and disgusting." I ignored my discovery and hurried them along to leave. I was hoping they would keep their new-found knowledge to themselves for a while. Later that day, however, Drew ambushed me with a head full of questions concerning sex. I am really wondering if children aged 11, 8, and 7 are ready to know this stuff. I know I'm not ready to talk about it. I'm aware the experts say to answer the questions honestly and give only as much as they ask for .... well, the cat is out the bag now... that damn library is just full of information. Drew wanted to know if her father and I did it and I said yes. Then, she asked where, and I replied no particular place. She then asked, can you do it in the water? I said I suppose so. She wanted to know why would you do it? That one was a bit harder, so I told her it was hard to explain and come back and ask me again in ten years. She happily skipped away without a care, so I guess all in all, it came off fairly well. I was sweating bullets, but she appeared to take it all in stride. I did consider it as a big step in their educational curriculum, one that I am not ready for obviously. Whew!

I loved the piece you sent by Dennis Rogers on snakes out of the paper. He's a man after my own heart. As to the "wildlife" here, that is the first question I asked in our culture shock class.... "Are there snakes in Sicily?" The instructor said there are no snakes in Sicily. Since then, however, I have learned that a man who lives near the hotel killed a European viper in his yard and the locals say there are a few, but rare. Don't worry I won't go poking around any poorly lit places until I know all the facts.

Well, I'll close for now, keep up the hard work on that outstanding "service-oriented" job and tell all hello.

Love ya,
Susannah, *Baronessa di* Phallic
Symbols and Sex Education

PS The sex topic was bound to come up eventually and maybe sooner here in Italy. The Italians seem to be much more comfortable with the topic of sex than Americans judging from the magazines and TV shows I've seen. Must be all those naked statues! We Americans are such prudes or hypocrites on the topic. We say it's wonderful, but don't do it. Italians say it's wonderful, and we do it. Ha!

The 4th of July, 1989

Dear Sue,

The house is quiet and I'm hoping it will stay that way until I get this letter written. Stephen just went down for a nap and the girls are at Melissa's house. We have received lots of letters from you and my birthday card arrived on the 28th. Perfect! Thank you! And, of course, the wonderful phone call. That was truly the best present I got. It made my day to hear all your voices and know you sounded the same and were thinking about us. Thank you so much!

Charles and I both took the whole week off. This is our vacation. It is nice to sleep late and stay up late without much of a schedule. On Sunday afternoon we took the kids, plus Melissa, to Jungleland. It was more fun than I expected. We were there for five hours. Stephen did fine, finally fell asleep in his stroller. The girls are a good age for enjoying everything that Jungleland offered. It wasn't crowded, no lines. We did the putt-putt golf course twice, which reminded me of *Alice in Wonderland's* croquet game with everyone picking up their balls and running all over. The only thing missing was someone yelling, "Off with her head!" The Jungleland attendants bent the rules and let Hailey and Melissa on the rides for younger kids with Laura when they wanted to ride with her. It made me think of your recent description of the Italian art of driving as I watched the kids crash into each other on the bumper cars with their little heads jerking around. Are there chiropractors on every corner in Sicily?

I am also happy to report that during our *vacation*, we got some baseboards down and some doors up. No doorknobs yet, but my standards for improvement are very low, so I'm happy. Our next goal is to plan how to get the rest of this remodeling done, hopefully, before you guys move back to the States in three years. Now that I am back to work, we will be trying to budget some of our money toward that end. After barely making it financially this spring, and we wouldn't have made it if you had not paid me so generously for babysitting, we have finally gone back to a fairly comfortable income.

Susan and Sarah came on Friday and stayed until Tuesday. We ate out almost every meal and did Jungleland, again. I've had quite enough of Jungleland, though the kids would go every day if they could. All in all, they seem to be enjoying their summer. Hailey and Laura both had friends spend the night. I kept thinking who would have been here if the Halls had been available for a sleepover. As a matter-of-fact, I kept referring to Clare as Drew because I am so programmed to say, "Laura and Drew."

Well, back to work next week. I'm sure Sigonella does a bang-up Fourth of July celebration. Thank you again for calling! The gift only you could give me!

Love, Anne

Up on Cloud Nine

July 6, 1989

Dear Anne,

We absolutely had the best weekend and the Fourth of July holiday. I hope yours was good. The base put on a huge carnival with rides and games and food of all kinds. It is a big deal and kept the kids thoroughly entertained. They won big prizes, stuffed animals, rode all the rides, and ran all over the place in bacchanal delirium all day having a ball, just finding us when they ran out of money. The point of the festival is not to make money but to treat the troops to a fun time, so everything was inexpensive. Saturday morning there was a 5K road race that Hillary wanted to enter, so she and her dad both ran it. She came in second place which was remarkable given her age and the number of entries. She got a big bronze medal on a red ribbon and was in seventh heaven.

On Friday we bought a *Fiat Uno*, a tin can little car which we hope is reliable, if not the safest, as it does feel like riding in a tin can. Everyone encouraged us to buy a Fiat as they are easy to get parts and service. We were told even Italian grandmothers could repair them! We are enjoying having wheels and the driving doesn't seem too bad, lots of horn blowing, and we certainly don't speed like demons like the locals, so they pass us left and right. I suppose we will get the hang of it soon. We drove to Catania to the market then to San Pedro Clarenza up further in the mountains. In Catania, you pay a little man a few *lire* to watch your car so it isn't stolen or robbed when you park it on the street. We are just trying to learn our way around and also trying to decide where we want to live. It is all really beautiful. The Italian towns and villages are so interesting...lots of peddlers selling fruits and vegetables out of their little three-wheeled vehicles called lizards by Americans, but called by Italians, *Ape*, which means bee...don't know why that is? The countryside is so beautiful and I don't think I will ever tire of these breathtaking vistas.

Tuesday the Fourth, we drove up to Mt. Etna, which we learned is the largest active volcano in Europe and one of the largest in the world. You drive up through the lava fields for miles, which look like a moonscape. Near the top, there is a parking lot with a couple of restaurants and souvenir shops. From there, you have to buy a ticket to continue up on a guided jeep or van. We rented jackets as we were told that it is very cold at the top due to the elevation. Our guide instructed us once we got to the top to stay in the designated area because there are thin parts of the crust that one can actually fall through. Believe me, I stayed right on that guide's heels. Once up there, we could see the crater and as we watched, it glugged up some brown-looking mud and rocks several times and wheezed and belched enough to make me ready to head back down. It was a unique experience and a great place to be on July 4th as I felt on top of the world with all of Sicily as my oyster. But I really don't trust volcanoes. The last big eruption was only two years ago. I was raised Baptist, so I know enough about fire and brimstone to not go looking for it.

We got back home in time for the fireworks show on base. The Italians love fireworks. Almost every night from the hotel window I have seen fireworks going off above the towns in the distance up on Mt. Etna as every little town holds festivals with a firework show. On a clear night, it is amazing to watch them light up the whole mountain like a big birthday cake. We walked over to see the show, following the crowd down to the soccer field, and sat in the bleachers. Little did I know, our seats were only about 150 feet from where they shot them off. The concussion alone was earth-shattering and the fireworks themselves appeared to come right down upon you. Hillary was in tears and buried her head in my lap for the full thirty-minute show. Even I was glad when it was over. Geez, Louise, I don't ever want to be that close again. Guess the Americans were not about to be outdone in the fireworks department but really, I'm just glad we are not all deaf now!

We really do have to get serious about the house hunting. I think I am in denial that this hotel life must end at some point, and I just can't decide in which direction to go. It is just so completely different from home that it is pretty shocking. At first it was such a far cry from everything I've ever known, it frightened me, now I am beginning to relax and adjust and I think it is beautiful. The towns aren't beautiful in the normal sense. There is trash and graffiti and the houses wouldn't win any Southern Living Award from the outside, but there is a gentle old-world charm that I am falling in love with. Italians may not try to show off the exterior of their houses but they sure are dressers. They dress up and keep their children dressed to the nines.

I may have to up my game in that department and shed the shorts and T-shirts. I hate to advertise that I am American, especially after what they taught us in our class about the Mafia and terrorism here. One thing for sure is if I get taken out, I will go happy.

I am falling in love with both the country and the people. While I was at the pool today, a seventy-five-year-old plus Italian woman came down donning a tiny bikini, showing all her rolls and glory. She was practically naked. She looked every day her age, with as many wrinkles as a Chinese shar-pei dog, certainly not a pin-up, but was completely comfortable in her own wrinkled skin. After sunning herself for a while, she then swam up to the pool bar and ordered a double espresso. Now, where on earth are you going to find that? They really are my kind of people.

Love you,
Susannah, *Baronessa di Sicilia*

Drew, Hillary, and Matt on top of Mt. Etna, July 4, 1989

Can of Worms

July 10, 1989

Dear Anne,

Got your letter and it made my day. Not much news here... we are going on a house-hunting trip arranged by the housing department tomorrow down to the south, supposed to be a beach area near Brucoli. Because it is summertime, there are fewer places available since many are rented by Italians for summer vacation. I hope we like it, as I'm starting to get nervous about nailing something down. Can't live in limbo forever...I think I have narrowed down the area as I like the beach better than the mountains. This is probably foolish, but anything in the mountains is just that much closer to Mt. Etna. Needless to say, an active volcano makes an impression. The last big eruption was in 1985 and the crust opened up and swallowed an entire hotel. About 300 people were killed...think that might keep me up at night. They say that robbery is a bigger problem in the beach area because there are empty homes that make easier targets so I'm trying to weigh out the options.

Robbery is a problem everywhere here with Americans. Many Sicilians are so poor and they all watch "Dallas" on TV and think all Americans are rich so it is sort of a Robin

Hood mentality. They know that we get reimbursed if we lose valuables. They have said there is little to no violent crime and if they do rob you while you are home, they just lock you in the bedroom, eat everything in the frig, and then strip the place. Oh well, that should be an experience. They watch your patterns and know when you are gone so it is a problem. Housing suggests that if we move to the beach area, we hire vigilantes who will offer security protection. That spooks me out as I feel like I'm sort of involving the Mafia to watch over us. So many people here have these horribly fierce guard dogs chained up in their yard, everything is fenced in with massively strong gates, many fences have broken glass embedded in the top….it sure gives one the feeling that everyone here lives in fear of robbers.

I have just finished a book on the history of Sicily and bandits have a very long history here. Robbers are partly responsible for the formation of the Mafia because a weak government left people feeling unprotected and the Mafia filled in the gap. Makes sense, huh? It is also probably why everyone lives in towns and cities…no one feels safe in the countryside.

So…volcanoes…robbers…new horizons…new dilemmas…it's always something isn't it? Like Rosanna Rosanna Dana says "It just goes to show you, it's always something--if it ain't one thing, it's another." Ha!

Much Love,
Susannah, *Baronessa di* Quandaries

PS Just finished a biography of Queen Victoria, nine children, so much for her statement of lie back and think of England...talk about doing your duty!

Looking for Home Sweet Home

July 12, 1989

Dear Anne,

Such excitement! Such glee! Such tremendous tearing of paper and squeals of delight!! Happiness abounds! The children have received your presents. They were so excited. Thank you, thank you, it was wonderful. It couldn't have happened at a better time. Just minutes before, Hillary was in tears. Big tears of homesickness, the first we have had from her. They started seemingly without provocation. I don't know what triggered it, but I guess it should be expected, and secretly I've been dreading it cropping up at some point. However, your gifts have cured it for the moment. How is it that you can always do the perfect thing at the perfect time? They loved the gifts, especially the books, but are now busy popping the bubble wrap which they all agree is the best part. Surely receiving something from you is the *best* part. Now I'm getting sentimental, bordering on homesickness myself thinking of you wrapping the books... thank you, it was perfect...perfectly wonderful.

Yesterday, we looked at the house down at the beach. It's a large villa divided up into three apartments. The downstairs is used by the landlords in the summer, always vacant the rest of the time. The apartment we looked at is on the second floor and has a huge rooftop terrace. Overall, the inside seemed small to me. It did have three bedrooms, a fair-sized living/dining room but no outside storage for bikes, etc. It has a nice balcony with a view of the sea. There is a fireplace in the living room which is the only source of heat! Nice views, if we don't freeze to death, I guess. I do think it gets down into the 40s here in the winter. The yard is all unkempt sand. I don't think the Italians believe in lawns. I've not seen much grass anywhere. It never rains here from May until September, so I guess it would all die anyway unless there was an irrigation system. The whole roof is a giant terrace the size of the house where I suppose we could go up at night and gaze at the stars like the Romans or Egyptians or whoever used to do that. The whole place slightly creeped me out for some reason. For one thing, I don't trust the kids on that terrace, or myself entirely, for that matter. It would also mean lots of driving to get to the base for school, etc., about 30 minutes at least. We put a hold on it for two days, so we do have to decide something. Knowing us, that is going to be next to impossible. Another couple who was on the housing trip put a second hold on it, so they are taking it if we don't. So, the pressure is on.

All for now. Thanks again for the presents. They meant a lot, it reinforced the idea that home, friends, and the life we had still exists there, which is nice to keep in mind.

Love you,
Susannah, *Baronessa di* Rolling Stones

Thursday, July 13, 1989

Dear Sue,

I am back at work this morning and it is very quiet, only one student here. I just came downstairs from the library where I was reading magazines. I saw a flyer announcing that tomorrow is the first day of the big craft show at the Civic Center, so I'll have to schedule that into my day. I'll be thinking of you and wishing we were there together. Since coming back to work after an entire week off, I have realized that one of the positive aspects of working is appreciating time at home, for a change.

Big news at our house! Your pictures arrived! Both batches arrived on the same day. We have practically worn them out. It was wonderful and sad to see your faces. We miss you all so much. Only a month, you say? It seems like an eternity. The girls went wild when they saw the pool, their idea of heaven. The pictures help so much as we try to visualize your new home. Thanks a bunch! Glad you received the books. The postal system is pretty good. Thank goodness.

I finally met the new principal. He seems okay, fairly businesslike. Did you know the outcome of his medical tests at Duke? I can't remember if you told me or where I heard it. Apparently, the doctors decided his problems were stress related! He surely has the wrong job, wouldn't you say? This should be interesting, watching him come unglued.

Beth asked about you and said to tell you hi. The drop-out prevention effort seems to be going well with many students completing their hours and earning course credit. One student who started with you finished yesterday. I enjoyed him. The students are each completing a questionnaire as they finish and I was joking with him to add something good about me. He wrote that I was a good replacement for you. I think it's funny when people don't realize that we're practically the same person! You were a hard act to follow, though. Another of your students, who had failed two courses, also finished her hours. I didn't know, however, until she was almost finished that she completed about fifteen hours more than she needed to. Clearly, I need to be more compulsive about my record keeping. They are an interesting group.

I think about you all the time and can hardly stand not being able to talk to you. I went back over to the cosmetology lab for conditioning and styling ($1.50) but the results were, to put it mildly, hideous. I was embarrassed to go back to work; there was no question where I'd gone during my lunch break. I guess I may let them do manicures, facials, etc., and leave my hair out of it. I'm getting uptight about this upcoming 20th class reunion. I don't have any idea what to wear, don't have time to lose thirty pounds, and, now, my hair!

Sunday evening

It must be nice writing a letter in one sitting. Finishing a letter to you seems to take me days. We are all fine. Got some more pictures from you. Beautiful! Your house prospects sound great! I love second-floor dwellings. It will be like the first place you and M lived. I'm sure it will be a relief to get it settled and not have the weight of that decision hanging over you. How luxurious to be able to live that close to the Med with no concern about the price. And it should be more enjoyable after *the season* is over, like it is here.

I got your "burn" letter and all that remains of it is what's stored in my rapidly failing memory. I know just what you're talking about. Maybe somewhere there are secure, well-adjusted men, but I'm afraid you and I didn't pick them. I feel that I, too, am resolved to make this marriage work. My biggest concern is the effect on the kids. It is a vicious cycle. I can see where Charles' problems came from and am afraid the dysfunction will be passed on unless big changes are made.

I can't believe how much of your letter struck a chord with me, the clothes business. Charles has complained for months about the state of his wardrobe. He, of course, could go anytime to shop, but will not consider going unless I go with him which is much easier said than done. His therapy with Rose is helping a wee bit, or I thought it was, until this weekend when we had a big fight. Anyway, I am scheduled to go with him to see Rose on August 7 and bring the girls. Bringing the girls was Rose's request. I'll let you know how it goes.

Stephen is finally crawling. I just *have* to get some of his milestones on video. He has an interesting three-legged crawl on one foot with one leg tucked under him. Needless to say, it's slow, thank goodness! He's so proud of himself. We took him to the beach today where I spent my time worrying about water getting into his ears and sand getting into his mouth. Whew! Remember when? Can you believe he'll be ten months old this week?

Laura and Hailey are going to be taking their second round of swimming lessons starting tomorrow. Laura has two loose teeth (bottom center). They really grow up so fast. Hillary, especially, looks so grown-up in the pictures you sent.

Thanks for all your letters. I love the "I Miss You" card. Would you believe (yes, you would) that I bought the same card at DeeGees to send to you? So one day when you least expect it...Meanwhile, take care of yourself and let me know your new address. Hi to all.

I love you, Anne

Ship of Fools
July 18, 1989

Dear Anne,

Things are better here. I'm in a lighter mood and His Majesty seems in a better mood, too. Much of the improvement can be attributed to the amazing weekend we just had. I know my words are not going to do it justice, but I will try. Edith Wharton, a consummate traveler, described being "drunk with seeing and learning" and that's exactly how I feel. It is hard to take it all in. We left early Saturday morning and drove north about two hours to the port city of Milazzo. Milazzo is the major port that connects Sicily with a chain of islands called the Aeolians, from the Greek god, Aeolus, God of the winds. Supposedly, Aeolus resided there and kept the winds trapped in a cave. I would scoff at this myth, but actually, I am so blown away, pun intended, with the splendor and beauty that we found there, I'm inclined to believe they are enchanted. There are seven islands in the archipelago and Vulcano is the closest one to mainland Sicily. From Milazzo, we took a hydrofoil ferry to Vulcano which takes about 30 minutes, my first experience on a boat with fins, like flying over the water. We had made reservations at a *pensione* in Vulcano and really had few expectations as this was all new territory to us. Well, it was like nothing I can compare it to, remote, undeveloped, and natural.

Vulcano is part of an active volcanic chain and rises spectacularly out of the water in a rugged landscape with a little beach and boat harbor. It is famous for the sulfuric mud baths and the whole place smells like rotten eggs. I've washed all our clothes twice since we got home and they still reek. I'm afraid they are irredeemable casualties of our wild weekend. So be it! The mud baths are literally mud basins that are super-heated by the volcano underneath. People wade into them carefully, as it is super-hot in places, and soak or just cover their bodies in it and bake on the hot rocks, very much like a mud pack. The sulfuric mud, supposedly, has healing qualities for a myriad of ailments. It dries and you see people all over walking around. mud smeared and looking like mourners covered in ashes. After a good soak or bake in the mud, you can go down to the sea and wash it off. There are tiny fumaroles, little bubbling hot steam jets, like a natural jacuzzi streaming up from the bottom of the sea. These are really hot and Matthew stepped on one directly and burned a blister on his foot. You sort of position yourself between them and just relax in the sea. A very unique experience, indeed. I noticed on Sunday that the sulfur fumaroles had eaten substantial holes in the bottom of my bathing suit. Must have been a reaction with the lycra! Judging from the strong smell of the place, there are some powerful chemicals in the mud brew. Strange and otherworldly.

The whole island is picturesque, remote, quaint, and simply mystifying. Most of the Italians are topless, even old grannies, and appear perfectly comfortable with their bodies. Two-piece bathing suits for little girls are sold with just bottoms, they don't even bother with a ludicrous top! How civilized.

The *pensione* was rustic. It included all meals but no air conditioning and we left the shutters open so we were up at 2:00AM swatting mosquitoes! The food was good and the view was amazing. All meals were served outside under a canopy and one Italian man dining there had a trained pet magpie that did tricks. I learned later robbers sometimes train magpies to fly into open windows and bring back any shiny things, like jewelry, etc. Not sure about the one we met, but he was entertaining.

The following day we decided to rent a boat and cruise around the whole island. It was not my idea of what to do but the water was so calm and beautiful, I didn't balk. So, the five of us set off with Hubby at the helm. At first, it was fine, but the further we went the rougher it got. Captain-Know-It-All did not anticipate the winds, no thank you, Aeolus, on the leeward side. The four-to-five-foot swells kept coming and we were grabbing the rails to hold on. Drew was prone in the bottom of the boat throwing up and the other two were panic-stricken, holding on for dear life. I was trying not to panic while frantically searching for life jackets, which I was sure must be stowed somewhere. NOT! I couldn't decide who I was more upset with, the Italians who rented us a boat without life jackets, or the lackadaisical parents who didn't insist on them, and just how big is this damn island anyway?

The sun was beating down and at each point we rounded, we thought we would be back out of the wind and waves. But believe me, it's a pretty large island and I've seen it up close and personal. After some major cuss words from the captain and he, who doesn't smoke, had smoked three cigarettes, which really did signal to the kids that things were serious, we finally reached the windward side and calm waters again. We were all weary and traumatized, to say the least, but so glad to be back in tranquil waters. We recouped and the beauty of the island soothed us back to normalcy.

The whole trip had taken about two hours and we were all so relieved to be back out of danger, we just stopped and anchored for a while. We snorkeled and swam and I saw an octopus. After we regained some composure, we were able to laugh about our foolishness and the fact that we had seen Vulcano like few other tourists! Chalk that up to a little greenhorn overconfidence, but we survived. The island itself is so beautiful with high cliffs and beautiful vegetation and a naturalist paradise. There are a few shops in the village and small businesses that offer all kinds of treatments. I saw one that advertised "aerosols, baths, beverages, mud baths, humages, inhalations, vaginal irrigations, intratubal insufflations, aesthetical treatments, and massages." Needless to say, I wasn't brave enough to try out any and just treated myself to the mud baths and sea jacuzzi and one *very* wild boat ride. However, I must say some of the above-mentioned treatments did pique my curiosity. Maybe next time.

We returned late Sunday back in Milazzo, tuckered-out and a bit wiser. We were relieved to find our car where we had left it on the street and not stolen. Guess the old Fiat is not a prime target and just goes to prove another good reason to buy a tin can.

We are learning, but it is difficult with the language and lack of experience. Everything is hard to navigate, but I am proud that we are game for it. I'm glad the excursion worked out as it gave us the courage to do it again. All in all, it was a wonderful weekend.

I'm starting an Italian class this week, so if I can learn the language things should get easier. We have just spent the entire weekend without hearing a word of English spoken. We have picked up a few words and phrases, but I am committed to breaking this language barrier. In most bars, you pay first, then take the receipt over to the counter to get what you paid for. It's hard when you can't even say what things you are asking to pay for. And besides, you know holding my tongue is not my forte. I have to crack the code of these people.

All else is fine on the home/hotel front. We, of course, could not commit to taking the beach house, so we are at square one in that quest. Day after tomorrow is Matt's 8th birthday. We are going to the Sicily Zoo, which should be interesting. Keep those letters coming...I'm definitely up for a trip... we can meet somewhere...anywhere. I suggest London at Thanksgiving. I will do anything to escape that slave holiday...I'd like to know what masochistic man thought that one up!

Love you,
Susannah, *Baronessa di* High Seas

Lady Madonna
July 21, 1989

Dear Anne,

How damn far do you have to move to get away from home? These grandparents aren't making it easy on me. Two years is starting to sound like a long, long time. I know the grandparents mean well and want to wish Matthew a happy birthday, but I'm also sure they have no idea what a hailstorm of the blues they are stirring up! Last night my mother called and cried on the phone the whole time. She choked out a few words to the kids, then they started crying and that lasted for about 30 minutes after the call ended. Drew said through her tears, "Just mail me home in a box." She said she misses everything... especially Hailey, Laura, Stephen, even, Petey, your parakeet. She wanted to know how many more days before we could go home and how big everyone is going to be by the time we get back. Sometimes it is tougher than others, as there is not a mother alive who wouldn't question if this is worth it and for whom, during the tears. After everyone cried themselves to sleep, I thought we have to get out of this hotel and away from the phone lines if we are going to make it.

I've got three house-hunting trips planned this week, so I am really going to try to get us an abode of some kind as soon as possible. It is just very hard to decide how much driving and what security risks I am willing to take on. It really has made me think about homeschooling the kids and then we could live anywhere. I don't know if I am going temporarily insane? We will probably get the Volvo next week and it will be great to be a two-car family again. Pray that we get a house soon or I might have a mutiny on my hands.

I think it is hitting us all that there is no St. Andrews School here. We all loved that school, and I already dread missing it when school starts. Too much change is too much change. How do you know where that line is? I really don't want to damage the kids permanently with all this. I am starting to question my flippant statement that this was a grand experiment to see if the nuclear family can survive unattached to a larger community…without the grandparents...without the norms. I didn't actually think I was turning my rug rats into lab rats, but I guess I have. Can we survive this total change of circumstances undamaged? If children crave stability, then I have totally screwed up as there is nothing normal about our lives here, from the food, the people, the language, our home, our lack of friends and relatives. I want them to be comfortable and content and those tear-streaked faces shook me to the core last night. Guess we will see how things go today and hope that everyone is in a better mood. Kids do seem to shake things off easily…it is mothers who agonize forever...Help me, Mother Mary.

Ciao for now,
Susannah, *Baronessa di* Mood Swings

Home Fires

July 24, 1989

Dear Anne,

I am deliberately writing on Friday so I don't fill up this letter with a description of a weekend trip. I don't want every letter to sound like a travelogue. We are all okay, but have all had a bad case of sickness, the worst kind, homesickness! I suppose I should have seen it coming, but it just jumped on us all of a sudden and we have all been teary-eyed and sad. We are coming out of it and have tried to stay busy to fight it. We did celebrate Matthew's birthday at the *Parco Zoo*. It is a sweet little zoo nearby and the animals look well taken care of, but the security is questionable. Good that you can get so close to the animals, but a little spooky at the same time. Jackie and her daughter, Candice, went with us, then we all went to Baskin Robbins for ice cream cake. Jackie is a blast. They are military and she said this is her thirteenth move in fifteen years! Nothing intimidates her and her sharp sense of humor is remarkable. She keeps me laughing nonstop. Hillary and Candice have become fast friends and we are all becoming chums. I think Hillary has had the hardest time with the homesickness, but it sure helps to have a friend. Jackie is helping me too as she can turn any situation into a riot of hilarity.

We are all getting a bit tired of this hotel life, even luxury gets old eventually. Once we get a house and the kids get their toys and things, I think life will feel more normal. No luck in that department yet...Matthew had a good birthday and he seems fine. He has made some new friends and loves the pool. He remains his usual complaining self, but that is not hot off the press news. Ha! He swims like a fish and I have started occasionally letting the children go down to the pool by themselves, as there is a lifeguard and all the hotel employees treat us like family now. The kids have really taken over this place and are on a first-name basis with all the hotel employees. They have befriended Alessandra, the beautiful young Italian who works behind the front desk, and she has taken them for ice cream. Did I tell you the manager's last name is Corleone?

Drew is her happy-go-lucky self, playing babies much of the time with her "hotel friends." She has charmed everyone here, and today is dressed in a striped shirt, knickers, sunglasses, and, of course, her hat. Always the fashionista. She's humming, "I'm cool, I'm rad. I'm a little bit bad." All in all, I'm a bit scared to say it, but I think the worst of the adjustment is behind us. I'm sure we will face challenges, but I can say that the thoughts of Morehead City are slowly being pushed out of our immediate consciousness and we are beginning to feel quite comfortable, and even starting to think of here as home, at least for longer periods of time.

My Italian classes are wonderful. The instructor is a local Sicilian who is a wealth of information and doesn't hesitate to tell all. My Italian is coming along and I take every chance to use it as often as possible. I am also thrilled with the new hairdresser that I have discovered. Her name is Monika. She is German, hip, young, and beautiful. She speaks excellent English and fluent Italian and is good at her trade. She cut my hair asymmetrical and I think I look very European.

I have started to give the kids an allowance of $5.00 a week. There is a lot to spend money on here, movies, bowling, shopping and it is easier to keep them on a budget that I can use as a threat if needed. Ha! They have a running tab at the pool so they can get sandwiches, ice cream, and drinks whenever. I am sure they are doing a good job of running that up.

Ray and Lib called us one night last week and probably helped to spark the homesickness. The children all took their turns talking to them and each one was so brave and tried so hard not to cry that it broke my heart. When it was my turn, I could hardly get a word out. It was not so much that I missed them, but the brave performance the children had put on for their grandparents was so dear. Such brave little soldiers. But I'm pretty sure the phone calls were the source of the homesickness epidemic.

One funny thing did happen this week. Sometimes we eat lunch or dinner in the military mess hall because they serve fairly plain food that the kids will eat. You have to sign in with lots of information, but it's free and convenient. Last week, we went in for dinner, got signed in, and started the buffet line. There was some golden-brown fried meat that I thought, at first glance, was chicken. As I scrutinized it closer, I did not recognize any of the usual pieces, thigh, leg, breast, etc., so I asked the Italian server, who was standing there, what it was. He answered, "*Coniglio.*" I shook my head to indicate I didn't understand. He said, "*Coniglio*," again, a bit louder. I still didn't get it, so he thought awhile and with his hands drew big ears over his head and said, "BOO

KNEE." The kids were mortified that they were serving bunnies for dinner and I was in stitches but didn't want to insult the cook or his attempt to explain it. It was an hysterical moment. The looks on the three children's faces were priceless. Needless to say, we moseyed on down the line for another choice, but the kids spent the rest of the night drawing bunny ears and saying, "Boo Knee" in horrified amusement. I have seen skinned rabbits hanging in the market for sale. Butchers leave a little tuft of fur so you know it's a rabbit and not a skinned cat or chihuahua, but I did not plan to come face to face with it as menu fare, especially with the children.

The girls have been dressing up in my clothes and pretending to be gypsies while I sit here in the room writing. They are fascinated with the gypsies we have seen each time we go to Catania. We have seen many of them downtown on the streets and they all look like they have a very hard life. The ones sitting on street corners with sleeping babies are rather shocking, as the babies look drugged. They leave me wondering if it is all part of their uniform to incite pity or reality. Either way, it seems a hard way to make a living. At each stoplight, they rush your car and want to wash your windshield for payment or sell you tissues or just beg for money. Surely, times must be very hard for them here as the unemployment rate for all Sicilians is 24 percent.

I have almost finished *The Shell Seekers* and I love it. Please read it so we can discuss it. I think it is excellent. That is about all our news for now. Settling in …growing a bit more confident daily...seems like a lot of things they have told us about possible robbery, terrorists, and other dangers are exaggerated but maybe I'm just still naive and have to see it for myself, which I can surely do without, thank you very much. For the time being, I am keeping my rose-colored glasses on as it suits me better to think it is all fascinating and enchanting. Sicily is very hard to describe; it is such a mixture of old and new, good and bad, beautiful and ugly. A lot like life, huh?

Love Always,
Susannah, *Baronessa di* BOO KNEES

PS 11:00PM Well, just got home from the hospital and Matthew is sporting four new stitches on his face. They are about 1/8 inch from his right eye, so it could have been worse. Long story, but he is going to be fine. I'll write more about it later. He's asleep now, in his bed, with his Batman pajamas on dreaming of riding in the Batmobile...God love us all and keep us until we meet again.

Monday, July 31, 1989

Dear Sue,

I knew I'd get mail from you today. That's how spoiled I am becoming with your regular and newsy letters. And I did, a letter and a card. It sounds like Matt's birthday was a great success, with so many activities. I thought about him on the 20th and felt especially sad to miss a Hall birthday celebration. They have always been celebrations I have looked forward to and have taken for granted. Maybe we will be in Sicily for Matt's next birthday! Thanks for the card and letter.

Well, the twentieth reunion of the Class of '69 is behind me! It was fun and I really enjoyed going, but it had its moments when I felt reduced to the emotional insecurities of a 15-year-old. Oh, the memories. The week before, I got anxious about going and even scheduled an appointment to get my hair cut at the last minute. I told my hairdresser I wanted a cut just like hers and I loved it. Can you believe it? I think I had neglected my hair for so long that any haircut would have been an improvement. She styled it and I didn't wash or comb it until Monday. That in itself makes me sound middle-aged. At least I headed to the reunion feeling like it was a good hair day.

There was a good turnout both nights and it was so interesting finding out what everyone was doing. Of course, quite a few classmates were parents and there were even some grandparents. On the flip side, one classmate was on the verge of having her first. She seemed apologetic for her late start but, hey, I say more power to her! There's probably an advantage to being senile when your kids are teenagers. Of course, you know me, during the weekend I had to give my speech on the virtues of breastfeeding.

Most everyone looked really good and seemed happy with their life choices so far. Our former homecoming queen and her husband were there. She looked good but different, very understated. I enjoyed talking to her. Her husband, on the other hand, looked like a serial killer. What a terrible thing to say, but honestly, I've never met anyone who seemed angrier and more miserable. He clearly didn't want to be there. He's bald, bearded, short, and stocky. You'd never put the two of them together. Chris' old boyfriend was there with his live-in girlfriend. They both work for that internet whatever and have an apartment on the edge of Harlem. Carol didn't come. I wish she had. You may enjoy reading what everyone is up to, so I'll get an extra book and send it to you. Be sure to send in your information when your reunion committee asks for it next year. I'll make sure they have your address.

I'm into my last week of Parallel High School and have signed my contract for next year. That's the good news. The bad news is they are not going to hire an at-risk counselor for the other high school. I talked to the assistant superintendent and he does not think it would be a good idea for me to do both, thank goodness. The plan is to start a pilot program and see how it goes. Bad idea. Number one, I'm afraid I will be asked to do more and more for the other high school, and number two, I don't think it is fair to those kids and faculty not to have a program, especially after getting a taste this summer of how helpful it is for failing students. I have gotten to know several of the students at the other high school and feel they would benefit from follow-up support. The parents, of course, may raise a fuss about the lack of services. Why does Carteret county have to do everything backward?

I'm in the process of writing a report on the program at Dick's request. The results are going to be very impressive, I think, with the number of students finishing successfully. I also got interviewed today, along with community college staff, by the *News-Times*. The reporter went on and on about how when she wanted to do the first story about the program all she had to do was publish your letter. It was so clear and well written, she said. She took pictures for this article. Yikes! I'll send you copies. The interview made me a little nervous because I have no idea how what I said will come across in print. And you know me, give me an audience and I'll talk! It's not hard to be positive, though, because I have really enjoyed this summer.

I just reread your letter. I hope the house hunting ends soon with a perfect place. I can understand not wanting to be cramped. I'm sure you'll find something just right. The pictures are spectacular. The mountains are amazing! I'm tempted to find someone to teach me Italian. Is it easy? We got the letter and pictures of the trip to Volcano. What adventures you're having! Life must seem really dull in Morehead. Well, it is.

It's time for bed so I'll close. Kiss everyone for me and tell Drew we will all look just the same when she sees us!

I love you, Anne

The Accoutrements of Life

July 31, 1989

Dear Anne,

I loved your last letter; it was just like talking to you. I could actually hear your voice in it. I was beginning to think you didn't miss me too much. I've told myself at least 5,000 times that you are fine and not missing me that much…what with all your cheerful letters...guess mine have sounded pretty upbeat too, for the most part. Why dwell on the dark side, huh? I think we were both just trying to keep it chipper, but as for me, I miss you and secretly want you to miss me too. There is a line in *The Shell Seekers* (Have you gotten that book yet?) that says if you love someone you are always a part of them. There is a spot in my heart that only you can fill and hope that is true for you, too, maybe. Please get that book. Get two copies and make Charles read it with you. I think it is worth a hundred sessions with Rose, not that you shouldn't do that too. The author touches on some things that are so pertinent…at least to me, maybe because of the turmoil I'm going through with my mother. Anyway, it is a lovely book and worth reading.

Enough of that, everyone here continues to be fine. I've felt better because I haven't been watching the news. I can't understand the local news and have made a conscious effort to skip the world news too, at least keep that stress out of my mind. So, I guess if any earth-shattering news happens, I'll be the last to know.

Well, I just came in from my Italian class and the news that was playing on the TV was the story about the hanging of the American hostage....so much for tuning things out. Sicily seems like the end of the earth and I'm wondering how far you have to go to get away from the madness of the world. But I've noticed that the world just keeps turning and life goes on amid each crisis, ours seems to anyway.

We went Sunday to a beautiful beach called Fontanarosa, south of Syracusa. It was a sandy beach with water the color of a swimming pool, crystal blue. Italians wall off access to the beaches and you have to pay an entrance fee, but it comes with an umbrella and chairs. The beach was spotless, which is a real find in Sicily...have I mentioned the trash everywhere? Another story there! While lounging in my beach chair, I was entertained by Moroccan salesmen coming by selling all kinds of items, including beach blankets, sunglasses, hats, clothes, watches, jewelry, and more. Shopping and sunning altogether, now that's what I call multi-tasking! I loved it, but can't say the same for You-Know-Who. He pouted awhile, but then realized I was not going to give in and humor him and relaxed and enjoyed himself. He was upset because it did not measure up to his idea of seclusion, etc. I told him to learn to go with the flow...maybe one day he will. Try as he might, he could not spoil the day. He really is no match for the splendor of Sicily. He seems to be giving it his best effort, though! Ha!

Later that night, I was giving him another lesson on how to enjoy life and it was falling on deaf ears, so I went downstairs to get a drink and missed a call from Susan. She said Lincoln has made it to Nashville.

I went to Catania shopping and bought your girls' Christmas presents. How's that for the early bird? I couldn't resist, so I'll save them awhile, or maybe I'll send them on with a sticker saying DO NOT OPEN TIL CHRISTMAS! The way they talk about robbery here, I might better do that! That is about all the news from Lake Woebegone for now.

Love ya,
Susannah, *Baronessa di Cie La Vie*

PS Get *The Shell Seekers*
PPS Matthew's stitches are healing nicely. No additional bloodletting or boo-boos!

August 6, 1989

Dear Sue,

Well, the summer job is over and I have until the 16th before I head back to work. I would rate the summer a big success! Fifty-four students restored 122 courses. And, that doesn't count the seniors who finished the week of graduation. I enjoyed being at the community college. I was able to help out at the Guided Studies Lab while the staff took vacations, so they're feeling indebted to me. I enjoyed the students and am looking forward to working with them next year. As you said, everyone, parents and students, were so appreciative, as if it were all my idea. I feel *in* with the college staff. There was only one staff member who, I thought, was consistently negative. Go figure it would be the minister's wife. Dick seemed to drop out of sight the last couple of weeks so I felt more relaxed. I feel I can make a difference with this group of students, so I'll be starting this school year very optimistic. The five-minute commute to work will be a nice change for sure.

Charles and I have been at each other's throats, so I was looking forward to going to Rose this morning. Taking the girls was okay, but I really think that it was just to satisfy Rose's curiosity. They kind of got in the way, if you know what I mean. It's a little hard to call your husband a bastard with his two adoring daughters sitting right there. We made another appointment and have orders to divide household responsibilities, etc., something Charles wouldn't even discuss. We go back, without the girls, in two weeks. He and I agree on many things, but there are also a lot of areas of complete disagreement. I'm sure we can make our marriage better; it will just take some change and work.

It's now Monday evening. Stephen just fell asleep at Melissa's house, so I have a few minutes. Got two letters from you today. I knew I would. It had been awhile, not that long, but for a time I was receiving letters every other day so it was nice to hear from you. Sicily does sound so idyllic. Did I tell you Charles has already asked for three weeks off next summer in June-July? Did it on his own, so plan for us. I can hardly wait! I must tell you though, I've been fantasizing about you and me pulling off a rendezvous in London or Paris. I started thinking about traveling with the family, which I would still do, but then I thought, "Why not just Sue and me, our Christmas presents to each other, a long weekend in London?" Wild, huh? Is it just a wonderful fantasy? It does make nice daydream material.

Sicily sounds so wonderful! We've had some high 90-degree weather here. I think your Southern origin, with hot and humid summers, has prepared you for summer in Sicily. Without the humidity and mosquitos, it is probably much easier to bear. Our electric bill was really high this month at $242.

Laura got her card from Drew today and was so excited. She lost a tooth this week and has another hanging by a thread. She is growing up fast. I loved hearing about the children and how well they're adjusting. With one good friend like Candice, they'll do fine and not feel isolated, and I'm sure they'll have more friends in no time.

I'm going to stop and put this in the mail. I really do miss you; can hardly stand it. As you can see by the card, I'm not the only one. Take care.

Love to all, Anne

PS I am anxious to hear what you think about our rendezvous Christmas present.

Boll Weevils

August 10, 1989

Dear Anne,

I haven't written for a few days as I could not even face putting my feelings down on paper. If I put my thoughts down in black and white, I might be forced to just jump off the balcony. Self-inflicted agony is the worst kind. I anticipated that this would not be easy, but I did not anticipate the overwhelming amount of angst I would feel carrying the weight of the decisions that affect the children, as well as, the grownups. The weight of it all has pushed me to the edge and resulted in depression and my second-guessing this whole thing. Here's a partial list of what has me hanging over the cliff by the proverbial twig:

1. Can't find a house
2. Withdrawal from St. Andrews School and normalcy
3. Got Lost
4. Had an anxiety attack
5. Matthew and Drew had the longest, sweetest conversation about whether or not a seed they planted under

Grandma Jessie's tree was growing (tug of the roots)

6. Read Garrison Keillor's *Leaving Home* (big mistake)
7. Matthew's stitches
8. Being the real grownup is very hard
9. Can't find a house
10. Writing a new chapter in your life means in some ways the old chapter is finished.
11. Can't find a HOUSE!

Just to name a few!

Maybe I am not cut out for this kind of lifestyle. At least, that is what it has felt like when I am crying into my pillow. Once the boll weevils of my mind start singing their song and the voice of my mother whispers, "Told you so," I imagine Ray's heart going bad and the children never seeing their beloved grandfather again or my mother shuffling off her mortal coil. I see my lovely home on Evans Street and long for the warmth and security of it. Now it has become very clear to me how important the relationships between the kids and extended family and friends really are to all of us. I see the kids two years older, distant from their former friends and relatives, not being able to pick up where they left off. I see us here in Sicily in a horrible house being robbed at gunpoint in the middle of the night and much, much more! Thank God, the kids are not on the same depression cycle as I am and seem to be okay with things at the moment. They inspire me to keep trudging on, otherwise, I don't think I could withstand this pressure. They are looking forward to school starting and I can only pray that it is not a big disappointment. Sending them out from a hotel room for the first day of school is not what I imagined but barring a miracle that is looking very likely.

The house, or lack thereof, is depressing. Security is the issue, the lovely places with yards and space are prime targets for robbery, and I would like to avoid that trauma for the kids and myself, if possible, and yet, I don't want to be cramped in an apartment that is too small and depressing. We found a beautiful place with steel shutters and an alarm system but were advised not to take it as the previous renters had been robbed. We are running out of the 90 days allotted by the government to find a house, and we have to find something or start paying this hotel bill ourselves. So, I really do have to be brave and smart and pick something soon, for better or worse.

We finally got the Volvo and it feels like an absolute tank after that tin can Fiat and it seems so much safer driving the kids around. Not much other news. I registered the kids for school and it starts at the end of the month. That was a bad day as I kept thinking of the idyllic St. Andrews School that we had forfeited, and God only knows what this will be like. Also, I had just read that darned *Leaving Home* book by Garrison Keillor, with all the quaint lovely scenarios of small-town life. I kept thinking of home and how it is a beautiful place to live and raise children. Oh well, I hope I can scrape myself up off this tile floor and get it together and get on with things. Once I get focused on the positive of being here, I can see that too, but at the low times, I just want to go home and stop having to adjust to every new thing. Trying hard to keep my mind going in a positive direction. Wish me luck.

Much love,
Susannah, *Baronessa di* Mental Breakdowns

August 13, 1989

Dear Sue,

This is a PMS letter, so if it sounds gloomy and rather depressing, that's my excuse. I've been telling myself I need to write but that I'd wait until I had some wonderful news to tell. Now I've decided to face reality and write anyway, otherwise it could be months!

We did, however, have a wonderful, exciting, happy time last week when your package arrived with the miniature Dr. Scholl's sandals. The girls were thrilled and are hard to live with as they feel *so* grown-up. They are completely sold on Sicily as being the best place in the world with the best friends in the world living there! Thank you so much for sending the sandals. It makes you seem closer somehow. You should see them clip-clopping down to Melissa's house.

Well, as I said, I have no news. Everything I've done is completely predictable. I'll take you at your word that you want to hear every boring detail.

I registered Hailey for another year of dancing. Laura decided dance lessons are not her thing. Laura, by the way, has lost her two bottom teeth and they are now in the hands of the tooth fairy. Hailey, against my wishes, had told Laura the whole nitty-gritty about the tooth fairy. But there is something innately protective about being an innocent age. Laura couldn't quite buy it, and tells with wide-eyed wonder how she woke up in the middle of the night and saw the tooth fairy. In addition to now having no bottom front teeth, she also has a huge goose egg on her forehead from falling off her bike face-first onto Melissa's driveway. It's quite a bump. I'm glad that I didn't witness it happen. She's fine, but I felt weak-kneed seeing it.

I finally went to Harriet's trunk-showing of children's clothes, knowing full well I'd probably buy something. Part of the reason I went was my curiosity to see the inside of her house. I did order outfits, times three: two blue cotton knit long sleeve mock turtle neck dresses with red and white leggings for the girls. They were the cheapest and least dressy outfits she had. Then for Stephen, I ordered a red corduroy romper with a blue rocking horse appliqued on the front. And, if that weren't enough damage to the checkbook, I came home and made an appointment to have Benners Photography take their picture on September 30. I guess that's how I justify the clothes. I hope it turns out. The clothes are photogenic, at least. It's going to be hard to top the one Benners did of Hailey and Laura. I'm anxious, though, to get the three of them in a picture together. So now you know what one of your Christmas presents will be.

I did a real first today...went on a solo yard sale outing. It seemed almost sacrilegious to go without you, and it was no fun. I was on my way to the grocery store and saw the signs in front of a Williamsburg-looking house east of Country Club apartments. I want to start going to yard sales again because I ended up with two coats, a pair of shoes, and some odds and ends. But it was hard without you.

Now for your *News Times'* summary: Marie had a baby two weeks ago and her father-in-law is in the hospital recovering from a stroke. He's reportedly doing well with some numbness, but no major problems. Sylvia's father died, natural causes. He attends our church, so I heard that way. And the photographer who always does the class reunion pictures died suddenly in his sleep. I just saw and talked to him two weeks ago at my class reunion. He took the big group picture, went home, printed it, and brought copies back to the reunion. I remember being surprised that he hadn't retired. He was 62. See what I mean about this letter being gloomy? You'll probably wish I hadn't written it.

We now have two parakeets. Gilda at CCC had one to give away, cage and all. So now Hailey has her own, a blue one. He was also named Petey, so rather than having "Petey One" and "Petey Two," his name has been changed to Angel. And now, I have two cages to clean.

Speaking of cleaning, how's life without housework? The only way to go, I bet. I've just hired two people who work together to come every week. Of course, they can't do everything, but it should help a lot. They were impressive their first day, so I'm excited that we are embarking on a new way of life... clean.

Charles is hot and heavy into tennis. I haven't seen him this excited about anything in quite a while. He's been playing three and four times a week and, of course, had to buy a new racket and new shoes. I think he is getting pretty good. There are several people from the lab who play, so they play doubles. We went to mass tonight because he has a game tomorrow morning. I wish I could get excited about something that was also good for me.

I'm going to close for now, although I may add on an addendum if a big story breaks tomorrow. Chances are I will have to wait until I am back to work for some real news. Take care of each other and keep those letters coming. I hope that you have found the perfect villa by now. I love hearing about all your travels. You are so adventuresome! We miss you and think about you every day. Thank you again for the Dr. Scholl's.

Love always, Anne

PS Do you have access to American magazines? I'm sure you do. I just bought *Life* magazine with an article on the 20th anniversary of Woodstock. Interesting. Shall I send it?
PPS Things keep popping up, so this letter goes on and on. About homeschooling...Are you crazy?!

Hold the Phone

August 14, 1989

Dear Anne,

Got your card yesterday about rambling on when lonely, just another example of our brains in sync. I bought a card for you with a lady on the front that says, "You would have gotten this card sooner"...when you open it says, "But I died four days ago"...I've been too superstitious to send it as life here does seem strange and full of danger, not to mention my state of mental health. Did I tell you that we can't drink the tap water? All drinking water is bottled in big liter bottles that come in six-packs that weigh about ten pounds. That should be fun to buy and stock up on in the kitchen. I sure hope we don't have a plethora of steps but I imagine we will. Still no house, not in a complete panic, but the tension is rising.

On Saturday we went to Messina, about an hour and a half north of here, to a world trade fair with vendors from all over. It was interesting. Of course, we bought some things. The largest purchase was a twenty-pound wooden carved turtle. We must have really wanted it, as it was a heavy item to carry around. Funny, I imagined putting it on our hearth back home which is pretty ridiculous since we sold that house and won't be going back there. Hope it looks stunning in our place here if we ever get one, that is.

About calling...once we leave the hotel in September, we will be strictly on snail mail to communicate since we are not going to have a phone and probably won't have one for the entire two years. They are too expensive, and so far, our phone calls usually turn out pretty disappointing and a major cause of homesickness...besides I wouldn't trust the kids to not be tempted to run up a tremendous bill. So, I think not having one is just easier. A clean break with the outside world.

Do you think we can stand it? The letters are a good substitute and I hope they can continue nonstop. I have decided that writing is my therapy, so I am glad you are willing to be the vault of all my rants. I am also writing Carol, Ray and Lib, and my mother so if I tell you something that I've said before forgive me as I get confused at what I've told everyone. Not to mention that with you I can be totally candid and bare all and not worry that I'll be committed to a nearby asylum. With the others I tone it down somewhat, trying to keep it upbeat, as they must think I'm questionable at best, in the finest of times. Ha!

Things got pretty exciting here last Wednesday when all the circumstances surrounding the hanging of Captain Higgins by the terrorists happened. Extra troops, pilots mostly, were flown in here and this base was full of extra military personnel. Security was beefed up at the base and security checks on all vehicles have been really tight. With increased security, you have to get out of the car, open the trunk and hood, glove compartment, open all bags, stand aside and wait until they check with mirrors underneath the car, show identification and registration just to drive on base. Usually, you just have to flash your ID card. It was a bit unnerving to me and I am glad Bush decided not to bomb anyone, but the US was definitely ready to strike judging by the activity here. Sigonella is a NATO base designed to serve the American fleet in the Mediterranean. They refer to this base as the "Tip of the Spear" and the motto displayed in every office is "To Serve the Fleet." I hope things calm down as my peacenik soul cannot take one more ounce of stress. Rigamarole such as this is putting a dent in my *la dolce vita*. Any more *incidentes* and I'm likely to lose it. My literal sanity is hanging in the balance at this point. I don't imagine President Bush knows my mental marbles are in his hands? Ha! Well, I'll close for now. I have some new film to drop off to be developed, so new pictures should be on the way.

Much love,
Susannah, *Baronessa di*
Fleet Readiness or Not

PS I need a house!

August 15, 1989

Dear Sue,

I miss you! I start back to work today by going to the orientation for new teachers and then a pig pickin' given by the superintendent. Kind of a hard thing to turn down, although I would rather skip it. Wanted to send you this newspaper article hot-off-the-press so you'd know *your* program was doing okay. Gale felt they should have put your name in the article, too. So do I!

My other disappointment was no "e" on Anne, even after I told the reporter, specifically. Oh well, such is life. As Anne Shirley would say, having a bosom friend will get you through anything, even no "e" on Anne.

Well, more later when I get back into the job. I'm sure there will be some news.

Take care, Anne with an "e"

PS I got your card. You certainly get movies fast. I've been trying to rent *The Accidental Tourist*. I'm glad it's good.

August 14, 1989
The Carteret County News-Times

New Program Reaches 110 Potential Drop-Outs
by Cheryl Burke

One hundred ten at-risk students have completed "parallel high school," a new program in Carteret County designed to prevent students from dropping out of school. The Parallel High School Program is a joint effort by the Carteret County public school system and Carteret Community College, Morehead City, to help potential dropouts. It is helping those students who are at risk, likely to drop out of school, because of credit loss from excessive absences or lack of success within their classes.

The program, which ran from April 4 until August 4 on a trial basis, helped students who had lost credit because of they had more than 12 absences, with one or more of them being unexcused. They also needed to have a C average or better to qualify for the program. The Carteret County public school system will allow only 12 absences each school semester. Students are allowed to make up their missed hours while enrolled in the parallel program. It also offered individual or small group tutoring services and counseling for students who were in need of extra help in order to be successful during the regular school year.

To enter the program, a student must enroll at the guided studies lab. He must sign a contract along with a parent or guardian, which clearly states how many hours he owes. The student agrees not to have any more unexcused absences for the semester. If he does, the contract is automatically invalidated and he is not allowed to return to the program. Enrollees work on materials in the guided studies lab, materials that have been specially designed for them.

Counseling and assistance were provided by the college guided studies staff and West Carteret at-risk counselor Ann Krouse. Mrs. Krouse served as a summer school teacher for the program.

Dr. Donald Bryant, president of Carteret Community college, and original designer of the parallel high school concept, said he was pleased with the early success of the program. "I attended high school graduation this year. A couple of the graduates told me they had gone through the program, and that was the reason they were allowed to graduate."

Mrs. Krouse said that the number of hours per student required to restore lost credit over the summer ranged from one hour to 109 hours. "Because the Parallel High School Program will be available next year with an at-risk counselor located at West Carteret High School, students will begin the program before excessive absenteeism has occurred," she said.

The guided studies staff along with Mrs. Krouse rated the program an overwhelming success. They said the participating students were motivated, well-behaved, and adjusted well to the college environment. The students were able to work independently on the prepared study packets and computer programs.

According to guided studies coordinator, Gale Swann, several students have expressed their appreciation of the new program. "We had a wrap-up session at the end of the spring portion for the stu-

dents who had completed the program. We asked for the students' opinions. Students said they liked the individualized attention from the staff. They felt a sense of responsibility and of being adult. They felt the attendance policy was strict and this was the first time an alternative had been offered. The students I dealt with matured while attending. Some of them set future goals by attending classes at the college."

Mrs. Krouse said students had told her they benefited from attending classes at the college. "I had students tell me they had developed good study habits by attending the program. I've had students suggest that a support study group be continued, even though they have completed their hours. Mrs. Krouse intends to follow the progress of the students as they begin a new school year. She wants to catch students before their absenteeism gets out of control.

What causes students to develop such a high rate of absences? Mrs. Krouse said there were several reasons. Some students lose motivation at the beginning of the school year and let absences build up before they realize the seriousness of their actions. One of the major problems is in scheduling a student's classes. It's a difficult task when you have a lot of students. Students' schedules need to be looked at on a more individualized basis."

"One student failed a grade twice because of one class and kept getting the same instructor. He felt intimidated and that caused problems. Some students are placed in classes over their heads and they become discouraged."

Mrs. Krouse is hoping to instruct students at some point on having better communication skills with their teachers. "Misunderstandings between students and instructors can cause problems." She hopes to help students learn how to approach their teachers in a more sensitive manner.

Ms. Swann said she was surprised by the types of problems some of the students faced. "Some students live on their own and basically support themselves while attending school. They work a full-time job and try to attend classes. There are some almost insurmountable situations."

The program will now be evaluated and future plans made.

Dr. Bryant said he was pleased with the program and hoped that more definite guidelines would be established as the program continued.

August 17, 1989

Dear Sue,

I don't know how to start this letter, I have so much to say. Oh, where to begin? I just know that I have to start it, finish it, and mail it or you'll start wondering if your best friend has forgotten you. Well, rest assured, she hasn't. Far from it! It's getting harder for me to deal with the geographical distance between us. I miss you so much. Your last two letters didn't surprise me. They did sadden me, but I knew somehow that you were going through a homesick phase. It is just a temporary stage, I'm sure, but while you're in the middle of it, I know it's hard. It's a tribute to your parenting that the children are handling it so well. I underestimate children. And it's not surprising that the house hunting job has begun to take its toll. With M working full time, I'm sure the lion's share of the hunting falls squarely on your shoulders. What else is new? You are an old pro at finding the perfect house, for sure. I hope by the time this letter reaches you, something wonderful has turned up and you can put that stress behind you.

Matthew's stitches! I guess knowing Matthew's energy level and love of adventure, not having his first stitches until age eight is remarkable. I hope that he has completely recovered by now and that it wasn't too traumatic for you and M. How were the base medical resources? I'm assuming that is where you went. Love you, Matthew!

I have lost track of when I last wrote and feel so badly that I have waited this long. I'm back to work, of course, at the high school and the two weeks of teacher prep have gone fine. I like the two female counselors that I work with and, wouldn't you know it, the solitary male is a deadbeat. I think he may be an alcoholic, too, from the way he talks. We all just tolerate him. Typical, right? Token male.

I spent the workdays trying to get proficient with the scheduling system, dealing with the drop-add requests, going to meetings, and completing the state-required drop-out form which was due June 20. I was happy to see two of last year's drop-outs, whom I encouraged to try high school for one more year, enroll and seem pleased with their schedules. That is rewarding.

When I got to school, Jennifer had moved back into your office, so now I'm in the office which you had last year next to Rosa. I like it better, I think. Beth moved to the other assistant principal's office since he is now a principal at one of the elementary schools. Beth's old office and Karen's office are now conference rooms. The principal moved to Mike's office. Mike moved to Brenda's office, Brenda has the principal's old office and Karen is in that extra room right next to the principal's old office. The teachers' mailboxes have been moved to the ISS room and Cherry has a desk in there. It's now a teachers' workroom. ISS is in another classroom. Whew! Were you interested in all that? Sally is back at the front desk and starts Monday.

I have already poked around in the records room and read the teacher comments in my cumulative folder, first grade through high school. Amazing what teachers wrote about students at the end of each year. Good, bad and ugly.

Charles' cum folder is in a drawer up near the very high ceiling and I'm too chicken to climb up to get it. Someone got shocked doing that; not by reading what was written in Charles' cum folder, but from accidentally hitting the light fixture! I have felt really good now that I am among the gainfully employed and going to work. A visit to Dr. Harker, resulting in a nice low blood pressure reading, confirms that this job is a good thing. I know you understand. Some people look at me like I'm nuts when I say how much I am enjoying having this job, but you and I know that being home with three kids is a very stressful life-and-death job with lousy fringe benefits.

Everyone has asked about you and I have a little speech I give telling them how much you are all enjoying yourselves, how comfortable and luxurious the hotel is, and how hospitable all of Sicily is. I usually include a little summary about your travels to Mt. Etna and Vulcano and snorkeling, etc., saying how glad you all are that you went on this adventure. Everyone looks so envious and I usually end saying, "And we are planning to visit them next year" (even if I have to indenture my firstborn). Your letters won't change my presentation, except to add updates as far as various travels, fabulous villa, dips in the Med, and gourmet meals go. Everyone everywhere has ups and downs, but overall, you have really made a good choice. Your family has already experienced so many neat things and the children are learning so much about the world. I just heard a 1989 high school graduate say that he got 12-hours credit at NC State University for placing out of German. He lived in Germany for a year as a freshman and never took German in high school. Hillary, and maybe Drew and Matt, will be like that with Italian!

It sounds so idealistic to be able to travel and teach them on the trip. Maybe I spoke too quickly and home school will work out beautifully. The kids are all good ages to do it...no geometry or chemistry...heavy on the history and creative writing. Give it a try. The nice thing is you can change your mind. Matthew might really like it, too, when he realizes he can work at his own pace. Just think, *no* PTO!

I'm going to stop and put this out for the mailman. I really do miss you. I can hardly stand it.

Love to all, Anne

School Daze

August 30, 1989

Dear Anne with an e,

The school year has begun and I passed the first week with flying colors! Ha! Actually, the kids have handled it well, too! Monday was the first day and I marched them to the front door and let them go. I blew them a kiss and said, "Okay kiddos, sink or swim," and turned on my heel and practically ran back to the hotel to have a good cry. I had no idea who their teachers were and felt I had thrown them all to the wolves for the first time in their lives, but it has turned out to be a tolerable start.

Drew's teacher, Ms. Schultz, is rather a no-nonsense type about our age, a bit Yankee for my taste, but Drew says she is fine. She says her classmates are fine. She says the work is fine and "Fine" is all I can drag out of her so far concerning school.

Matthew's teacher, Ms. Wells, is an elderly lady who looks like she should have retired ages ago (or maybe has a serious drinking problem). She had lost her class list and was all to pieces and had the shakes. Needless to say, she does not look like a match for Matthew, but I think everyone deserves at least one teacher who is totally out to lunch and I think this may be his lucky year. He hasn't brought a book or paper home all week and is delighted about school, which makes me highly suspicious. Maybe a lighter touch is just what Matthew needs. We will see.

Hillary, thank God, got the pick of the lot, named Ms. Krouse, can you believe it? She is very nice and very on the ball and Hillary likes her a lot. Seems she is up to challenging Hillary who thrives in that climate. Hillary can leave school for lunch and she comes over to the hotel and has lunch with me. How's that for civilized? Hillary has signed up to play flute in the band and is excited about that, too. All in all, I am fairly well pleased with the school business.

AND DRUM ROLL!! We have a house! We are supposed to sign the contract on Tuesday and can move in on Wednesday. Good thing, as our 90 days of free hotel life runs out on that day. It certainly is not exactly what we wanted, in many ways the complete opposite, but it will have to do. It is close to the base in the town of Motta Sant' Anastasia. That is the very medieval-looking town in the photo I sent you with the castle on top of the huge rock. The apartment is roomy and bright with three bedrooms, a large kitchen /dining combination, and two bathrooms, but it actually had me at the front door with the six deadbolts! You have to turn the key forever to unlock it. It is a four-story, stand-alone house divided into three apartments. Ours is on the third floor sandwiched between our landlords Signore and Signora Santanocito who live on the second floor and their married daughter who lives above us on the fourth floor. I shudder to think of the movers struggling to get our heavy piano up to the third floor.

The apartment has a wrap-around balcony on all four sides. There is a gated yard/garden in the front which is a formal rose garden that is pretty to look at and should help keep me cheerful. Not exactly a space that the children can play in, so there will be no yard for them. The whole bottom/first floor is a communal garage and we can park the cars and store the bicycles there. No grand views, no real yard, but it is about as safe as it gets in Sicily. In the end, I could not risk having the kids or myself face a robbery, so I opted for security. It is close to the base and the kids can ride the buses that run every 30 minutes, so that should be nice. I can walk to the *panificio* (bread store) and the bar and it is safe, safe, safe. The outside driveway gate locks, the outside doors lock, and then there are the six deadbolts on our front door. So as long as I don't lose my keys, I should be okay in this fortress. What pushed me over the edge was I heard last week that a family was stopped at gunpoint on the Syracusa beach road. They robbed them, took their car, and left them stranded on the side of the road. Call me naive, green, culturally unsophisticated but I just did not want to add an experience like that to my list of travel souvenirs. With this house, I can come and go in relative safety, so I am pleased. My thought is that we didn't come to Sicily to house sit and guard our stuff. I came to travel and mix with the natives.

Motta Sant' Anastasia is a real Sicilian town with an outdoor market every Wednesday. There is also the daily bread man, fish man, vegetable man, and Fuller brush man who come down the street hawking their wares, and you can shop from their carts as they pass by. Just call from your balcony and they will stop and wait for you to come down and shop. I am happy with the local color and can't wait to explore every street and alleyway.

The apartment has twelve-foot ceilings and white tile floors so it is a bit of a blank canvas. Each room has a set of double opening doors onto the balcony and the living room has two sets. Lots of light streams in so I think that will be cheerful. There is radiator heat and we were informed that by law it can only be run four hours in the morning and four hours at night during the months of October through February. We have to pay an extra heating fee that is based on the amount of fuel that is used. So, this winter, at least, we won't freeze. I am not looking forward to hoisting all the groceries up three flights of stairs, but hopefully, that is about the most inconvenient thing I will have to deal with. Anyway, for better or worse, it is done and we can get our household goods and start living like a real family again. I have to buy my own kitchen cabinets and my own stove, which is normal here. The apartment comes with bare bones and bare light bulbs hanging from the ceiling, so it really is a BLANK canvas. I'm ready to put my spin on it for sure. Hotel life is grand, but it does get old.

The only other news is that Mt. Etna has put on quite a show lately. The first night I saw it, I called the hotel front desk and asked if we should think of evacuating and they laughed at me. The whole sky was red and lava was pouring down the mountainside and shooting up into the air. Hubby accused me of being afraid of everything, and I told him no, just snakes, lightning, active volcanoes, robbers, airplanes, plagues, earthquakes, boogeymen, etc., etc. Just the normal stuff we chicken-hearted folks steer clear of.

The weather has cooled off and is delightful. Monday is Labor Day and we are going shopping in Taormina. It is a real gem, a quite famous tourist destination, and the shopping is just the best. Taormina is the "Rodeo Drive of

Sicily" and has been a hot spot for the rich and famous for many years. Vivian Leigh had a house there along with lots of other celebrities.

Well, I'll close for now. By the way, I'm pretty sure I am permanently over the worst of the homesickness. I feel fully recovered. The kids starting school has really helped me get back into a more normal routine and now with a house to keep, decorate, and to practice my domestic arts upon…I'm feeling more myself. Dear God, am I actually longing for housework? Guess that comes with the territory, at least I'll have a home of my own. Write when you can.

Much love,
Susannah, *Baronessa di Casa Mia*

PS Can you picture the concerned crowd that gathered this week when Matthew got stuck in the hotel elevator for over an hour? It made for great drama throughout the hotel. Leave it to Beaver! He was a little shaken up when he was finally liberated, but all was fine afterwards. I think he finally learned not to push all the buttons at once. Ha! The Italian hotel workers took it harder than I did; they were wringing their hands and showing great concern but then, I have nine years of Matthew experience!

September 5, 1989

Dear Sue,

I've written a dozen letters to you in my head and have wanted desperately to sit down *alone* and clear-headed and write you. My life is on fast forward! I was *so* glad to get your card. An answer to my prayers that your mood would swing (although if it hadn't, I was prepared to come and get you...my passport is good until March 1990!) Nothing like a good dose of depression to make you appreciate our normal manic stage.

The job, the children, the house, the husband are keeping me busy. Susan and Sarah spent Labor Day weekend with us. Charles always gets so weird and needy when they are here. And if one sibling wasn't enough, Peter and Aurora were also in town. I keep waiting for a *normal* routine to set in, but am afraid maybe this is it.

Hailey hates school this year. Laura seemed to be adjusting well, but then today, she mentioned something about being hit by a girl in her class and hitting her back. Yikes! Stephen is fine. Walking like a pro and now climbing stairs. A couple of times I barely grabbed him before he headed back down. And he's biting the boob that feeds him. Drawing blood! Really! I've been yelling, "No! No!" when he does it, but he hasn't let up much. He's taking milk from a bottle part of the time. He still wants to nurse but it seems like that option may be on the way out.

I plan to write you a real letter very soon. Hope you'll understand if there are lulls in my letter writing schedule. I'm thinking about you all and every day.

Hugs and kisses all around, Anne

PS Your letters are wonderful! Susan brought *The Shell Seekers* back this weekend, so I'll be reading it soon. I loved the Garrison Keillor book.

September 6, 1989

Dear Sue,

I can't believe it's already Sunday night. I'm not sure where the weekend went. The girls are asleep with their clothes laid out for the first day of school. Thank you again for sending Garrison Keillor's book. I really liked it, but do see how it might be a difficult and emotional reading choice for you. I've noticed that I always experience a combination of nostalgia and melancholy this time of year. I don't know why. It doesn't always seem to match up with the current comings-and-goings but is probably an end-of-summer thing. I know part, or maybe much, of it this year has to do with not having you around to talk to. I have had *no, none, nada, zip, zero* social life since you left, especially in terms of a good heart-to-heart conversation. I miss it so much! And the thing is, I don't want to unload my deepest, darkest thoughts on anyone else, so there is no point in pursuing that angle. The letters will have to do. Keep them coming. They keep me going.

And something else that will keep us going...our rendezvous in London! We owe it to ourselves. It's settled. Of course, I initially mentioned it casually, but I knew you'd take the bait...remember, we share the same brain. We'll do it! Now to start *The Plan*. Thanksgiving is good. I was going to quietly investigate flight dates and prices and then tell Charles, but the opportunity arose so I went ahead and told him. Later that night as I was getting ready for bed, I found out that, unknown to me, he had already called Piedmont Airlines to check the schedule. Here's what he found out: Pay a month in advance, no refund, must stay at least a week, $500 round trip from New Bern to Charlotte to London. Not bad. I'd have to go on the 21st and return on the 28th. There are seven seats left for the return flight. All flights to London after the 21st are fully booked. Can you get free flights anytime from Sigonella? How does your deal work? I wonder if I can get four days leave from work around Thanksgiving. I'll check tomorrow and call Delta. Also, check early December, although I'd probably have to take too much time off to make that work. As I am writing this, Charles is calling Delta...6 days $348 and it has to be booked by September 14 for travel November 23 through 28. Write. What shall we do?

Love, Anne

September 10, 1989

Anne,

Book that ticket. I will make it work on my end...dates sound perfect.

See you in London!
Sue

September 11, 1989

Dear Sue,

Well, I've done it! A non-refundable, non-returnable, full-speed ahead ticket has been purchased! London, here we come! I sure hope everything is as easy on your end. I am sending my reservations so you can try to match them. I will write my friends in London for help with a hotel. If they offer to put us up, I may take them up on it...for a few days anyway. They both work, so we'd still have *our* time. I don't want to spend too much time with them or have them feel they need to entertain us. I want you all to myself so we can talk nonstop about everything!

So here is my schedule:

Depart on RDU Delta flight 6270 6:30 p.m.
Nov. 23 Turkey Day!

Arrive Gatwick 9:00 a.m.
Nov. 24 Friday

Return trip from Gatwick Delta 6091 1:45 p.m.
Nov. 29 Wednesday

Back in RDU 8:00 p.m.

Note that the airport is Gatwick. I've never heard of it. If I get there first, I can go over to Heathrow or vice versa. Also, note that I leave on the 23rd and arrive on the 24th

Well, I'm going to close for now. I'm too excited to write about anything else. Let me hear from you soon. I don't think I can wait two months!

Lots of love, Anne

PS Small detail...I haven't asked for the days-off from work yet. I'll let you know how that goes.

Bombed Out Beirut

September 11, 1989

Dear Anne,

Thanks for the call today. I was really needing some good news. Using snail mail to arrange a time to call is difficult, but we managed it. My trip down to the hotel was fraught with perils…more on that later. I really can't believe that we are meeting in London. It seems too good to be true...I needed to hear your confirmation that it was real. Moving has been a lot of work and I hate to use this word...I've used it so much…*stressful.* I think I may be too old to start this kind of lifestyle…maybe twenty years ago, but bumping forty is just too old. I will be glad to see you in person and get your opinion on how much this experience has aged me. To be honest, I know it has only been three months, but I feel like Sicily time should be measured in dog years. I think I've lived an entire lifetime since I've seen you. I am pretty gray and I'm expecting to be good friends with Lady Clairol before I get back to the states, if I live to see that day.

The furniture was delivered on Wednesday and I have been digging through the rubble ever since. Whew, it is a lot of work and I'm the only one doing it. Wouldn't you know it, the ink wasn't dry on the contract before His Majesty informed me that he hates the place. He says it has no view, is not a grand villa, and is just too ordinary. It certainly is not what we had in mind, but I think the positives outweigh the negatives by a long shot. So, it is up to me to turn this place into something that meets his standards, and unless I can magically change this downtown apartment into an isolated villa by the sea, I'm afraid I'm never going to make any headway there. Go figure!

Buses run all day, to and from here to the base, every thirty minutes and the children have a short bus ride to school and back. The apartment is unquestionably safe, with those landlords poised to react to every little peep, and we can leave to go traveling anytime and not worry about being robbed. I'm satisfied and not too worried that Hubby is not. I have had eleven years of experience on that front too!

He called up to me on the balcony this morning as he was leaving for work and was slamming the outside gate, "Well, unless a huge condor swoops down and plucks you off the balcony, I think you're safe!" He is so cheerful in the mornings! I wish he could see that with the kids in school all day and him at work all day, I would not feel safe alone in the middle of nowhere. This apartment does allow the children easy access to the base for extracurricular activities. Besides, I came here to mix with the locals and not just gaze at the Mediterranean Sea. Did I tell you that the people who took the beach house that we turned down have already been robbed and moved out in fear for their lives? They weren't home during the robbery, but the whole house was destroyed. The robbers even cut the head off their daughter's doll. They had to pay out-of-pocket to be moved out and find a new house. That could have been us, but he doesn't see that. We are both disappointed that we didn't find the perfect Italian villa, but I was tired of looking and just ready to try to get back to some sense of normalcy.

Our last few nights in the hotel were highlighted by a spectacular show from Mt. Etna. He insisted on grabbing the camera and driving up to get a closer look. We went as far as the *polizia* would allow and he got his photos, and boy was I glad to put some distance between me and that natural wonder. The kids were fighting in the back seat and he was accusing me of being afraid of everything...I told him yes, it was fascinating…so is Pompei, and I hope to live to see that ruined city soon.

The move-in day was taxing, to say the least. Whew, what an arduous operation. Luckily, most of our household goods made it intact. There's a huge gouge on the top of the pine dining table, but other than that, it's all here. What was I thinking to bring so much? Guess I don't travel light. The movers were nice young Italians, but they did have a devil of a time getting that piano up three flights of stairs. They put a small scratch on the stairway wall and the landlord came out and screamed for about an hour as the movers were about halfway up to a landing with the piano strapped to their backs. His wife came out and joined in. The movers screamed back and this went on and on. You have never heard such a hell raised in your life!

Signore Antonio Santanocito wasn't too friendly the first day we met. He was wearing one of those black buttons pinned to his lapel that Italians wear indicating that he was mourning someone's death, so I had chalked it up to that. But NOOOO. He's a certified #1 grouch and his wife is, too. Leave it to me to pick the only cold-hearted Italians in Sicily as landlords. Score one for Hubby.

After that crisis passed, everything else went alright. Then Sunday the kids were bouncing a ball on the balcony, the only place outside they can play, and Santanocito came out and screamed at them and told them to stop. I learned a new Italian word, *BASTA*! Which means stop, enough! He tried to explain that during *reposo* (rest time) from 1:00 to 4:00 PM everything has to be quiet. Well, that's a crock with three kids.

Today was the icing on the cake. I was headed to the hotel to be ready to receive your call at our scheduled time and I accidentally let the Fiat roll into a garage pillar. I had opened the Fort Knox doors to the garage, which weigh 500 pounds each, and backed the car out and had gotten out of the car to close the doors. I had pulled the emergency brake on the Fiat as the driveway is on an incline and almost had the doors closed, when I realized the car was rolling right toward me. I pushed the doors as hard as I could to open them, turned to run, and try to jump in the car to stop it. I fell and ripped my pants, skinned my knee and foot, lost my shoe, and thought I was going to get run over by the car. I scrambled out of the way, stood up, and tried to catch the car, but it had gotten away from me and was rolling right into the garage and right for Signore Worst Landlord Ever's new car! Well luckily, the Fiat veered off just enough and hit the huge garage piling instead, which did sound awful, I will admit. The impact actually rocked the house but it could have been so much worse. Within seconds, both the landlord and his wife were screaming at me at the top of their lungs. I was standing there, bleeding and crying, and trying to explain in my woeful broken Italian what had happened. I was also thinking I was missing your phone call and these people hate me and have now labeled us as the "Home Wreckers" or "Worst Ever Tenants." Eventually, I got the nerve up to try to get out of there again and get down to the phone call. If I sounded a little shook, I should have. I need a nice quiet vacation in London. Let's don't plan anything too demanding, as my nerves are shot. No wonder my hair is graying. I am thinking I will try to make the landlords some chocolate chip cookies, but they better be powerful good cookies if I think I'm going to mend this relationship. This is so very disappointing to me as I imagined a good relationship with them and it is off to the rockiest of starts. I hate to say it, but I think it's not even salvageable at this point. Fate is against me here or they are impossible people. I'm not really sure which. That is unfortunate because I genuinely do like our apartment.

We get one American channel on TV, using an antenna that we move around the living room to get a sharper image. We get the *Today Show* live at 1:00 PM and CNN several times a day. Most of what is broadcast on this one station are old last season's reruns, but they show some CNN, the *Today Show*, and *Nightline* live. If we lived further away from the military base, we wouldn't get any American TV.

I am liking Motta Sant' Anastasia too, my new hometown. It is a horse of a different color. Get Sister Gretchen to look up St. Anastasia and see what she is famous for. Her remains (or at least a part of her) are here in the church. The legend is that her remains were being moved on a donkey and the donkey stopped here and refused to move. They then put the remains on another donkey, and it refused to move. When a third donkey was tried, it laid down and died. So, they were pretty sure she was supposed to be buried here. Thus, the town was started. I've researched her a bit and it appears that the early church powers horse traded in the human parts of deceased saints like currency. Some churches got a finger, some an arm. One day, as Jackie and I were out in town shopping, we stopped to watch a very solemn church processional through the streets. They were carrying a huge statue, candles, and a box containing whatever relic that is vaulted away in the Sant' Anastasia Cathedral here. It must have been a special Saint's Day, and we paused to observe it pass by and Jackie said, "Wonder who got her clitoris!" Ha! As I said, she is a rip-roaring companion to have around.

The first time I rode through this town, I thought it was shockingly ugly because many of the houses are unfinished on the outside. Seems the Italians don't have to pay taxes on their property until it is finished, so they never, ever finish them. Jackie refers to it as "bombed out Beirut" and in places, it does look like what you can imagine unfinished re-bar and concrete would look in all stages of construction or destruction. Ha! But on the whole, I find the town charming, especially the oldest section, and the whole place has really grown on me. I love the bars, the bakeries, the total atmosphere.

Well, the house is quiet, they are all asleep. Hillary didn't win president of her class, but she took the loss well. She got accepted into the school band and is drawing cartoons for her class newspaper. Matthew cried tonight and said he missed his friend MJ. Drew's teacher sent home a bad report saying that she was talking too much and she cried over that. I told her to not worry over it, just try to listen more, and to know that the art of communication when used wisely is a lovely gift.

Love to you all,
Susannah, *Baronessa di* Pilgrims

PS Nov. 23 is just ten weeks away. I think I can hold on until then!
PPS Don't invite anyone to join our trip, please. I want you all to myself for uninterrupted therapy!

Sue and children on the balcony of their apartment in Santanocito's house

September 17, 1989

Dear Sue,

I've been waiting for your *after-the-phone-call* letter because I wanted to *read* in black-and-white that we were going to do it! I am so excited about our trip! It's so neat how things turn out. I miss you so much, but your trip to Sicily is going to be a gift in so many ways. You and I would never have been bold enough to schedule a trip for two while in Morehead. And it's going to be worth the six months apart to be together for six days with no one else. *I repeat*...no one else to worry about. No one else to try to keep happy. Have we ever had that luxury? No! I feel like I lead a charmed life. It's so wonderful having you as my best friend! It was interesting that you mentioned my inviting my sister Susan in your letter. No, of course, I didn't. But we (Susan and I) had mentioned her coming here for Thanksgiving and I did feel guilty telling her about my change in plans. She said she understood, but felt left out. She's having a hard time letting go of her past with her ex and I'm her biggest support right now. She's been wanting me to go on a trip with her and I just haven't been able to consider it. It's just not the same as going with you, but I shouldn't have to feel bad about it. Anyway, I never for a moment considered bringing someone along. Although speaking of sisters, Chris was all ready to come with me and go back to Sicily with you when I told her. She likes to plan and talk without much follow through, so I wasn't really worried, and my good deal for the price on the airline tickets ended on September 15, so we're on our own. I can't believe it! Please, please rack your brain to see if you come up with anything, and I mean anything, that you, M, or the kids want from the here. I'd love to do that.

This week of work went better than last, maybe because of the trip, or maybe because I got paid. It's a difficult job working with these kids. It's the type of job where you may spend all day working something out, only to have the student drop out or, if not that drastic, repeat the same mistake that got him or her into trouble in the first place. I'll bring you up-to-date on the job when I see you.

We had our first group get-together for the returning drop-outs. A representative with Community Action which focuses on helping drop-outs was there. She is very positive and I like her a lot. Her job involves going to homes, county jail, anywhere the drop-outs are, so I don't have to do that right now. A lot of kids are enrolled back in school but are already cutting class and skipping school. Many are already having to do in-school suspension. The teacher who has the in-school suspension program full-time was promised a coaching job this year but, instead, the-powers-that-be hired a new coach. He seems really bummed about continuing the in-school suspension position, which to me is a bad way to start the year. I really feel sorry for him. I hope this county doesn't screw me.

I know you're glad to be settled, but what a job getting settled! Thank goodness your stuff was okay. An exchange student who was here last year, whom Sister Gretchen had befriended this summer, wrote that on her return trip to Spain all the new things, such as gifts, were stolen from her suitcase with everything else left untouched. It's not just Sicily...the world is full of thieves and she wasn't even

American. I would love to see your apartment and meet your wonderful landlord. It must be strange to be under a landlord again. The kids will win him over and, before long, he'll be a pussycat.

Several people at school mentioned Mt. Etna's activity to me. You're making international news! But just think, you don't have to worry about hurricane season. Is that an even trade-off?

Alice stopped by this afternoon just to say hi and bring two shirts she had bought for her boys which they think look too much like girl shirts. She didn't know you were in Sicily and was she ever jealous! She said that she would give anything to live overseas for a while. I told her, like I tell everyone, that all of you are loving it and living it up. Can you believe she turns 45 this month? She looks great!

Well, everyone is in bed, so I'm going to wrap this up. I hope your knee has healed, and that it is a little more soothing living in your own place with school started and a schedule for the kids. We are more or less getting into a schedule. By the way, when are you going to tell the kids about our trip? I'm scared to say anything until my bags are packed and I'm heading out the door! Even if the trip isn't fabulous and, of course it will be, I've felt so good since I started planning for it that I've already gotten my money's worth! Aren't we great?

More later. Charles has been perusing tennis magazines to find a week or weekend-long tennis camp in Southern Pines or Hilton Head that he can schedule. Fine with me. Is M going to try to get even, too? Actually, Charles has really been positive about this whole idea. Take care.

Love to all, Anne

September 22, 1989

Dear Sue,

Well, I guess you've been hearing about good old North Carolina on international news this week. That was quite a hurricane and we were extremely fortunate here. It was hardly even stormy. We only lost a few small tree limbs and one day off from school. I thought of you a lot and wondered what the news sounded like halfway around the world.

I'm sending you the *News-Times,* mainly because of Carol's award, but also thought maybe you'd like to read the paper for old times' sake. The superintendent initiated that award at the beginning of this year to honor an educator every week. Carol is the second recipient, which doesn't surprise me. What does surprise me, however, is that I'm the third recipient...that's right, Old At-Risk Annie! Dick nominated me and, lo and behold, I got it. I've been interviewed by the Board of Education's publicity person and I guess the article will be in the paper next week. Actually, it's been embarrassing. I really don't feel like I deserve it. I hope that the teachers don't hate me, being so new and all. Oh well, it is flattering, probably says more about Dick's persuasive writing ability than my a*ccomplishments.* Yes, you will be getting a copy of that paper, too. The interviewer asked me if I had any plans for the $50 award and I did, but was hesitant to tell her because I wasn't sure that I wanted that information printed in the *News-Times.* I am planning to use it to take you out to dinner in London. I feel like it's your award, too. You would be getting it if you were still in this position. I told the interviewer the whole story about our trip, off-the-record. I love telling people about our plans.

Work was better this week. I keep remembering what you said about being so busy all day in this job. It's true. I am getting to know these kids and I really like them, but they are so mixed-up and have so many conflicting sides to their personalities. Of course, this school has problems, too. The principal has an incredibly short fuse and a real need for power. I'm sure it goes along hand-in-hand with being a principal, however, sometimes he reacts too fast and too harshly. I've witnessed a shouting match between him and a student in the front office. I feel that there are more effective ways to deal with (and model for) adolescents. He jumped all over me on Thursday and, if I hadn't been expecting it, I would have probably burst into tears. The encounter did shake me up. I had told a chronic skipper and in-school suspension regular that I would be willing to throw a party for her to celebrate her last time in ISS if she agreed to make it her last. It was one of those things that just evolved and my gut feeling said, "Go with it." I told her to make out a *guest list* and we scheduled the celebration for 9:00 the following morning. I wrote passes to teachers and got Cokes and Better Cheddars, etc. There were only four girls present, two who were serving in-school suspension and two who were being excused from class. We were in the conference room in the office. It went great. The girls all decided not to skip or get ISS for thirty days and, if they were successful, we'd celebrate again. I think it made them feel special and empowered to chart their own future actions.

The four students were safely back in class when the principal stopped me and asked about *a party,* insinuating that I was undermining ISS by pulling the two girls out and that the other two needed to be in class. He had not yet mentioned my award and I am not sure if he even knew about it, but my having just received it gave me confidence that I was in the right. I answered his questions, using phrases like *peer support, peer witnesses, behavioral contracts,* and *positive approaches to changing behavior.* What could he say? This is my job. This is what I was hired to do. It is hard, though, because I think the criticism initially came from some teachers. I am still really glad that I got this job. Isn't it something the way it worked out? Clearly, he is not handling the stress of his job very well. I recovered from the confrontation on Thursday but realize, too, that he and I see things very differently.

Saturday morning

I want to get this letter mailed today, so I will close. I hope that you are feeling at home in your apartment.

Charles just got back from playing tennis and it just started raining. My turn to go out, wouldn't you know it? But I'm going. After yesterday home with the kids, I'd happily go out alone in a blizzard...or a hurricane! Take care.

Love, Anne

Working out the Kinks

September 25, 1989

Dear Anne,

We had a great weekend, another island excursion. This time to Lipari, which is the next island over in the Aeolian chain. We took the car and went on the slow car ferry, a big steamship-looking vessel where the cars are stored in the belly. We got to Lipari and had a reservation at the Hotel Poseidon. We asked several people who should have been in the know, but no one had ever heard of it. We searched for almost an hour and no one had a clue. We were pretty exasperated. Finally, we got the bright idea to write it down, and of course, everyone knows the Hotel PO-SID-EE-ON. Our pronunciation was throwing them off. So much for feeling like we aren't dumb Americans.

Lipari is marvelous, lots of amazing shops and restaurants and is about as picturesque and charming as can be imagined. Nice sand beaches and a huge pumice quarry that is right on the water. It's about 80 feet high and people climb to the top and surf or roll/slide down. The kids loved it because it's like skiing and the pumice is snow white. Sure hope it's not harmful to the lungs or something. There is a nice archaeological museum and park. The Hotel Poseidon was lovely and full of "Calgon moments," little alcoves, and as beautiful as I could imagine. I really want to meet the person who designed and decorated the place.

We met a lawyer from California and had dinner with him. He travels all over but said he made a point to spend a month in the Aeolian Islands every year. He doesn't have to convince me that they are unique. I'm sold. We want to see Rome, Venice, and Florence, but right now we cannot get enough of these islands. There are five more to go and they are all stupendous. This one, Lipari, is just full of charming shops. Oh, to be rich...I could do some major shopping here.

I am liking our apartment more and more and seeing the wisdom of having chosen something simple and secure. The kids seem content, the decor is taking shape, still a bit sparse, but I am adding to it daily. I've purchased a small wooden table and chairs for the kitchen, a bookcase, a small hutch, a rug for the living room, which is berber like your carpet, and a red and white art nouveau chair for the living room. We had to buy a gas stove and some kitchen cabinets, too. It has been fun seeing it all come together.

Well, the biggest news is we had to do battle with the school system here in defense of Drew. Remember I said Ms. Schultz was the no-nonsense type when I first met her? Well, that's the understatement of the year. More like a Nazi, Simon Legree type, or Attila the Hun. Every day for the past few weeks, Drew has come home in tears saying she hated school, hated her teacher, and hated Sicily. Ms. Schultz had sent home a bountiful supply of unhappy faces all over her work. On some papers, clearly partially completed and correct, she had written great big red zeros. She had also sent us several bad reports saying Drew needed to learn to follow directions. It was puzzling, as we both know sweet, cooperative Drew never received an unhappy face all through kindergarten. When Drew finally opened up, after saying she was planning on throwing herself off the balcony, she proceeded to tell us that Ms. Schultz had hit students over the head, refused to let anyone go to the bathroom, one poor boy wet his pants, and took up Drew's paper before she was finished, tore it up in her face, and threw it in the trash can. So even though I did not want to intervene and be one of those complaining parents who pretend their child can do no wrong, I thought I better try to do something.

We called the school and requested a meeting. They wanted to know the reason and we told them. They scheduled a meeting with Ms. Schultz, the principal, the vice-principal, the guidance counselor, and a union representative. We started off by sharing some background on Drew, that she had been in a small private Catholic school for kindergarten, but had always been an easy child and a happy one, too. We stated the rigid practices that Drew had informed us of and…get this… Ms. Schultz admitted to all the offenses and was very belligerent with us. The guidance counselor suggested that Drew work through her problems. I stated that in my opinion, the problem did not lie with Drew. I also stated that I was not flexible on any idea other than removing her from that classroom and placing her in another, otherwise, I felt I had no choice other than to home school her. I would not abide any more stress for Drew as she had left her family and friends and loving school back home and at six years old needed an opportunity to feel safe and untroubled. She was new to this lifestyle and was doing her best to adjust to the culture shock and I thought

Ms. Schultz was one area of stress that could be eliminated. Anyway, to make a long story short, WE WON! They moved her to another class and she now has the sweetest teacher, Ms. Webb, and we now have our sweetest of all daughters back, loving school and loving life. Sometimes you have to break some eggs. I'm just so glad it is over and Drew is out of that crazy teacher's clutches. Talk about having issues. I just felt sad for the other students.

We went to school's open house and I really like all of their teachers. Hillary has band, music, art, computer class, Italian, PE, and six other subjects. That should keep her busy. Matthew's teacher Ms. Wells, the one I said might have a drinking problem, is really a hoot and right down Matthew's alley. Whether he learns anything or not, he is so happy I wouldn't rock that boat for anything.

I am counting the days until our trip. I have broken the news to the kids and they took it fairly well. They don't understand why I get to go and they don't. They think I'm a little mean, and I guess I am, but nobody is going to rock that boat either, Lord willing! I feel a little guilty, but not enough.

I had an article on dropouts that I was going to send you, but Hillary needed a current event article and there was nothing in the house but that one, so I had to sacrifice it to her education. Basically, it said teenagers are working all these low-paying jobs and not studying. Car insurance and clothes budgets are making them stupid and sleep-deprived. How true! America better take stock and value education or we will probably end up with a moron for president one day! Well better close for now.

Much love.
Susannah, *Baronessa di* Kinky Stuff and Problem Solvers

All the News That's Fit to Print

September 28, 1989

Dear Anne,

I saw Carol's picture in the newspaper and am delighted to hear that you will be the next recipient of the outstanding teacher award. Both of you deserve it, and more. I sure do have the best friends and that statement is documented by the *Carteret County News-Times.* Can you believe that my mother has paid for me to receive a weekly subscription to that paper all the way here in Sicily. Hint, hint…much? Boy, that's not very subtle propaganda. Little did she know, I could hardly stand to read it when I lived there. Anyway, I look forward to seeing your smiling face in the upcoming edition.

I am glad that the job is turning out well for you. That principal does leave something to be desired in the area of positive feedback. He always seemed stingy as hell with any kudos, so I don't think you should expect any. The whole staff is such a fruit bowl. I hope they like you better than they did me, as several made it plain that they thought my job, helping students, was a waste of time and money. I think the in-school suspension program is a waste of time and money. I wish I had a dollar for every time I walked in there and all the students were asleep or staring off into space. Not only a waste of time, but also, I am not sure that the message it sends doesn't do more harm than good. All I can think to say is "*Illegitmi non carborundum,*" which translates to "Don't let the bastards grind you down!" Good luck, go forth, and save those kids! But enough of work stuff!

Everything here is settling down into a routine. Each morning when the kids leave for school, I turn on the TV and watch *Nightline* with Ted Koppel which comes on at 7:00 AM. It's broadcast live, so I guess it's 1:00 AM in the States. Doubt you're up watching it but it keeps me abreast of world events. Another plus of this Motta apartment is that we are close enough to the base to get the one American television station called SEB, Southern European Broadcasting. Jackie's husband, Rex, is the chief engineer there.

We have an intercom system on the front street gate so visitors can buzz us from outside. An Italian just buzzed trying to tell me to move my car out of the garage because they are tearing up the street and I won't be able to get it out later on. He was yelling and flailing his arms and it took me forever to decipher that conversation. Boy, this language barrier is killing me. Just went out and moved the car to a side street for now and Mt. Etna just burped out a huge cloud of smoke. Must go take some photos of it. It has been putting on a remarkable show lately. The Italians say Etna is their friend. I am still not on a friendly basis with her as of yet, only an acquaintance...not sure I trust her completely.

We have met an American family down the street with two girls the same ages as Hillary and Drew and they are becoming fast friends. Drew's birthday is next week and I am planning a little birthday party here at home with cake and ice cream then down to the base for bowling and then out for dinner for everyone. Drew likes school now and I am so thankful I stood up to the bully Ms. Schultz. Her new teacher, Ms. Webb, is wonderful. I am so very glad that I marshaled the nerve to nip that in the bud early on because now things are going very well. You win some of the time, it seems. I'll close on that positive note.

Much love,
Susannah, *Baronessa di* Fourth Estate

October 1, 1989

Dear Sue,

I can't believe how hard it's been to find the time to write you. I imagine it's the same for you now that you're in your apartment. Are you eating out a lot or have you switched over to the housework/cooking track? It's a drag. I have never lived in a hotel for three months, so maybe being able to cook again is a welcomed change. Do you do all your grocery shopping on base? What are Italian grocery stores like...little neighborhood stores?

We all sure miss you. I have, especially, this fall. Maybe because I was pregnant last year, but daily I remember what I was doing a year ago and I get very nostalgic.

Saturday Charles and I drove to New Bern to take the kids to Billy Benners' studio for pictures. I thought about you so much and wanted to talk to you about the mundane, piddly, everyday things that we used to talk about. We went to the mall afterward and I saw two women with their daughters, both girls under two, and they were talking about this and that, just like we would have. I am relying more on Charles, but it sure isn't the same. After the picture-taking session, he told me that he didn't like the outfits that the girls wore (although truth be told, he didn't really care). He had not laid eyes on them until Billy was taking the picture. Not earthshaking either way, but I know you understand the time and effort I put into getting three children ready for a studio portrait and how insulted and dismissive Charles would have acted if I had asked for his input and involvement ahead of time!

We had Stephen's birthday party Thursday night. It ended up being quite a crowd and went on rather late. Charles' mother brought fried chicken, potato salad, green beans, and biscuits, quite a southern feast. Stephen showed off his walking skills and the girls were a big help keeping him occupied. You'll probably get a letter from Chris describing the scene. She started a letter to you during the party and had several people add their greetings.

The superintendent is going to present me with my $50 check Monday at the faculty meeting and I'd rather be beaten. I hate the attention. I'm glad for the vote of confidence, but I feel the other teachers will resent a new person, with no classroom, getting singled out for recognition. I'm glad to get the money, though!

Is being in Sicily as lucrative as you thought it would be? It doesn't seem to matter how much money Charles and I make, we are always broke! Now we have these extra things, like therapy with Rose twice a month and housecleaning four times a month, plus a new car payment. We must really like being pushed to the edge financially. Saturday in New Bern, Charles bought $300 worth of new glasses and I bought some clothes for the girls and Brownie stuff for Hailey. One of the second-grade mothers has started a troop for second graders at St. Andrews. It just seems like every year, it's more and more.

I've written my friends in London so maybe they will come through and offer us a place to stay. Have you made your arrangements? I'm anxious to hear when you are getting there. I hope it's working out. I've decided to take four days off work and spend the night in Chapel Hill with Susan when I return on Wednesday. I'm afraid it would be too much to land at 8:00 p.m. on Wednesday at RDU and plan to be at work on Thursday.

I've missed getting all the letters from you. I was really spoiled! I'm so looking forward to hearing how you've settled in. How is M reacting to our trip plans?

Charles just left the house to get the classified section of the Raleigh paper. He's ready to quit his job. It drives me nuts when he talks like that. I wouldn't mind moving if, number one, we could handle it financially and, number two, I was sure Charles would be happy with a new job. I think he just wants an ideal that does not exist for him right now. Oh well, I just have to learn to let his complaining fall on deaf ears.

I'll close for now. Hugs and kisses all around! I miss you all. Got your pamphlet on London. "Lady of Shallot" here we come! See you soon.

Love, Anne

Laura, Hailey, and Stephen, Fall, 1989

Wreck and Ruin

October 6, 1989

Dear Anne,

Where should I start? The bad news or the bad news? Don't panic, the trip is still on, it's just that things here have taken a turn for the worst. Remember my telling you that Etna has been putting on a show, well now, expert volcanologists are expecting a major eruption. There are plans afoot on the base to maybe evacuate us and we have been told to have a NEO pack ready at all times, a bag with all passports and important papers, packed and ready if the need arises. What the heck next? I am really surprised that I haven't taken to drink. There are scientists here from all over the world monitoring the activity. An eruption could be anytime between now and March. So, do I Christmas shop this year or what?

The dust and ash are a daily nuisance and the balconies are covered each morning with ash that looks like black sand. They have restricted outside activity and said to keep children from playing outdoors since the ash is like silica, tiny glass particles. That can't be good on the respiratory system. Geez, just what we needed to thwart the routine we were settling into. I am glad I don't live any closer, as our friends who live up on the mountain say their windows shake day and night and the belches are a constant reminder that things are rumbling deep inside the earth. There was a huge eruption in 1649 that covered parts of Catania, which is 30 miles away. Etna is a Strombolian volcano, which means it constantly erupts and does not build up the pressure into a gigantic explosion like Mt. Saint Helens, thank goodness. This type is much safer and most lava flows are rather slow-moving, but I really did not need any more suspense in my life. Thank you very much, Mother Nature.

The other bad news is that I missed the very tight turn in the driveway and managed to cream the right side of the Volvo pretty badly and put a scrape on the corner of this house. I swear I do not think these evil landlords are human. Within seconds, they were there, screaming at me and I know full well that there was no way possible to get to the scene that quickly unless you walk through walls. The Volvo got the worst of it, but of course, these loathsome landlords will probably charge us enough to build a new house. They screamed at me and rolled their eyes and wrung their hands as if I had done it on purpose. Oh well, *mi dispiace*, I am sorry, not exactly how I planned to ruin their day. I do hear that the court system here is backed up for years, so I guess we will be back in North Carolina by the time they try to squeeze that out of us.

A bit of good news, Drew's birthday party was a great success and everyone was well pleased. She had one overnight guest because that friend lives so far away. But a good time was had by all.

I should be able to give you my travel plans for London soon as I have about gotten them nailed down. The best deal for me is to take the weekly charter flight that leaves on Wednesday and returns on Wednesday. That would mean I arrive a few days ahead of you, but I am fine with that, and I will meet you at the airport with bells on when you arrive on Friday. That will put me on my own for Thursday, which will be Thanksgiving Day, the first time in my life to be alone and not celebrating with turkey. I think I will try to find a McDonald's for a variety of reasons. A nod to my American roots and to not having to prepare the feast, besides I am dying for a hamburger. I will say, the Italians make the best french fries I've ever tasted. You can buy them on the street and Italians put mayonnaise and ketchup on them. Yuck. I stick with just ketchup.

Don't be concerned because nothing is going to interfere with our trip. I'll be there come hell, high water, or volcanic eruption. Don't worry about us, either, as I am doing enough of that for everyone. The kids seem to be coping well. They take everything in stride; they accept that volcanoes erupt, that's just what they do. As for me, my nerves are shot. Maybe it is menopause or maybe there is just a new host of Italian worries to go along with all my regular American ones. You offered to bring me something from the States; bring me Valium. Just kidding, I can get that from the *farmacia* anytime, without even a prescription. Just walk in and ask. If you can pronounce it, you can buy anything. I just got some Retin A. It seems so strange to be able to get drugs so freely. Odd, but very convenient. If you need a penicillin shot, just ask. You can get them to give it to you in the store or you can take the syringe home and do it yourself...seems civilized to me, cut out that doctor visit. Well, let's hope they are wrong about Mt. Etna erupting or I will be visiting that *farmacia* daily just as soon as I learn how to pronounce Valium in Italian.

All for now. Love you,
Susannah, *Baronessa di* Cataclysms

October 8, 1989

Dear Sue,

I can't go to bed Sunday night with a clear conscience unless I've written you, so while Charles soaks in the tub, I'll write a quick note. Hope all is well. Morehead had the Seafood Festival this weekend and Charles worked at the St. Andrews' booth the entire weekend. It was very successful. Their Cajun shrimp pita pockets were delicious and a good profit margin for the school. Of course, I was less than thrilled to be a single parent this weekend. I also think I'm jealous of how enthusiastic he gets about helping everyone and working nonstop on these projects. Just once, I'd like to be on the receiving end of that enthusiasm and have my project receive the same degree of dedication.

I saw several people this weekend who asked about you. Miss Kitty and Mr. DB for two. I've started telling people about our trip. For a while, I think I was afraid it wouldn't happen if I talked about it.

I'm so glad you and M bit the bullet about Drew's teacher. What a terrible experience for Drew after having such a wonderful kindergarten teacher at St. Andrews last year. I'm so glad Drew is enjoying school now. We loved the picture of the kids getting on the bus. The only things I want you to bring for me are lots of pictures of your apartment.

I'm enclosing the latest article on me from the *News-Times.* It was nice to get some recognition, but I'm certainly glad that is behind me.

Chris was planning to leave Carteret county for Atlanta and/or Florida but has changed her mind. She quit her jobs in Beaufort several weeks ago and had moved back in with Mom where, I'm afraid, she is wearing out her welcome. Last week she told me she had taken a job at My School daycare for the one-year-old class. I nearly dropped my teeth, then I started laughing! A dozen one-year-olds from 10:00 a.m. until 6:00 p.m. for $3.40 an hour... she had lost her mind! Not surprisingly, she quit after one day. Too much responsibility, different child rearing philosophies, and too much work, I think. I don't know what she will do next. She wants to come to Sicily. She wants to tag along to London, but that's out of the question. She and Mom are driving me nuts!

Charles' grandfather had a stroke and isn't expected to live. He's really suffering. He's 85 years old. Saw Bennie and Vickie this weekend. Bennie and Tommie are going to build a house at East Shore Estates for Tiffany and Stanley. At first, they were going to remodel, but Tiffany kept changing her mind. Now, they are going to build on two lots. That should be interesting.

Well, that's the news. Please give everyone a kiss for me. Two years is certainly a long time. I feel like it's been two years already! Let me know your reservations. I got my new passport. Did I tell you already? Take care.

Love, Anne

Carteret County News-Times
September 29, 1989

At-risk Counselor Named Winner of Excellence Award

Anne Krouse, at-risk counselor at West Carteret High School, has been named the winner of the Educational Excellence Award for the week ending Sept. 22. The award is presented as often as weekly to a school system employee (a non-supervisor) for a specific activity that contributes to educational excellence. Ms. Krouse was nominated for organizing a special guidance session for 20 students who have returned to school after having dropped out last year.

Ms. Krouse said that she was pleased by her recognition, which includes a check for $50. "I was very surprised," she said, "because I know I'm working in a school system with a lot of educational excellence. That makes (receiving) it even more special."

In discussing the meeting she organized, she said, "I was trying to reinforce their returning to school and let them know as their teachers we respect them for taking that step. We also wanted to get some input from them on school and how it's working for them. I wanted them to know their teachers are here for them." Ms. Krouse said she hoped that initial session would serve as a springboard for having the students meet regularly as a support group for one another.

The students did appreciate the meeting, she said, along with other kinds of encouragement they are receiving. "One student told me it made him feel good when a teacher said he really respected him for coming back. That meant a lot to the students. They've kind of gone against the odds coming back."

Through a support group, students will be able to discuss any difficulties they have experienced in returning to school. "I hope I can be a sounding board for that kind of thing," the counselor added.

Ms. Krouse is new to the school system this year although she did work this summer at Carteret Community College in the parallel high school program, which is offered cooperatively with the public schools. She also worked previously as a regional school psychologist in Carteret and Onslow counties.

"I graduated from West Carteret 20 years ago last summer," she said, "so it's been really fun to be back here. Some of my classmates are teaching here now," and so are some of the teachers who were at West when she was a student.

Daily Life in Modern Motta

October 16, 1989

Dear Anne

Got your letter yesterday and was so glad to hear all is well. Our mail has dropped off some now and I'm not writing as much either as some of the new has worn off. We are just coasting along with an ordinary routine of home, school, and daily life. We do have more family time now since we have no friends, to speak of, no TV, to speak of, no social obligations, to speak of, so we are all together in this apartment with time to interact. I like this aspect since we did seem to be all over the place back home with much more going on. Friends, family, school, soccer, and the community really do keep things spinning back in the USA. I spend some of my extra time planning meals and shopping daily for fresh ingredients. There are two little grocery stores here in town called *supermercatos* about the size of a very small Zip Mart, tiny aisles, with lots of pasta, oils, and mainly staples. Vegetables and fruits are at the greengrocers, the meat at the butcher shop, the bread at the *panificio,* so it takes several stops to get it all together. Each neighborhood has its local bakery and there are about four or five different ones in this tiny town. I have found one that still uses a wood-fired oven and the bread is amazing.

Every town has its own market day; here in Motta Sant' Anastasia it is every Wednesday morning, so I try to go there. It has all sorts of food, cheeses, meats, and household items, cleaning supplies, clothing, even some furniture and occasionally live animals, etc. There are about fifty vendors who set up stalls early in the morning in the soccer field parking lot next to the cemetery. There are usually flower vendors there because the cemetery is always unlocked on Wednesday mornings and open for visitation. At 1:00 PM they pack it all up and disperse. The market is fascinating to me and changes each week.

We still eat out frequently as pizza is cheap and delicious. Did I tell you each person gets their own plate size pizza uncut and it is eaten with a knife and fork? Most restaurants offer about 25 different types. The kids love the *Margherita* which means daisy in Italian and is just cheese. I'm hooked on the *Norma* with eggplant and the *Rustica* which is salami and mushroom. Our favorite place in town is called Valentinos and we are on a first-name basis with the staff there. Pizza is their specialty, but they also offer pasta, meat dishes, and the very best spinach I have ever tasted. It is cooked with butter and garlic and melts in your mouth.

Several places in town sell spit-roasted whole chickens called *giarosta,* and they are delicious. The chickens are roasted on large rotating spits with potatoes banked up underneath in a large pan. As the chickens cook, all the juices drip down onto the potatoes. A whole chicken with a generous serving of potatoes costs $3.50. We absolutely love them. An Italian version of fast food. Beats Colonel Sanders in price, taste, and quality, for sure. Another convenience you won't see back home are self-service pumps by the side of the road that look just like gas pumps and you bring your own containers and can purchase wine by the gallon.

But my all-time favorite here are the bars, hands down. The Italian bars are neighborhood affairs much like the *panificios* and are sprinkled all over town. There are five bars in this tiny little town, the Green Bar, Bar Paradise, Old-Tyme Bar, Bar Centrale, and the Mondial Bar, there seems to be one on every corner and I've tried them all. My favorite is the Green Bar. My standard order is a *cornetto marmalade* with a *cappuccino*. I've finally learned how to order those without just pointing and hoping for the best. I've heard that Sicilians only drink cappuccino for breakfast then it's strictly *espresso* for the rest of the day. They sometimes give me strange looks when I order a *cappuccino* at 3:00 in the afternoon. Bars also serve *gelato* and my favorite, as of today, is coffee and hazelnut, *café e nociola*. Everything is made on the premises so each bar has a little different fare and its own sort of flavor. The fancy bars in Catania are a true feast for the senses. I'm a total bar junkie now and may never be able to kick this habit. Guess I'll just have to stay here forever.

Your description of the Benners Studio photoshoot was a hoot and I know what it is like to orchestrate something like that. I remember it well. But the pictures will be great, at least I was really pleased with mine. Also, I got a good laugh from your description of Charles looking for a job! I needed a good laugh because this Mt. Etna thing is no joke. It's funny to me that while my biggest concern is that Mt. Etna might erupt and kill us all, Hubby's biggest complaint is that life here is boring with nothing to do but shop and go out to eat. Typical male mentality, he thinks it's boring and I think it is living on the edge. Oh well, the male mind will never cease to amaze me. Tell Charles I understand the ideal he is looking for and it doesn't exist. At least, I haven't found it yet.

There are days I am thrilled to be here and days I wish we had never come. So, I think that is just life in general. As for us, we are learning so much and traveling and experiencing so many new things, however, the sweet calm picture of home still lingers in our minds and we know that we have given that up for the time being. Sometimes it's worth it and sometimes it's not. We all like it here (except for the bored husband) and we all miss home too. I don't think that will change. It is to be expected. I'm glad we know we can return there eventually. We are just getting our world travelers' sea legs and it is going to take some time to adjust, I think. I am pretty sure Drew is a farmer and not a pilgrim like me, so I think she prefers putting down deep roots and staying in one place.

Our trip to London is pretty much settled now. I pay for my ticket on Friday. The charter flight will cost $184 and I will arrive on Wed. Nov 22nd and return Wed. Nov 29th. Just a month away! Yeah! Can't wait. I sent Ray a prescription that I need refilled and asked him to give it to you to bring to me. Wow, just think, I said bring to me. Can't believe we will be face to face soon.

My language course is still going well and I'm in the second level now. Once I get the basics down, I intend to break into the larger society, if I can. At the moment, I sound like a perfectly fluent three-year-old. For now, I am just a novice, but give me time. I plan to dive deep in this lovely place and wring the essence and suck the marrow before I leave.

Love you,
Susannah, *Baronessa di* Italian
Housewives Extraordinaire

Jackie and Sue at the Motta market, October 1989

Boom Goes the Dynamite

Oct 20, 1989

Dear Anne,

How are things on your end? Mt. Etna continues to smoke, belch and pour out lava. The only town threatened right now is Zafferana Etnea, up high on the slopes of the mountain. The lava has taken over some orange groves and fields but now they have Italian army troops and NATO helicopters dropping dynamite and digging new channels to hopefully redirect the flow. They have volcanologists from Japan and other countries monitoring it. I guess if all else fails St. Agatha's veil will once again be held up by the priest to stop the flow...it has worked in previous eruptions. They are still saying that expectations are for a major eruption between now and March. Not exactly a tight timeline. Unpredictability seems to be the guide word for this place. Part of the charm and the pain.

Motta Sant' Anastasia is really growing on me. It is truly a one-horse town. There is a tiny ancient old man known to everyone as Zunino, the shortened form of *Zio* Nino, meaning Uncle Nino, who drives his horse and cart all over town each day. He picks up things along the road that he finds of interest...Jackie calls him the original recycler.

Most of the time Zunino appears to be fast asleep however the horse knows all the streets and just carries on. I took a photo of him today as he passed by the house. He is a true slice of local color.

The kids have just arrived home from school with the exciting news that they get to wear their Halloween costumes to school on the Friday before Halloween. They were in a frenzy for me to find the costume box from years past and there was considerable shock and grief when I told them I didn't bring it. Matthew said, "Gee Mom, you didn't bring the costumes either!! You only brought the stuff we didn't need." I guess he was referring to all the furniture and household goods, clothes, toys, practically everything we own. Ha! So now everyone is in a mad scramble to come up with ideas. I think Hillary can pull together a cowboy/girl outfit. I now have Matthew dressed in boxers, a bathrobe and high tops, and he is practicing his lines "Float like a butterfly, sting like a bee." Drew is still undecided, but there's always the mummy, gypsy, or hobo that can be pulled together.

I have my ticket in hand for London! I arrive at Gatwick at 16:45 on November 22nd and have reservations at a Bed & Breakfast called Radford Farm for the first two nights. Then I will meet you at the airport Friday morning and we will take the train to London. I could not be more excited. A whole week of you and London; it's combining my two favorite things. Be still my heart. Can't wait!

Much love,
Susannah, *Baronessa di* London Bound

Sunday, October 22, 1989

Dear Sue,

I've broken my pledge of at least one letter per week, so I'm trying for two letters this week. I'm so glad the dates of your reservation correspond so well with mine. Are you flying into Heathrow? My friends wrote and are looking into places for us to stay.

When I got your Mt. Etna letter, I must admit that I felt like writing and telling you to pack up and bring everyone! Charles saw Elizabeth the other day and she said something about London and how M was going there to take a course and you were going with him so I was meeting you both there. Wonder where that idea came from? Is it that hard for people to imagine two women doing this totally on their own?

I am so looking forward to it. I'm going to bring as much money as I can scrape together. I hope that I can pay half of everything, but I do appreciate the offer you made. In an earlier letter you said you'd be clinging to me, begging me to take you home with me. Well, since you are clearly over that desperate phase, it may be just the reverse. I feel my life has reached a frenzied pace and I don't know how much more I can handle. One minute the girls are both angels and the next minute...brats! I feel guilty and worried that they are going to grow up screwed up. Sometimes I think Charles and I just reside in the same house with the same mounting debts. Also, I have traded in a one-hour commute to Onslow county for a rat race here. The job is so big! I have done nothing yet with the Parallel High School for this year and, even without that, I stay at a dead run all day. I can give myself credit for probably keeping half a dozen drop-outs in school, but several others have left. I am trying to be an active member of the guidance department, so I am involved with some of their stuff, plus Dick keeps calling me about generating state reports and statistics for Raleigh. To top it all, I went to the county office on Thursday because I knew my paycheck was in error only to find out I am one of the *few employees* whose salary is lower this year than last year on the *new and better* pay scale! What a bummer! I am still glad that I took this job and that I am not commuting two hours a day and I don't know if I could have handled being a school psychologist in Carteret county.

Charles' grandfather died Friday following a stroke two weeks ago. We all went to the funeral home last night for the visitation. The funeral was today, but after going church this morning and dealing with the kids, it turned out that Charles was the only one who attended the funeral. Stephen, Hailey, and I took a nap and Laura went down to Melissa's (under the threat of a nap if she came home early).

Thank you so much for Stephen's cow suit. It fits him perfectly and looks so cute! Bless his heart, he really is the child of the hand-me-downs so having something new for him is a real treat. I'll try to send you a picture. I wish we could exchange videos. Any chance of that?

The girls have gone round and round about Halloween costumes. I even bought material and started making a Batman outfit for Hailey. Laura looks cute in the Drew's old Peter Pan outfit and may wear it to kindergarten, but then when the girls tried on the two mice costumes from your "Three Blind Mice" last year, that was it. So, two mice it is. Maybe Beatrice Potter's "Two Bad Mice" (I just thought of that). You will be getting my very thankful vibes between now and Halloween because of the work you have saved me. And really, Sue, without you here, it hasn't been enough fun planning Halloween costumes to make it worth the effort. Stephen will be going as a cow, no doubt. Or should I say, bull?

I am going to close for now. If this letter sounds depressing, it's because it is. I'll do better about writing. Let me know about Catherine and Mike in London and your arrival. No other news. Chris moved out of Mom's house and is moving in with friends for a few days at a time. See you in a month!

Love and kisses to everyone,
Anne

October 26, 1989

Dear Sue,

Got your letter today answering some of the questions that I asked in my last letter. Isn't everything working out great?! I can see the headlines now, "Two Mothers of Three Disappear Together on the British Isles. No Foul Play Suspected." I can dream, can't I?

The girls got Hillary and Matthew's letters and have read and reread them. Did you read Matt's? It was wonderful! I miss them so much!

Got the letter with the school pictures and Drew's birthday pictures. Everyone looks so happy and well. I can tell Sicily agrees with them. Hailey, who has been lamenting about growing her bangs out again and her hair to her waist, took one look at Hillary's picture and insisted on immediately going to get her hair cut just like Hillary's, so we did. Thank you, Hillary! Drew's haircut looks cute, too.

I was so excited about your letter with the reservation information. I feel better with all the great arrangements you've made. I'm enclosing my plane reservations. In looking back over both our plans, it seems you will have a longer wait than I thought. Hope it's okay. Keep the reservations at Radford Farm for two nights and then we will plan on somewhere else when I arrive. Although I leave Raleigh-Durham on Thursday at 6:30 p.m., I don't arrive in Gatwick until Friday at 9:00 a.m. I plan to get a good night's sleep on the plane and be ready Friday morning. We will have all day to find a place.

Let's do try to talk before the trip. Send me Jackie's phone number and the time you will be there and I'll call then. If it's 6 or 7 a.m. here, which is a good time for me to call, I think it's around 12 or 1 p.m. in Sicily. Is it exactly seven hours? Your letters arrive a week after you write them, so give me a date about ten days ahead. It will be really easy for me to call you someday around the 17th or 18th. Everything is working out so great. Charles is going to be gone the week after next, so I'll really feel ready to leave him with the kids, as if I didn't already!

I'll write again this weekend. I am exhausted and am afraid this letter isn't going to be very coherent if I go on. See you soon.

Love, Anne

The Good Life

October 30, 1989

Dear Anne,

Got your latest letter and think I'm clear, but not sure. Do you arrive at 8:00 PM or 8:00 AM? We just got back from a shopping trip in Catania and had a big long lunch at the wonderful *Cafe Caprice,* so I've sent the kids into the theatre to get their dinner. I just picked them up from soccer practice. Life is so simple here. I picked up in your letter on all the stress you are feeling with juggling work/home and three children. I know what you mean because the pace was killing me when I was in your shoes. We have traded that for a whole different pace here and I seriously think we have gotten the best end of the bargain. We have to think up things to do on the weekends and evenings. It is wonderful. We have time to think and have a conversation, a luxury that was not possible before moving here.

I know first-hand how demanding that job is. Preventing drop-outs is a big order. There is only so much you can do to change the trajectory of their lives or alleviate the stress that is complicating their access to education. Principals must think you have a magic wand, but really, I think they wonder why everyone can't just be a model student and make *their* lives easier. Ha! My only advice is you must let some things go/slide and not feel guilty about it. Don't go to PTA meetings, cut out anything that is not life-supporting, and give up trying to do everything. I have learned a few things being here, and that is daily life is not all that serious. It seems to me that folks back home take everything way too seriously. Little fish in a little pond. Once your pond gets bigger, you do realize that every little thing is not that critical. Besides, feeling that way sure does take all the fun out of life. Living in that little pond makes you competitive and judgmental. Funny, I don't know anyone here, so when I talk to someone, there's just conversation, like ships passing in the night. No past, no future. I guess that is what is meant by the advice to live in the present. It is hard to do in a small town as everything has such long roots and tentacles...I do know that, but take my advice and say NO sometimes. And don't try to save all of the high school's 1,200 students. Do a reasonable amount and disregard the rest. Life really does go on, regardless of us. Well, got that off my chest....

We went last weekend up on the mountainside and picked up chestnuts. The trees were changing colors and we hiked for a while. I love looking down the broad vistas of the mountainside meadows with sheep grazing. The view stretches for miles, all the way to the seaside. Sicily offers such amazing views and is a feast for the senses. Mt. Etna was puffing out clouds of ash and smoke against the trees and the blue, blue sky. It was lovely and peaceful and a treat for the soul.

Tomorrow I am going to help Matthew's class put on their costumes for the big base-wide Halloween Parade. All the students wear their costumes and parade around all over the base, then have a school-wide party and carnival, and then on to trick-or-treating. The kids are excited and it should be a blast for them. The whole atmosphere here is so different from home. The number one objective of the school here, seems to be, that it must be fun, and they really go all out, and it shows! Amazing that happy kids really do seem to learn better and feel more confident. It does help everyone, students and parents alike, to enjoy their school. I'm so impressed.

Well, better close and hustle these kids into homework mode. I am sorry that the job is overwhelming. I knew it was...just pace yourself and brace yourself as it will probably get worse as the year progresses, with students falling farther behind. Sometimes, I wonder if we are creating problems that don't have to be there. Anyway, hope it helps you to know that I'm happy on the home front. One less thing for you to worry about. We are in Halloween Heaven.

Love you,
Susannah, *Baronessa di Dolce Vita*

Saints and Souls

November 3, 1989

Dear Anne,

Everyone here is coming down from the Halloween sugar high, but I must say the children had a great holiday and really the best of both worlds, Halloween on base, then the Italian All Saints and All Souls Days. There are special skull and bone cookies in the bars and children are surprised by gifts left, according to tradition, by dead ancestors. It is my understanding that Italian children receive more gifts now than they do at Christmas, so I got a few things and surprised the children. I did not tell them they were from dead relatives. That part was a bit too far for me, but the Italians told me that it was not strange for their children because they frequently visit the graveyard to converse and commune with the departed. When in Rome, huh?

Only a few more weeks until I see you in London. I'm counting the days and just hoping that Etna doesn't blow her top before I make my escape. My reservation is confirmed for Radford Farm for my first night. A friend just came back from London and saw two plays and had great fun, but she said everything was expensive and advised me to bring lots of money.

My sidekick friend Jackie is leaving today for a week in Germany. Jackie is so funny, literally the best sense of humor and so outrageous. I probably would have had several mental breakdowns without her. Meeting her in the hotel when we first arrived was a real gift. She keeps me laughing. She and her husband, Rex, are stationed here for three years and she hates the place. Her take on everything Sicilian is so amusing. She can't understand why I would like to live here at all. She is a very positive person and keeps me entertained, especially how she characterizes Sicily and the Sicilians. Her depiction of Sicilian life is hilarious, as she really does think it is a third-world country. She sees her stay here as punishment and prefers a more four-star lifestyle. What I see as rustic and charmingly provincial, she sees as backward and savage.

I was with her at the Motta market on Wednesday and we were looking at all the cheeses. There are whole stalls dedicated to at least twenty different kinds, soft, hard, grated, in wheels, some shot through with peppercorns and spices. I was remarking how the Italians seem just crazy about it and she said, "Yes, they put it on everything, even their cereal." Gullible me said, "Really? That's amazing," and of course she laughed and said, "I'm just kidding." The funny thing was I believed her since I wouldn't doubt it; they liberally put it on almost everything else. She is an amazing woman who can make any situation funny. I am so glad I met her. Jackie is a beautiful soul, but she doesn't see what I see on this island.

On Sunday we went to the Pantalica Gorge about halfway to Syracusa from here, about an hour's drive. The cliffs contain prehistoric tombs that are carved out of the side of the white stone mountains. The whole side of the gorge is honey-combed with them and it made a very interesting hike. The area is referred to as a necropolis, which literally means city of the dead. Our hike was our tip of the hat, I guess, to All Souls Day, November 2nd, the day of the departed.

My latest big find has been an antique store in Misterbianco. I bought two amazing canvas paintings. They both are mounted on brass hangers and look like something that might have hung in a pope's bedroom in the 1500s. The dealer said they actually date to the 18th century and they do look that old. Both depict a woman and child. One is definitely a Madonna and the other is a reproduction of the well-known painting "*La Zingarella,*" the gypsy Madonna, patron saint of travelers and the homeless. Seems appropriate for me, I think. Anyway, I love them both and I am now thinking of starting a Madonna collection since I don't collect anything. I doubt I will get very far with that idea because I think I am more of a sieve than a vault. You are the vault.

No other breaking news, so I'll close for now. Be careful and please don't sprain an ankle or anything to hinder the trip. I'd just die of disappointment.

Love you,
Susannah, *Baronessa di* Gypsy Souls

Hiking the Pantalica Gorge

November 4, 1989

Dear Sue,

It won't be long now! It's hard to believe I'll be on my way in less than three weeks! I am so excited! I think planning this trip has kept me sane. This fall has been so hectic and unsettled. I don't feel I am handling things here too well. Are you enjoying the distance from your mother and in-laws or do you miss their support? My mother, Chris, and Charles' family are really getting under my skin. If I could blink my eyes and be relocated, I'd do it. It is clear to me, however, that I'm not strong enough to actually orchestrate a move. Oh well, more of this complaining when I see you. I can hardly wait!

I'm sending you Catherine and Mike's letter because they gave some London hotel suggestions you may want to check into when you're there. I'm sure that we will want to be close to central London. I wish I were getting there on Thursday instead of Friday morning. Please make any plans for us, such as plays, concerts, and hotels. I trust your judgment completely. As you know, we are kindred spirits.

I'm glad you mentioned the B&B not taking Visa. I'll have my Visa and travelers' checks. I'm all for staying in cheap places and just using them to sleep. Also, I don't mind shared bathrooms. Did you see in the *News-Times* that this is London's sunniest year?

I saw Ray and will get the medicine. I thought I should let your mother know I'd be seeing you in case she wanted to send something, but I don't want to make her angry. Does she know about the trip?

I can't even focus on anything else, so will go ahead and mail this letter. Since I'll be seeing you in person, I will fill you in then on work. Halloween went fine. Beautiful weather. Costumes were a snap, thanks to you. The Carrolls and Mom came over for dinner. For a change, everyone on our street was at home and well prepared for trick-or-treaters. Glad it's over!

We only have time for a few more letters. Everything about our plans seems great. I wrote to Catherine and Mike saying it wasn't necessary to meet my plane since you'll be in the neighborhood by then. I expect Mike may anyway. Hope you don't mind if we see them for dinner one night. You'll like them and I promise, we'll keep it minimal.

See you soon. I'll be the frumpy, middle-aged redhead with a copy of *The Shell Seekers* under her arm humming, "Free at Last."

Love you, Anne

Christmas is Coming
November 8, 1989

Dear Anne,

The kids went off to school today in coats and sweatshirts as today is the first chilly day we have had so far. It is bright and sunny and cold. Mt. Etna is wearing a blanket of white snow on top. That is an amazing sight to see at dusk, the white snow and the top glowing red. An incredible image, to say the least. Guess it will be colder in London than here. I'm starting to pack, are you? Things here are quiet. The kids had a soccer match on Saturday and then we went to a fall festival. On Sunday, the bicycles finally got put together and the kids rode around and around the paved driveway, happy as Christmas morning. It was really a bit sad because they will never be able to ride outside this gate, but they were happy for a day.

Drew came in from school yesterday with a question which was, "Why aren't we going to move into our old house when we go home?" I told her we sold it and were going to buy another one. She said, "Well what if we don't find one before it gets dark?" I laughed and told her we would be staying in a hotel until we do find one. I think she has been house hunting with us before and knows our limitations.

I have finished with the stateside Christmas shopping already. I am pretty proud of this, but it was because I had a steep deadline as we need to get them mailed by November 15th to ensure they arrive by Christmas. It was hard to decide what to get everyone. I hope they are not disappointed. I have visions of everyone unwrapping their gifts and saying, "This is what she sends from Italy??" Oh well, what's done is done. Mark that off my list.

Got your letter and did choke up at the end when you described yourself as the middle-aged redhead like I wouldn't recognize you at the airport. I've been leafing through a book from the library called *The Pasta Diet*. It promises 10 pounds weight loss in 14 days. The recipes look too good for any hope of that! I suppose if you only eat a spoonful. I am desperately fat now and think I am beyond help. I am thinking of having my face liposuctioned. So don't expect me to look slim and stylishly European when you see me at the airport. You will recognize me, I'm sure. I'll be the fat dark-haired lady snacking on Cheetos.

See you soon, Hurrah, hurrah! Whoopee!

Susannah, *Baronessa di*
Middle-Aged, Overweight Women

Death in the Family

November 12, 1989

Dear Anne,

We have been here exactly five months today and I've survived it. There has been so much to learn and adjust to, and I think I've barely scratched the surface. But I have survived and the surprises keep coming. As a matter of fact, last Thursday night we got a great big one. Better sit down for this one. We had an earthquake! The real live thing! We were all sound asleep at about 4:15 in the morning and there was an ungodly explosion. Now we know it was an underground explosion. I thought Mt. Etna had blown her top from the way it sounded. We both sat up immediately in bed. That in itself was remarkable for sound sleepers, but it was like no other sound I've ever heard. Very loud, like the center of the earth groaned. Actually, I think the geological plates that push against each other slipped and made a noise that was unearthly and indescribable.

After we sat up, we both tried to get out of bed but strangely we couldn't. The concrete walls were moving back and forth in a way that was so disorienting, we couldn't move. It was so foreign to our orientation that we were really unable to function, like being frozen. Strange beyond strange. Everything was shaking, glass rattling, water sloshing, sounds coming from everything moving around. It lasted only about twenty seconds but felt like a lifetime. We never did make it out of bed until the moving had completely stopped.

We are certainly thankful that as earthquakes go it was a small one, but it was enough for me to know I never want to be in a big one. It did no damage to our house. Other people in town had cabinets turned over and things knocked off the walls. It was extremely frightening and that was damage enough. It really shook me up, to say the least. To see the solid concrete walls moving back and forth to that degree was startling. We had referred to this house on many occasions as the concrete vault and I kept thinking, "Is it a good vault or a bad vault?" After things quieted down a bit, Hillary called from her bedroom and asked, "Mom, was that an earthquake?" With a very heavy heart I had to say, "Yes, darling, I think it was." I had so much guilt at that moment that perhaps I was risking the lives of my children in this folly. All kinds of thoughts went through my mind. How do you tell your daughter to just go back to sleep after that?

We made an inspection of the house and by that time the whole town was up. Many people were in the street since most Italians know enough to leave their homes and get in an open area in case of other quakes or after-shocks. All seemed okay in the house, except our one goldfish was floating belly up. I found that strange because he had been fine earlier so I think the explosion frightened him to death; I know it almost did that to me. I think another casualty of this episode may be my sense of humor as I did not find it amusing in the least.

We probably need to do earthquake drills; however, I don't think there is much chance of getting out of here alive if there is a big one. Just turning those deadbolts six times to get that door open would probably finish us. Anyway, I'm still pretty upset and disheartened by it all. This may be the last straw for this place. The landlord is so hateful and living here with earthquakes is no pie-in-the-sky. Why is it always something? Funny, easing into our new lifestyle had me worrying about so many things…and earthquakes were not even on the list! We are all okay, all systems are still a go for the trip and, by gosh, rain, sleet, snow, volcanic eruptions, or earthquakes will not delay me. See you soon.

Ciao for now,
Susannah, *Baronessa di Pesce Morto* (dead fish)

PS You will be able to recognize me at the airport. I'll be the fat, middle-aged, *white-haired* woman pacing nervously, biting her nails.

Monday, November 13, 1989

Dear Sue,

Got your letter today reassuring me that you had gotten my schedule. I wish I were arriving a little earlier, like a day, but considering it all, I think we've coordinated this trip very well. And do I ever need an R and R! I'm really taking a beating at work. Each day tops the previous one, from the principal. angrily asking me (his at-risk counselor, I might add), "What's in it for you to help these punks?" to the wrath of the department heads when I appealed to them for course-related parallel high school material. All in a day's work. By the way, one of our counselors was physically attacked at school today by the estranged husband of one of the teachers when she attempted to interfere with his trying to pick up his daughter from school. The counselor knew he did not have custodial rights. It is crazy around this place. Nobody in the school is in very good shape. I am not sure that I can save this job for you. I may have to head back to school psych work. Carteret county's special education department is looking good at this point! Of course, what I really need is an escape. A trip to a beautiful European capital with my best friend. This trip is keeping things in perspective for me.

I read and took to heart your letter on leading a simpler, slower-paced life. Of course, it came after I had volunteered to house two teenagers coming to a four hundred delegate high school student council convention here this weekend. They were sweethearts, two black males who were from Elizabeth City and Raleigh. I really enjoyed them and the girls were so excited about having them as guests for the weekend. Although before they came, Hailey asked, "Do they do drugs?" We were only responsible for a couple of meals, overnight accommodations, and chauffeuring them back and forth to the high school. Just another example of my taking on something else. I do worry about my kids' views on other races and nationalities, so I feel it was a nice opportunity for a closer look and some first-hand experience. You certainly have tackled that challenge with your family's immersion into the Italian culture!

I enjoyed looking at the article on the London markets. Will bring it. I have no idea how much money to bring. I'll have my Visa cards, but realize they may be hard to use at some places. I also wish I had a stylish, new raincoat. I've decided that instead of rushing out and buying something acceptable at Belk, I'll wait and we can raincoat shop in London. We are going to have so much fun! It's a good thing you leave home before I do because that leaves me no other choice but to down my Valium and hop on board!

I still have to make the final decisions on what to pack. I'm going to work on that this weekend. I can hardly wait! I'll see you soon!

Love, Anne

In-Flight

Dear Sue,

I'm writing you from 35,000 feet. I know by now that you're safely home in the bosom of your family. I keep having to remind myself this wasn't a dream. I had such high hopes that our week would be perfectly wonderful and it was, in fact, wonderfully perfect!

The time didn't drag too terribly for me at Gatwick. I walked around, bought some chocolate oranges as gifts and a *TIME* magazine and an *English Home* magazine. Since I was pushing that trolley around with my luggage, in and out of the bathrooms, I went, as soon as possible, to check in, about 11:00 a.m. It turns out my flight has "extra security" according to the woman who helped me, so she walked me over to a line in a room where a very nice young man proceeded to take everything out of my suitcases! Can you believe it!? Emptied it completely! Dirty underwear and all. I was afraid it wouldn't all go back in. The English are so cute. He commented on who was getting the doll, as he took the box to get x-rayed, and I ended up telling him the whole story of our rendezvous. I'm so proud of it! It wasn't customs, just security, so he didn't care what I had as long as it wasn't dangerous. Everything went back in and the suitcases were taped shut to indicate they had been inspected and I was rid of them. Actually, the extra precautions made me feel a bit more secure.

The plane is fairly empty. I'm stretched across two seats and it's been a lot more comfortable than the trip coming. Right before take-off, I decided that the more I fly, the less anxiety I have. I was feeling quite smug and a little guilty that you didn't have the Valium. As we were taxiing down the runway, however, I began searching frantically in my purse and swallowed the bitter pill with no water! So much for bravado. The trip was fine and smooth. I watched a movie and tried to sleep.

I was glad I had made the list of purchases for customs. Although they didn't look in my luggage, the customs officer did question me. I had written down everything I was bringing back and came up with $313. The allowance is $400. He asked me what the most expensive purchase I made was and I proudly said, "The shoes I'm wearing!" These are the cutest little lace-up leather boots. So glad you got some, too! Some passengers did get searched by customs. It sure wouldn't have been hard to spend more than $400. I didn't count the gifts from you, which I probably should have.

Well, if I hadn't downed the Valium, I would order some wine and drink to our amazing trip! Just know that I'll be toasting the two of us, in my heart, for quite a while. Here's to friendship! We did it!

Love, Anne

Merry Old England
December 4, 1989

Dear Anne,

Well, how does Paris in the spring sound? I just bet Delta will be running a special. Can't stop thinking about what a perfect week we just had. I have been trying to recreate it in my mind so as not to lose any of the details and trying to decide what was my favorite thing. What was yours? Was it shopping in Portabella Road, Covent Garden, Harrods, or Selfridges? Enjoying the plays *Aspects of Love* and/or *Cats*? I'm glad we did all the tours, even though we had both been before. We had never done them together and that is what made it all so special. I've narrowed my favorite parts down to three things and that will be as far as I can go. Ducking into pubs for warm drinks to fight the cold, drinking tea while having our hair done at Harrods, and of course, our last meal at the Crown Pub which was "British to the bone" with the fireplace blazing. But above all, I think the most special moment was at the Tate Gallery, standing side by side seeing "The Lady of Shallot." Could we have even imagined that experience when we were sharing the *Anne of Green Gables* books and pinching pennies as stay-at-home mothers on Emeline Place trying to budget for diapers and baby food? Well, we did it, and it was real, and it was thrilling. It was perfection for me. It was the best trip I have ever taken and I wouldn't change one minute of it if I could. I wouldn't even change the fact that I arrived a day earlier than you and spent my very first Thanksgiving on my own in a foreign country. I felt so mature, liberated, and cosmopolitan. Like the independent woman that I'm not, but wish to be. Overall, London was our oyster and we did it justice in my book. I kept thinking on the flight home that we couldn't have improved a single aspect of it.

Arriving home was not as big of a let-down as I imagined. Everyone was really happy to see me and I have been getting the royal treatment ever since I got here. It is nice to be appreciated and they really did miss me. I was told that Drew was found several times hidden in the closet, clutching a picture of me and sobbing, but that seems to be the worst of the damage. Hillary helped out by making lunches for everyone while I was gone. I could see by the look in all of their eyes that they now realized that they had better be nice to Mom in the future because she does serve a purpose in this family. Some collateral benefit of the trip, I think.

Another godsend of the trip is that it has decidedly improved my mental state. I can't stop chattering about how great it was. It has inspired me to get busy and plan to see as much of Europe and the world as I can while we are here. We have booked reservations in Berchtesgaden, Germany, for two weeks in February for a skiing trip. And in a few weeks, we are headed to Rome by train to spend part of our Christmas vacation time there. The children get out of school on the 15th and we leave on December 16th. We will be taking the day train which will be safer, I think. Did I tell you that robbery on the train is a real problem? On overnight trips, I was told that thieves actually gas the sleeping compartment, sedating everyone while they sleep, and steal everything, including your clothes, even the earrings out of your ears! When I heard this, I vowed to never ride the train, but Jackie says, "One hasn't fully lived unless you've been robbed on a train." So here we go forewarned, but just hoping we are not underprepared and overconfident, as usual. There is some bliss in being ignorant ...might as well take advantage of it.

I'm hoping a Roman holiday will ward off any homesickness that might crop up during the holidays. I am dreading the holidays a bit, as we are pretty isolated and it might be hard to create a holly, jolly Christmas, given it is just us. We are getting our tree soon and have been making all homemade ornaments since I put all of our Christmas decorations in storage, too... more additional important stuff according to Matthew, that I failed to bring. I did bring the stockings so there is something from home. We are stringing popcorn and cranberries and I'm thinking of making a gingerbread house, Italian villa style. Ha!

It has started to rain here and everything has turned so green. It is the orange season and the trees are loaded. The groves are beautiful and the blood oranges and tangerines for sale all come with green leaves attached and are as delicious as they are beautiful. The weather is fairly cold, but we like the radiator heat that we get for a few hours a day. Can you imagine the government telling you how much heat you are allowed to have? Sicily is strange and beautiful, and if I can tune out the robbers, the litter, the volcano, the earthquakes, and the Mafia, I think I might just love it. Well, all for now.

Much love,
Susannah, *Baronessa di* Hopes and Dreams

PS Everyone here is all excited about the Bush/Gorbachev meeting. The President's helicopter is here and Raisa Gorbachev is supposed to be shopping in Taormina and Messina today. No doubt there will be an entourage and the traffic will be worse than usual, if that is even possible.

Anne and Sue at Portobello Road, London, 1989

December 13, 1989

Dear Sue,

It was truly wonderful, wasn't it? I am still floating, too! My excuse for not writing sooner is that I had decided it was so perfect that it must be a dream and if I wrote you, you wouldn't know what I was talking about. It has been hard, actually impossible, to describe to people what a marvelous trip it was. I think it has been the talk-of-the-town. I did decide in my mind that seeing the "Lady of Shallot" at the Tate was at the top of my list of superlatives, with *Aspects of Love*, the Crown Pub, Harrod's hair salon, and the Italian restaurant following close behind her. Actually, our evening at the Italian restaurant was what I had at the top of my pre-trip list...eat, drink and talk. Oh gosh, remember going to the movies and seeing *The Rainbow* our first night? Oh Sue, everything made our trip the absolutely best time of my life! We did it!

As wonderful as it sounds, I'm afraid Paris this spring probably won't work out as well. I promise, though, we will do a trip again, and it won't be too far in the future. As a matter of fact, I was ready as soon as I got home to begin plans for trip number two. Everything seems to have gone well on the home front with Charles and the kids. He thanked me for going. He says he now feels closer to the kids and has a better understanding of their needs and the ins-and-outs of parenting. I don't know why fathers can't just roll up their sleeves and jump right in the fray of parenting. Is it our fault? Do we stand in the way?

Stephen is completely weaned, although he is now heavily into bottles. After a *little* sadness for the end of our nursing relationship, I feel quite relieved. He is a happy little fellow. Stephen and Charles are quite close. Charles puts him to bed and is now the one getting up with him at night.

I came back to full steam ahead with work, the home front, and at St. Andrews School, and must admit feeling depressed with the end of my brief *jet setting* lifestyle. The Saturday I returned I woke up with a terrible stiff neck which lasted a week. I'm sure it was from the seven-hour plane ride, the heavy luggage, the drive from Chapel Hill, and maybe some tension, do you think? This is such a busy time of year and I haven't done much Christmas shopping. The kids' gifts are done, but I am at a loss for Charles' family and mine. I ended up giving Charles the sweater, socks, and talc I had gotten for him on our trip. He was quite pleased with them. The girls loved the assorted little gifts that I picked up for them and were so excited about their art sets. You could not have given them anything they would have enjoyed more. And it's a blessing that they are not identical! I've been pleased with my purchases and the things I'm saving for Christmas. I've been wearing my shoes and always get compliments.

The girls opened their Christmas box from you, as well as Stephen's box, too. They were so excited about it when I got home. You have done an excellent job with gifts! So European and unique. No five-and-dime stuff here. I will take some pictures, though I'm not sure when. I'm enjoying displaying my hand-painted Italian platter in the kitchen.

Having your gifts early has given Hailey and Laura something to play with as they wait for Christmas. Thank you for everything!

Everything is wide open at St. Andrews with Christmas programs, parties, gifts, plus Haileys' dance recital and both girls' Brownies and Daisies parties. I am afraid I have now joined the ranks of the typical working mother, thanking the stay-at-home mothers for running the show, while I send in juice and money.

Last week I went to an all-day meeting at the county office for all the counselors. I left the meeting about 2:30, decided against going back to work, and thought it would be nice to pick Hailey up from school for a change and enjoy a little mother-daughter time. I arrived at the school a little early and went in to check on whether her class was dismissed in the front or the back for pick-up since it was my first time this year picking her up. When I walked in, the secretary said, "You don't have any kids here." It turns out that Hailey had gone home sick at 9:30! Charles had handled it all, and since Hailey wasn't very sick, hadn't called me. I felt strange, although I know I should be thankful he's so willing to take over and handle things.

I asked my sister what she thought the psychic meaning was of your affinity for hats. She thinks it represents your wanting protection. That certainly makes sense to me since you are living in the shadow of a very active Mt. Etna. Have you been wearing them?

I better close for now. Everyone else in this house has been asleep since 8:30. I can hardly wait to hear about your trip to Rome and your ski holiday. What do you think your plans will be this summer? Charles doesn't think we can afford to make a trip to Sicily and I don't think we can afford not to! I already have the girls' passport pictures. What did M hear from England? Let me know when you can. Most of these airline deals are nonrefundable and, of course, are better deals when made way in advance.

Give everyone a hug and a kiss. I miss you all. We all do. We talk about you guys every day. This has been like the break-up of a close family! The girls are already lamenting how Christmas just won't be the same. Take care, especially when you hit the slopes!

Love, Anne

Buon Natale 1989

December 26, 1989

Dear Anne,

Well, Christmas 1989 is almost ready for the record books. "Whew," said every American mother of three on planet earth, I bet. It is always best when it is behind us, I think. We build up Santa Claus to the point of making kids wild with expectation then always hope that it goes off well. We put pressure on ourselves. I have noticed that Italians do it a bit differently. They don't do many toys at all; you rarely see *Babbo Natale* (Santa) in the stores, but rather the focus is on family gatherings and food. Cakes called *panettoni* are mass-produced in different flavors and eaten all through the holidays. The stores are full of them. I think I like that version of Christmas better. No toys… just let them eat cake!

How was your Christmas? Ours went off pretty well, considering. It was quiet but Santa outdid himself and everyone seemed to receive their heart's delight. Who says you can't buy happiness? You can buy it sometimes. I made a big blunder which I won't repeat again by saving all the gifts from folks back home to be unwrapped Christmas morning, knowing that it would be just us together this year. Boy, that backfired bigly! Each gift made me miss each person all the more and I had a hard time not breaking down completely into a big old cry fest. I think the kids felt it too, but they had so many gifts they were distracted, thank God. The kids loved your gifts and I heard you had a white Christmas with a record snowfall. It was 75 degrees here yesterday. I, for one, am glad it is behind us. It really didn't seem like Christmas much to me, but I did try to keep the mood as jolly as my poor homesick heart would let me.

We did enjoy our Rome trip. Went up on the train and got to visit the Vatican and museum, Coliseum, Forum, Spanish Steps, Trevi Fountain, basically all the main attractions. The highlight for the kids was the new and recently opened McDonald's near the Spanish Steps. It was our first fast food since we arrived six months ago. It was so crowded with a waiting line of hundreds, they could only let a few people in at a time. The menu offerings were definitely Italian influenced with a big buffet fruit bar and also offered wine and beer. The Big Macs were similar and so were the fries. All in all, it was a very nice trip and the children enjoyed it, which was surprising as it wasn't exactly a kid-oriented trip with all the historical sights. I got to see Rome's Christmas decorations so that thrilled me. So glad you and I got to see the ones in London, also.

The train trip home was a real experience. Our compartment seated six and we had an older couple with us who had stored big packages of volcanic mud from the island of Vulcano which smelled, of course, to high heaven of rotten eggs. They broke out their lunch, which they generously offered to share, of salami and olives, cheeses, and many fragrant delights. Needless to say, we spent a lot of the trip standing in the hallway outside our compartment, mainly for the fresh air.

We are leaving for the ski trip in Germany on January 13th for seven days. The kids will be in an all-day ski program, so we can maybe get some side trips to Salsburg and maybe even Munich. I hope we all have fun as I could use a pick-me-up from the Christmas letdown. I haven't been able to fully shake the holiday homesickness, and I haven't heard a word from you. I sure am hoping you got home alright. You weren't hijacked, were you? The mail is probably just held up due to the holidays.

We have a new member of the family, a Christmas kitten, a present for Drew who has been praying for one. It is part Persian and part Siamese and is a darling kitten. Beautiful blue Siamese eyes with a sleek tan coat and brown points. It is a cute little thing but cries a lot. We smuggled him in past the landlords, but I don't know how long we can keep him a secret. We bought him from a lady in Syracusa, who is the sister of Mamma Elio. Mamma Elio runs a restaurant/brothel (seriously) here and is about four feet tall and two feet wide with a distinctive mustache and a rolled-up wad of cash stuffed down in her very generous bosom. I asked her if she knew of any kittens for sale as there are always cats around her restaurant and, luckily, her sister in Syracusa raises them and had a perfect kitten ready for a new home. Drew is crazy about him but hasn't named him yet. He is very affectionate and I hope he makes a good pet, especially because we might get kicked out of here if the landlord finds out. We didn't sign a lease that said no pets, but he is such a grouch, I'm sure he would try to charge us a tremendous pet deposit, which in Italy is never returned, or maybe use it as grounds to put us on the street. I know enough of him to bet that he is probably not a pet lover and wouldn't approve. I don't care. I've given up trying to win him over.

Besides, Drew really wanted a kitten and I thought, well, I could make her happy or Mr. Groucho downstairs and it wasn't a tough decision. So right now, our home rests in the paws of the soon-to-be-named new love of Drew's life.

I will close for now. I cooked the entire holiday dinner and it turned out pretty well. Some things were unavailable but we managed. That's a good way to describe our Christmas 1989...we managed.

Ciao for now,
Susannah, *Baronessa di* Homemade Christmases

January 2, 1990

Dear Sue,

Happy New Year! Yes, one of my *few* New Year's resolutions will be getting back into writing you regularly. I have thought about you, M, Hillary, Matthew, and Drew constantly. Your absence was definitely felt this Christmas. It wasn't the same.

I'm home today for two reasons, even though I should be at work. Mainly, I wasn't ready to face it and, secondly, Stephen has been running a fever (103 degrees last night) and I am taking him to the doctor. He had his MMR shot two weeks ago, and now I'm wondering if that's the reason for the fever, or his ear, or his cold. This is truly the worst part of being a parent. He is asleep right now. He was up a good part of the night. Our appointment is in about an hour and a half.

We got your postcard and Drew's letter. I'm so glad the Roman holiday was successful. I do want to hear more details. And now, you are gearing up for your skiing trip. As you probably know, we had a very white Christmas. It was quite an experience! Of course, the kids were ecstatic and are bound to be disappointed every balmy North Carolina Christmas from now on. The snow started Friday evening and did not stop until Sunday afternoon. I've never seen anything like it. We lost our electricity for about an hour

Saturday morning, which was a sobering moment, but never had any more problems after that. Our Jeep was quite handy. Charles was able to drive here and there, even when the roads were not visible at all. With the Jeep, he was able to take on the role of Santa's helper by delivering gifts to the Guerins, who were unable to get out of their driveway and who had left their Santa stash at Michelle's house.

On Christmas Eve, I was settling in for a very small, intimate family celebration (church services were canceled) when Sister Gretchen called. She was beginning to get anxious about being at home with Granny and handling a potential power outage. At that time, with at least six plus inches of snow on the ground, it looked like a blizzard coming down. So, she started packing up and Charles went and got them around noon. A couple of hours later, I was on the phone talking to my mother, who already had her mother at her house, when she noticed the heat had just stopped. So, to make a long story short, we had a full house. I felt like I was running a combination geriatric ward and daycare. They all stayed two nights. There was still quite a bit of snow on the ground when they all headed home and it was hard to drive anything that wasn't four-wheel drive.

On the 28th as the weather and roads cleared up, Mom, the girls, and I headed to Chapel Hill to visit Susan and Sarah and do after-Christmas shopping. The girls blew about $100 each of Christmas money in ToysRUs. I had convinced Charles that it was child abuse to put a 15-month-old in a car for four hours and then spend time in a house that wasn't baby-proofed, so he kept Stephen while we were gone.

We had a good time and ended up staying an extra day. We were so appreciative that Steve, Susan's ex, who is, of course, Sarah's father, agreed to take care of his daughter and her two cousins for a few hours so that Mom, Susan, and I could go shopping and out to eat. What a gem of a man! Why is it that when fathers agree to take care of their own children, mothers always feel so fortunate and grateful and can't stop lavishing praise and appreciation on the male parent? Something is wrong with that picture.

It is now Sunday, January 7. I did go back to work last week and must start getting the wheels turning for the Parallel High School. I've gotten into spending so much of my time doing counseling and crisis intervention that I haven't had time to set up parent meetings and check student credits.

Due to a blizzard delay, we finally had our St. Andrews Christmas pageant last Thursday. It went well. I helped with refreshments, so ended up being there late. Margaret asked me if Deidre and Henry were having problems. I didn't know but if they are, beyond the usual problems one would have married to a creep, I should have guessed since anyone losing forty pounds is probably anticipating some big changes.

I just realized I never sent you a Krouse family Christmas card. It's a good thing I showed it to you in London. I feel like I'm losing it. Charles and I are getting along better, but sometimes that worries me. There is definitely something missing, like a sincere, mutual desire to maintain a positive connection. I think we are just tolerating each other better. Thank you for all your Christmas cards.

We went and saw *War of the Roses* with Danny DeVito. A black comedy about a bitter and vicious divorce. I liked it, in my own sick way, but would not recommend it unless you are in the mood for that type of story. It doesn't have a happily-ever-after ending.

The Kafers are definitely moving this summer. I don't know how Margie does it with five kids and a Marine pilot husband and the constant moving! Her house will be for sale. I guess the Gapners will be putting their house on the market, too. That house would be closer. I am ready for you to move back!

I am going to try to do better about writing, but I feel I have so little control over my time or lack of it. Having a 15-month-old eliminates any free time. Can you remember those days? He is into everything and, heaven knows, there is a lot to get into. The stairs are his favorite toy.

I am going to close for now. The cleaning ladies come tomorrow and there is so much I have to do before they can clean that I better get started.

Give everyone a Happy New Year hug for me and keep me posted on your traveling. What did you hear from England and what are your plans for staying? Take care.

All my love, Anne

PS Stephen's fever was nothing more than an excuse for me to stay home. Just a cold, which he's over now. Hope all of you are healthy. Careful on those slopes!

Stephen at backdoor watching his sisters in the snow, 1989

Felice Anno Nuovo
Happy New Year
January 4, 1990

Dear Anne,

A new decade…I think that is the first time I've written this new year 1990. I am glad to flip the calendar, are you? It's funny, sometimes I want time to speed up and sometimes slow down. We talked about the fact that both Hillary and Matt will graduate from high school at the end of this decade. Wonder where we will be then?

We enjoyed our New Year's holiday. We drove up on New Year's Eve to the top of Mt. Etna and let the kids play in the snow. They rented sleds and had a fine time frolicking all day, capped off with hot chocolate on the bar terrace. It was our dry run to see what we might need for Germany. We have purchased snow-suits and boots for everyone.

Later that night, we made chili and waited up until midnight. Sicilians shoot off lots of firecrackers and their guns and we were warned to stay behind walls. The town of Motta Sant' Anastasia put on an impressive firework show over our heads and we did risk going out on the balcony to enjoy that. They also have a custom that you should throw something old out the window at midnight, so we all tossed something out with glee. I threw out the old calendar. I aimed at the street so it will just blend in with the other garbage.

Sicilians have the strangest idea on litter. All the houses are walled off and I've heard it said that once garbage is over the wall, it becomes a government problem. Whatever their thinking is, there is about two feet deep of litter along every highway and road. It is a shame as it is so beautiful but only if you look two feet above the ground. I've seen so many adults walk right out of a shop, unwrap a purchase, and drop the paper wrapping right in the street. At least in town, there are street sweepers who use these big witch-like round brooms and I guess it is job security for them. Apparently, they never heard of or weren't impressed with Lady Bird's Beautification Campaign message that beauty can improve the mental health of a society.

A crazy thing happened to us concerning garbage yesterday; we stopped to buy a crate of tangerines from a Sicilian man selling them along the road and got out and paid him. He lifted the crate and we opened the back car door. It was the day after we had been to Mt. Etna and we hadn't had a chance to clean out the car. The back seat floorboard had all sorts of trash and food wrappers left by the kids from our trip up the mountain. The man put the crate on the back seat, paused, looked at us, and shook his head. He then reached down and raked all the trash out of the car and onto the roadside. The look he gave us said, "Why would you drive around with all this trash in your car when you can just throw it out?" We didn't have the courage to disagree and just couldn't bring ourselves to pick it up in front of him, so we just drove off and shook our heads in disbelief. The man thinking that we were just more filthy

Americans, while we left feeling like litterbugs. A little taste of culture clash, I guess.

The Sicilians are double-minded on the trash and the tidiness issue. The Sicilian housewife cleans her house like a fanatic. I have heard that they remove everything from a room and start with the walls and floors and then clean every item before returning it back into place, and they do this once a week! I have seen so many intriguing cleaning items for sale in the market. It is plain that they take a very serious and scientific approach to a clean house. As most Sicilian women do not work outside the home, I suppose they see all that housework as a worthwhile task. I just see it as a necessary evil. So, all the trash outside is a startling contrast. I have also heard that Sicilian women think Americans are slovenly and keep a dirty house and by their standards, I guess we do. A clean house is a point of pride to a Sicilian woman. I'm sure there is more dust in my house than theirs, but I'm usually not a litterbug. Jackie, however, says that one of the few joys of living in Sicily is throwing trash out of her car window!

The kitten, now named Leonardo, has his first vet appointment this week and he seems healthy enough, but I would like to get him checked out. He is very affectionate and I think we should have named him Romeo. We all love him. He has brightened up our lives and seems right at home now.

January 6th is *La Bafana* day, the Christmas witch day, when Italian children get gifts from the witch. They have little effigies of her, riding her broom, all over in the shops and for sale in the markets. The story goes that she was out sweeping her steps when the three Wise Men passed by on their way to Bethlehem and asked her to join them. She replied that she was just too busy, probably doing all that house cleaning. Later, she realized that she had missed her opportunity to see the Christ Child so on Epiphany, January 6th, she goes and looks at all the children sleeping, looking for the Christ in every child. She leaves a gift for each one. I am going to pick up a few things for the children. I think that's a lovely story, but the kids are sort of double-dipping on this Christmas thing.

Well, the rain has brought everything back to green, green, green and it is startlingly beautiful. The wildflowers are beginning to bloom and I may never get enough of the beauty here in the countryside. One problem with the rain is that I don't have a dryer, only an outside clothesline on the balcony so drying the laundry is a challenge. I've purchased a wooden drying rack and with the radiators running a few hours a day, it is working out okay. Well, I'll close for now, it's time to go turn the clothes over on the radiators and rotate the rack.

Guess you are back at work, hope this is the best year yet for you. I am a bit concerned that my career status is null and void. I am hoping to start substitute teaching at the school soon. We were told that there are going to be scheduled flights going back and forth from here to Israel the first week of February so if we can farm out the kids, we might try to hop a flight there. I am waiting before dipping my toe in the work world right away in the hopes that we get to take advantage of a free flight. We want to be ready to grab the rare opportunity of a free trip to Israel if it materializes, as it is not a usually scheduled flight destination. Story of my life…can't afford to work and can't afford not to.

Love you,
Susannah, *Baronessa di* Christmas Witches

January 11, 1990

Dear Sue,

Wow! What a wonderful surprise to receive that beautiful scarf! I love it! Thank you so much. It will go with several things I have, but I think it deserves a new outfit of its own. It's also wonderful to be getting your letters again. As you can probably tell, I had the post-Christmas blues. Anything would have been a letdown following on the heels of our London trip. Reliving in my mind our adventures has kept me going, as well as emphasized the contrast with my daily life. I can still see us enjoying our English breakfast at our B&B served by Mr. Patel, wandering the Tower of London, and watching the street juggler at Portobello while buying my antique coin pin. I like remembering our B&B, which was exactly like hundreds of others all over London. My mood is picking up. We have a holiday Monday and exams next week, which will be interesting. It will be nice to start spring semester. The new beginnings are what I like best about working in the schools. You keep starting over, which, in itself, holds the hope of and the potential for improvement.

January 15, 1990

I am having trouble finding time to write. I really do miss

talking to you. And I am not at all getting accustomed to your being gone. It's actually getting harder for me.

I received my London pictures. I really didn't take very many, but I'm pleased with what I got. The girls love the one of you, as you stand guard at Buckingham Palace; the color of your coat is just right. If we had put our bags down for the one in front of the flower stand, it would be *suitable for framing*. Actually, I think it is now. I'm looking forward to seeing how your pictures turned out. Also, sending some pictures of the kids at Christmas. I've enjoyed the pictures you've been sending and realized that I had not sent you any of us. The kids are six months older, of course, so I know Stephen looks different, as does snaggle-toothed Laura.

I saw Rachael at Rose's office last week. Her appointment was right ahead of ours (everyone here is in therapy since you left). This thing with Harry seems to be getting weird. I'm not sure how often she is seeing Rose. We are going once a week, partly because of work pressures for Charles. It's helping, but we are still only dealing with the tip of the iceberg. In my opinion, we are not going often enough.

I spoke to Charles' sister about the piano and she agreed with me. It should definitely be left in Sicily when you leave. I wish I could come to your yard sale, but then I'd rather be with you here going to yard sales together.

I hope that you won't be too disappointed with me if I say we probably won't be able to come to Sicily. One reason is that even though it would be a very economical trip considering your generous hospitality, at this point, it would almost have to be a money-making venture for us to be able to swing it. I don't know how we manage to go through money like we do. I guess we just enjoy being in debt. The other reason is the possibility you will be back in the States during the summer. If I'll be able to see you in less than a year, I believe I can hang on. Also, I am not finished with school until June 16th and really, the last thing you need is visitors as you all are gearing up to come home. Since we will be traveling with an eight-year-old, six-year-old and 18-month-old, I think spending a week with you guys in a cabin in the mountains of North Carolina in July or August might be more our speed. I don't know what to plan for. I guess it's weird to have me say that. What an understatement for you and M.

By the way, what is administrative hold? Is it like being in limbo? With or without a salary? And where? Does it mean M would have to stay in Sigonella until they get a replacement? Please don't be mad if it sounds like I'm backing out. The trip with Stephen does intimidate me, too. When do you think that you'll know your plans for sure? I remember military co-workers saying they were never sure until they had the final paperwork in hand. Have you told your mother you may be home this summer? I haven't mentioned it to anyone. Charles and I have not sat down and had a heart-to-heart talk about going to Sicily, but that's because every time I try to pay bills and balance the checkbook, I lose my nerve, and also because getting Charles to sit down for any heart-to-heart is like trying to get a two-year-old to focus on a geometry lesson…without the use of manipulatives and M&Ms. Things may change. I did just send in our Publishers Clearing House entry. I may go ahead with the girls' passports. I have gotten their pictures made. I would so enjoy seeing all the places you have been writing about but, of course, you guys are the main reason we'd go to Sicily. Keep me posted on what your plans are when you find out.

Stephen is waking up, so I'm going to close for now. School starts tomorrow and the beginning of exam week. That should be interesting as I ferret out the status of my students, who typically don't even attend class!

Take care. You asked how I felt about entering 1990. I haven't really reflected much on this start of a new decade. Having a baby around, who is changing daily in a very active way (to put it mildly), is about all the change I can focus on right now. Most of the time I just feel I'm in a time warp, not really getting anywhere, just trying to stay afloat.

Well, I promise to write again soon. Take care of each other. I really miss you all.

Love, Anne

PS I bought an outfit for my new scarf!

January 22, 1990

Dear Sue,

I hope the skiing trip was a success. We loved the picture of Drew on Mt. Etna and, for heaven's sake, quit feeling guilty about those ski pants. I was so glad to find a Christmas present she would like and we wouldn't have used them much at all. I'm thrilled Drew is wearing them.

Beth may be writing you and M about her house. I told her you were interested in buying a house and she said they were between realtors. I encouraged her to write you. Then, she said that even without the realtor's fee, they were asking $140,000. Whew! I knew that was out of your price range. I heard that the Gapners will be asking $170,000 for their house. Can you believe it? They are living in a dream world if they think they'll get that much. There are so many houses on the market now in Carteret county. It is a buyer's market. I'm still looking for you.

We had a home school meeting on Thursday. Tiffany announced that the Halls would be back this summer. Then she looked at me as if to say, "Right?" Someone else (I couldn't see who) said, "Yes, they're coming back to stay." I just said that it was a possibility that you'd be moving back. I didn't know how to respond. Are you going to find out for sure before too long? You can't imagine how excited I am, but I'm afraid to let myself count on it. And as you can see, your family is the talk-of-the-town.

I began my CCC schedule this week. On Mondays and Wednesdays, I'm going to the high school at 12:30, then at 3:00 over to CCC until 7:30 p.m. I was dreading the change, but after Monday I feel much better about it. I enjoyed the morning at home, just Stephen and me. Some days I may have Charles' mother come and I'll be able to do errands. I should begin an aerobics class or something. I am enjoying my cleaning ladies, so I don't feel I should spend my Monday mornings doing housework.

Hailey is thrilled about getting her First Communion dress from Sicily! I can't begin to tell you how much I appreciate your generosity and thoughtfulness. We were to have a meeting of First Communion mothers after Christmas about dress details, but haven't met yet. I feel sure the consensus will be white dresses, but that's not to say there can't be any other color on them, like a sash or something. The traditional First Communion dress is all white. I believe the date is a couple of weeks before Easter. I can't remember exactly, April 1st or maybe the last Sunday in March

I really can't think of any other news. Since I know that you are getting the *News-Times*, I won't mention any *real news.* January and February are such quiet, or should I say, dull months around here. I do get such vicarious pleasure from reading your letters. Keep them coming! Hugs and kisses all around.

Love, Anne

PS I'm sure you saw the picture in the paper about St. Andrews Physical Fitness awards with Hillary's name. Later that night I said something to the girls about taking them and the Greenleaf girls to the movies at Atlantic Station and letting them watch a Disney movie while Cynthia and I watched another movie in the same theater. Well, Hailey didn't like that idea, at all. Too scary, she said. And she's probably right. She and Joan would end up having to monitor the younger two. Later, when she was getting ready for bed, she was cranky and out-of-sorts. All of a sudden, she burst into tears and began crying her heart out. I asked her what was wrong and she said, through her sobs, "I miss Hillary! If Hillary were here, she could take me to the movies!" I felt like crying, too. We are ready for you to come home. I don't know how we will be able to celebrate birthdays without you. We love you!

Vacation or Bust

January 25, 1990

Dear Anne,

I got two letters from you today. We haven't been here to check the mail because we were on our skiing vacation in Germany. Thanks for your snow pictures. Your snow was unimaginable, and we all could not believe both all the snow and how much Stephen has grown. Now, I really do feel guilty for talking you out of the snow-suit for Drew in London. Thanks for letting me get the only one for sale. Thanks for the London pictures, too. My photos are about the same, but I think yours are better. I will send copies of mine soon.

We got back from Germany late Tuesday night. It was an interesting trip for a myriad of reasons. Never a dull moment in this vagabond group it seems. We flew out on a MEDEVAC flight to Ramstein, Germany. It was my kind of flight, equipped with nurses, hospital beds, and medical equipment that I felt sure could handle most any malfunction I could throw at them. Ha! We landed and got a rental car and decided to spend the night in Ramstein village. We left the next day and drove to Dachau, which is right outside Munich. We went to the Dachau Concentration

Camp, which I learned was the first concentration camp established in Germany. It is well preserved and much of it is in its original condition. There is a museum and a theatre with actual film footage. I spent much of the time putting my hands over the eyes of the children while the film was on, and hoping it was not all too disturbing. I wanted to see it, but I must say it is a sobering experience and possibly too much for children. I will never forget the lingering smell of the oven room and the huge pile of shoes in the corner. Well, no one can ever accuse me of not being real when it comes to mothering.

We spent the night in Munich and drove the next day to Berchtesgaden. This region is called the Obersalzberg and was Hitler's favorite part of Germany. Because we have the military IDs we had reservations in the General Walker Hotel, which is part of the military recreational facilities and can only be used by military personnel. It has such an interesting history, as it was part of Hitler's complex of buildings for his personal and government use. Hitler rebuilt the hotel, named it the Platerhoff, and used it for his guests. Hitler's personal house and the houses of other government officials were located behind this hotel. All of those houses were connected by huge underground tunnels and bunkers. We went on a guided tour of the tunnels, fascinating to say the least. All the houses are gone now, bombed out of existence by the Americans so they would not become shrines, but the tunnels and bunkers and this hotel are in their original condition. Once the Allies took over the region, they decided to keep this hotel to use solely as a recreational site for the troops, some poetic justice there. This military ID is really paying off. For a history buff like me, it doesn't get any better than this. Most of the furniture used in our hotel was original and some even came from the Eagle's Nest. We actually dined in the hotel restaurant with a giant picture on the wall of Hitler giving a speech in that very room.

Well, amidst all this historical drama, we had some of our own. Drew had experienced several short nose bleeds before we left home but nothing that we were too concerned about ...well, Monday night she developed one that would not stop. We tried everything we knew to do, but to no avail, so at 5:00 AM we left Hillary in charge and flew down the mountain in a taxi to the nearest hospital in the village of Berchtesgaden. A hospital is called a *kranenhouse* and we had to ask at the front desk how to say that in German so we would know what to say to the taxi driver. At this point, the bleed had become a flood and I was beyond upset. Not speaking German made it all the more frightening, but the hospital staff was very understanding. They packed her nose and sent us to an ENT specialist in town.

We took another taxi to the office of Herr Dr. Heck (his real name) and he was simply wonderful. He was so very kind and spoke perfect English. He numbed her nose; I covered her eyes as he cauterized two open blood vessels deep within her nose. He packed it extremely tightly and told us it must remain that way for the next twenty-four hours. He had a nurse assisting him and her little schnauzer dog was following right at her heels. Not something you see at home every day back in the States. Herr Dr. Heck was so considerate and skilled. He really made us feel better because we were wrecks by this point, at least I was, totally. He gave us medicine to use for 15 days after the packing was removed. He asked us to watch her overnight since she would naturally try to pull it out in her sleep, so that meant another sleepless night for us. By this time, I was a nervous wreck and a sleep-deprived zombie.

When it was removed on Wednesday, she was fine and has remained fine since. She has had no more nosebleeds, but her traumatized, sleep-deprived parents may never be the same. The next day we were able to go ice skating in an outdoor rink and then we all fell into bed very early. The rest of the week we spent skiing and everyone but me, of course, got very proficient, turning and stopping with complete control. They made great progress and were zipping all over the slopes in no time. I stayed on the sidelines as I could not get the hang of it. The image of me on crutches kept me in the safe zone and one trip to a *kranenhouse* was enough for me on this vacation. But the rest of the family all loved it.

We left Sunday and drove back to Ramstein, Germany, to try and catch a military flight back to Sicily. After we boarded our plane, another passenger dressed in her military uniform was instructed to go back into the terminal to change into civilian clothes. I asked why was that an issue and they said the flight was going to Amman, Jordan, first and would be on the ground for a while there before heading to Sicily. After learning this, we opted to get our luggage back and try for another flight. A short side trip to Jordan did not appeal to me at this point of our vacation given the present climate in the Middle East.

There was a flight leaving shortly for Decimomannu, Sardinia, so we took that. It seemed safer, if not any closer. Not having learned much about Sardinia in geography class, I had a slight suspicion it might be the end of the earth and I was about right. Found it! But it did have a commercial airport nearby so we bummed a ride with a nice person who took pity on us and took us over to the commercial airport. We bought tickets to Palermo, only a thirty-minute flight away. Once in Palermo, we got a rental car and drove home. It is about a three-hour drive, but I got to see the whole breadth of Sicily and a tiny slice of Sardinia. All in all, I think we had a good time. Traveling on free military flights is always an adventure with lots of twists and turns. The price is right, but there are no guarantees that you can get from point A to point B without being flexible and creative.

Upon arriving home, the father figure announced that it was our *last* family vacation! But he always says stuff like that. He just does not adjust well to the fact that traveling with three children can be a challenge, just living with them is no picnic. My fault, I guess, for doing so much that he is shocked when exposed to the full force of it daily with no escape. We did have fun, and we did learn heaps and Germany is much more beautiful than I imagined. And maybe...he will grow into this parenting thing, eventually, I hope. If not, remind me to take all my vacations with you in the future!

Arriving home did not exactly give us the comfort and security we were hoping for as we found out there was a creditable terrorist threat against Americans here. We were told not to go on base, not to wear a uniform off base, to check our cars for bombs before getting into them, not to eat in local restaurants, and basically, stay home and keep a low profile. Well, that pretty much says stop living here, I guess. I think it has to do with Gaddafi being upset about something. My vacation brain has been out of the news loop. Oh, and get this, they are putting armed guards with bullet-proof vests on the school buses. It sure makes me want to go home! I swear it is always something, it seems.

I am starting to wonder if it's me or the world that is the problem. I hope the threat goes away quickly as it is a massive hassle and my nerves are not equipped. I'll close on that cheery note. Give me strength!

Ciao for now,
Susannah, *Baronessa di* Vexing Vacations

PS Well, when it rains it pours. I stepped out of bed this morning into about three inches of water. Seems a pipe burst in the night and our apartment was flooded. Apparently and luckily, I might add, our floors are not too level (maybe thanks to the earthquake) so at least, the children's rooms were spared. That would have been a nightmare with wall-to-wall toys and stuffed animals. So, it seems we are just a bit water-logged at the moment and I'm sweeping the water out with a broom. Wow, my floors will be as clean as any Italian housewife's!

Abandoned on a Crowded Island

Groundhog Day, 1990

Dear Anne,

February is here! I'm always excited to see time passing and realize I'm still hanging in here. Guess some of the "live in the moment" Italian style is rubbing off on me. I have had a bad cold since Germany and have had a hard time shaking it, which is the usual for me, unfortunately. Conditions here remain about the same. The terrorist threat has lightened up a bit. They tell us to remain vigilant but with no restrictions on our activities. The whole issue bothered me at first, but I've felt so physically bad with this cold that I couldn't give it too much thought. I think I might be starting to learn to take it one day at a time and to be thankful for each day, realizing we have no guarantees. I think the Sicilians really do live like that. Maybe earthquakes and volcanoes and robbers and stupendous car wrecks teach you to enjoy the moment. They do seem to have more fun and are more relaxed, in some ways, than Americans.

I have been emotionally up and down. It is very hard when your other half makes things worse than they have to be. He does not like it here and has made sure we all feel his pain. His complaining from day one has now evolved into an almost complete shutdown as far as communication. I even threatened that if he keeps it up, I would take the children and just go home. He has tried to be a little bit nicer since then, but it is very hard for me to handle everything and feel so alone. Not to mention that Sicily is the most romantic place I've ever lived, the scenery, the poetic beauty of ancient places, the men and women walking arm in arm, the lovers on the beach, the flowers, and landscapes. It all tugs at my heart and makes me feel more alone than ever. American wives don't expect much in the way of romance, but to bring me here and immerse me in such beauty and then reject and isolate me so completely seems beyond cruel. He isn't even speaking to me. I am not in a hurry to go home and that was pretty much an empty threat. I do wish things could be better between us but I feel I'm just grasping at straws now.

Not much other news here. Southern Foods seems like a good idea for you. I know that lugging all the groceries and water that it takes to keep this place fed and watered step-by-step up three flights of stairs is no picnic. That is my biggest chore, along with the laundry. I now realize why Sicilians shop daily…not only freshness, but it's all those stairs with big loads! When I make a weekly commissary run, it takes thirty minutes to haul them up the stairs and whew, what a workout! I will be glad when the weather improves so I can resume hanging the clothes on the line. That is tricky, too, because if you drop your panties, they go down three flights and may end up on the landlord's balcony. That can be a ticklish situation, especially with my landlord, as I would rather sacrifice my best pair of drawers any day than face them.

Drew has told me several times that she dreams of going home and living near you. But you won't ever want us living down the street. My kids have accelerated, in fact, they are ruined I'm afraid. I brought home movies this weekend and they turned up their noses at Disney and insisted on watching *Splash* and *Three Men and a Baby*. They seem to know everything about sex and in several languages, too!

Matthew says he never wants to leave. I think he feels delivered and in his element. Hillary was expressing the other day her worry over upcoming report cards. Matt piped up and said his teacher, Ms. Wells, told the class not to sweat it, "That a report card was just a report card!" I got a good laugh at that as it was so typical of her and a philosophy that Matt could embrace.

Enclosing a photo of us at Dauchau and also an Erma Bombeck article. Love to you, keep those home fires burning.

As always,
Susannah, *Baronessa di Solo Mia*

Sunday, February 4, 1990

Dear Sue,

Got your letter yesterday and I've read and reread it. I'm certainly glad I heard about Drew's ordeal after she was over it and back to normal. How frightening that must have been! It sounded like you were located near a very up-to-date hospital. I guess all you have to show for it now are a few more gray hairs. It will be good for a chapter when you write your book.

Now, the terrorist thing is another matter. Charles had heard on the news about bases closing in Crete, but that may be too much to hope for in your case. I guess they'd have to send you home then. Everyone here has been asking me about your plans, literally stopping me on the street. I'm sure it will work out. I just hope you'll have some advance notice so it won't be too hectic. As for the administrative hold, we'll just pray that nobody thinks that is a good idea! I've already bought your birthday present, but I am not going to send it because I would hate for you to have to turn around and ship it back. I'm operating under the premise that you will be home this summer. And of course, you are all welcome to stay with us until you find a place or build a place or whatever. Or send the kids home and I'll keep them while you and M tie up loose ends. I'm not sure what I'll be doing about work this summer. One of the home economics teachers has asked me to keep her in mind if I need someone because she does want to work during the summer. I think that she would be good with the at-risk students, so if you are coming home, I'll take the summer off and be at your service.

Your trip to Germany sounded wonderful to me! You'll never forget this year with all the amazing things you have seen and done. Your kids will always see the world differently now. They'll be so much more open and knowledgeable. And, when you get back to Carteret county, you can pick up right where you left off. Nothing has changed!

As I let you know in my last letter, I'm really stressed out! And in a way, it's gotten worse. Susan and Sarah visited the week before Sarah's birthday and I accompanied Susan over to Mom's and sat there, piping in every so often, while Susan told Mom how rotten her childhood was and how judgmental and self-righteous Mom is now. I felt used and torn between loyalty to Susan, who has been supportive to me, and guilt about depressing Mom more than she already is. After all, it's been barely a year since my father suddenly died. Mom and I have had one conversation, at her request, since Susan's visit, and that probably made things worse. I do, at times, feel angry at Mom. I feel she can be very self-centered and full of excuses. She's a first-class manipulator and I am tired of being manipulated. The guilt does make for sleepless nights, though. I'm sure Sister Gretchen is mad at me, too. She and Mom eat together every night, so I know she has heard it all. Susan and I both told Mom she needed therapy, but she'll never go. I know I probably should have listened to my cowardly instincts and not gone with Susan. I can hardly wait until my daughters are grown and turn on me! Ha!

Gosh, I hope you'll be here next year. I am going with Charles to Rose for therapy every other week but it's not the same, or nearly as good, as therapy with you. Maybe when you get back, we can both check ourselves into some nice residential nuthouse for a couple of months.

I am now going to CCC at night and happen to be there right now. It is a nice change from being at the high school. Mondays and Wednesdays are my half days at the high school and my evenings at CCC. I spent this morning at home playing with Stephen and watching daytime TV while my cleaning ladies cleaned the house. It felt very luxurious. Charles took the girls to the dentist at 3:00 (Hailey had her first cavity!) and then did dinner and baths. This working late is not all bad. I usually stop to get something to eat and then head home to tuck the little darlings in. Tomorrow Charles and I have our midyear conference with Laura's teacher. I have a feeling it won't be as glowing as Hailey's was, but then who can compete with a firstborn?

Well, I'll close for now and get back to whatever it is I do here. Hope things are calmer when you receive this letter. Please consider sending me a time and phone number so we can talk. I would love to hear your voice and, if it's early morning for me (between 5:30 and 6:30), I can probably talk uninterrupted. Though there's no guarantee I'll even be able to talk if you were to call. This place is a zoo and the phone ringing sets the animals off! Remember I'm working, so money is no object, especially for a phone call from you. Take care. You are in my prayers.

Love, Anne

The Mothership

February 13, 1990

Dear Anne,

Got your letter and Valentine's cards. My Valentines were not very good, not much to choose from here. Hillary cried when she read hers from you. The essay that Hailey wrote really touched her. I think she misses St. Andrews more than the others. She is the one who loves school in general and St. Andrews felt not only like her friends but family, too. Her last year's class from St. Andrews sent a large packet of letters, valentine cards, and pictures from all her classmates, which was so sweet. She hasn't seen them in a year and yet they remembered her on Valentine's Day, which to me shows their exceptional friendship. Giving up that school was the hardest decision I had to make to come here. We got the packet just before getting on the plane to Germany. We sat and read them all on the plane and they were so sweet and touching. We sent them a box of Sicilian items for the class yesterday, along with a thank you note and all the love we could pack in the box.

What is it with our mothers? I know you feel rotten about the trouble with yours and I think I know exactly how you feel. After reading your letter, I have thought a lot about my childhood. It was pretty idyllic...sort of Pippi Longstockings' style, on my own. My mother was always so busy she basically turned me loose to roam and do anything I wanted as long as I was not underfoot. She always stepped up for the showy things, like Christmas, cupcakes for the classroom, new Easter dresses, but had very little interaction with me. I just ran wild in the country, rode my horse all over, and was allowed to be completely free, as long as I showed up before dark. There were always good meals, clean clothes, and a lot of freedom. That continued through high school, and by the time I had my own ideas, I realized that she and I did not even really share anything or even know each other. Whenever I tried to converse with her, she shot me down. It was like we were people from different planets. Our big problems started when I tried to move out of the family unit. It was always clear that she expected a return on her investment in the form of my doing what she had in mind, not what I had in mind. She became downright cruel in her manipulation and we emotionally moved even further apart. She doesn't understand me, not surprising as she never had the time.

Now things are at their worst with her disowning me because we moved here. I tried to explain it to her, but to no avail. Not sure we will ever patch things up, which is not that disappointing to me as I don't really like her very much and do resent her total need to control everyone in her orbit. Funny that she could be so distracted when I was young but now wants to call all the shots when I am an adult.

I do know that I want a better relationship with my children and I am aware that words do have lasting consequences. I have promised myself I would not make the same mistakes. Guess I will make a whole new set. I do want to respect their choices, even if I don't agree. I don't want the relationship to be based on their always meeting my approval. My mother grew up in a black and white world. I think we grew up in a gray one with things not so simplistic. I want to be friends with my grown children. I wish my mother was my friend, but I am resigned that it might never happen with us. I am glad I came here. Flying the coop to Sicily has been a chance to spread my wings and stand on my own. I am fairly immune to her pain and to her ways of inflicting pain. I am much closer to Elizabeth and she is my mother-in-law. That says it all, I think.

I hope things improve with you and your mother but I am not expecting much change with my *familiglia*. I like your idea of the residential nuthouse. All mothers need therapy, why can't ours admit that? Motherhood sure is taking a toll on me and we haven't hit the teens yet...Yikes. I hope we can face that stage together, the thought of facing it alone makes me weak in the knees.

Love,
Susannah, *Baronessa di* Sainted Mothers

PS Went to the doctor yesterday and got medications for this cold and am feeling better already.

Monday, February 19, 1990

Dear Sue,

We want the dress from Sicily! I've discussed it with Hailey, even gave her *carte blanche* in the spring Wooden Soldier catalog, but she'd much rather have a dress from you. I'm sorry this has gotten so complicated. I hope the dress you described to me on the phone is still available. Hailey's eyes did light up when I described the petite wedding dresses. She thought that sounded wonderful, but I think that's a little much for me. I wish you and I had just decided, but I know you understand my wanting to ask her. When she has her mind made up, there's no changing it. I think she has been talking at school about her dress from Sicily (I asked her if she has been bragging) and would be disappointed if she had to settle for one that wasn't *haute couture*. Let me know what happens. I can always make other arrangements. I hate to put so much pressure on you.

I'm at CCC now. It's about 6:30 p.m. No students are here. I had one at about 5:00 and since then, I have been reading a magazine in the library. I really could spend this time working in my office but did not bring much with me tonight.

I took Hailey to the dentist for her first filling this morning. She did well, although she was dreading it. This week is also the science project, so you know Charles and

I (but mostly I) had a busy weekend! I had sworn I wasn't going to get involved this year. Ha! Ha! But, of course, I knew that if I left it up to Charles, I'd be stepping in at the last minute. He's been in the worst mood lately. He yells at the kids for any little thing, so then I try to compensate by being *Miss Congeniality.* He agrees to do things and then is mad he's overcommitted. I wish that he could enjoy our daily comings-and-goings a little more. I know it gets hectic, but it's our life now with three kids. It will be this way for a while! Right?! He will be going to Monterey, California, for two weeks in April. That will be tricky with my working two nights a week. I hate for him to take the trip over Easter break, but that week with no school would be easier for me to handle by myself. He opted for the week of Easter break.

I tried to call Ray and Elizabeth to see if they had Jackie's phone number so I could call you about the dress. They must be out of town. I saw Rachael and she said she had been going by their house for about a week and hasn't seen them. I'm going to look through your letters and see if I can find where you sent me the number.

I think I'll close up shop here and go home. I usually leave by 7:00 if no students are here. Hope all is going well. I'm trying to adjust to the idea that you'll be in Sicily next year. It's hard. Thank you for the valentines. We all enjoyed them.

Love, Anne

Life is a Cabaret, Old Chum

February 20, 1990

Dear Anne,

Sending you this book I just read, *Making Peace with Your Parents.* I read it and thought you might also find it helpful. The authors have some good points and suggestions that have given me some hope in this department, even in my chronic situation. I must admit that I had to muster up some courage to even open it as I was afraid that it might open up wounds and stir up emotions. I was fearful that it might arouse enough hatred that I might do something drastic, like send my mom a mail bomb. Ha. It did make me see that I was holding onto the pain, and not being very forgiving, either.

I am on the hunt for Hailey's First Communion dress in earnest. Seems in Sicily no one buys that kind of dress off the rack. I've been scouting around Catania and have found an entire street of seamstress shops and some have a few ready-made dresses. I hope to find the perfect one. Send me those measurements.

The weather here has been nice, but windy. It is in the 70s today. Things here are all calm and no great events to report. All is quiet above and below the earth for a change.

That is a relief because all this stress had us thinking we might try to return home early. Now we are feeling better and besides, I haven't seen all of Sicily yet, much less the rest of Europe. Also, my Italian is nowhere as advanced as I want it to be. I think we have made real progress in adapting and now that we have that skill we might as well use it, huh? It hit me the other night as I was cooking dinner how crazy, stupid, courageous, you pick one, this whole adventure has been for us. Talk about stepping off into the unknown...we did it. So far it has worked out well, I guess, but I will never again jump off into the unknown so flippantly. Another lesson learned. It always pays to do the research.

Luckily, Sicily fascinates me in so many ways. There has been a lot for me to love here. I love to watch people and here that is a regular national pastime. However, in Sicily, a look can be dangerous so you have to be careful. The Sicilians love to stare but don't necessarily appreciate it when you return the favor. Needless to say, I wear my sunglasses a lot.

I also love the language and I am practicing every chance I get. I am hoping to get a private tutor soon. I love it all...the food, the architecture, the meadows, the hills, the mountain villages, the customs, the people...and the bars! I told my friend Jackie that I think living here for two years is equivalent to a four-year college degree. There is so much to learn. The money and laws and customs, I suppose you could tune it all out, but I am soaking it all in as much as possible.

Speaking of customs, it is *Carnevale* here. We had a parade on Saturday in downtown Motta, a small one, but every town and city has a parade or celebration of some sort. Acireale, a town north of us, has a huge parade that is known for big floats and emphasis on sex. *Carnevale* is all about poking fun at yourself. It's the holiday before Lent, to let off all the steam. There are masks and silly string and streamers and confetti and people playing tricks. It is quite a party. Of course, there is special pasta, special cookies, special treats. Not surprising as they have pasta for everything and every occasion it seems. Did I tell you they have pasta for dogs and cats? There is penis-shaped pasta, too. Yum? No kidding. Also, it is not unusual in *Carnevale* for male /female role reversal and quite a few men dress up as women. Pranks and everything upside-down is the general theme. *Carnevale* goes on for a week or so and the children parade around the piazza in the evenings to show off their costumes, throwing confetti everywhere and having fun. They tend to go for traditional costumes. Cinderella, Snow White, Zorro, Pinocchio are all popular. The costumes are elaborate and the children are so cute. Sometimes I feel like I have gone back in time as the Italians like traditional things and I have the feeling, while watching the festivities, that it has been done in this timeless way for decades.

I'm enclosing a photo of Leonardo, our cat, and Uccello, our new bird. Leo is the most loving and good-natured cat. Drew dresses him and wraps him in baby blankets and he is completely indulgent to her wishes. He has made a perfect pet, except for the fact that we have seen him several times jump up on the one-inch balcony railing. It is about a three-foot leap up and then he walks the length of it, like a tightrope. We are three stories up and the tiny metal railing is perched between heaven and the earth with no safety net. I'm terrified he is going to fall. I know it would be the end of him, but I don't know how to stop him from doing it. It is both amazing and appalling and has caused my heart to skip a beat more than once. It would devastate Drew if something happened to him. Drew is doing great in school now. She has started to sign her name on her papers as Drewsy, her idea. She is still wearing her collection of caps every day.

In your last letter, you did sound a teeny bit depressed. I hope you're not. I do listen to my *Aspects of Love* soundtrack, but it doesn't make me cry. Our trip was one of the best times of my life. It was truly like I stepped into a dream, just perfection, so unlike my ordinary existence for sure! My favorite line from the song "Love Changes Everything" is "love changes everything… the way you live and how you die." Sometimes I think about the fact that we almost didn't meet for the trip, and that we only met at all in life by pure chance. I think about how much you have changed my life… enhanced it...enriched it. It really can't be measured. Thank you, thank you! As I struggle to co-exist in this marriage or build a relationship (or glue it together), I realize that only a few things in life are genuinely valuable and good and precious. Truthfully, our friendship is one of the most precious things in my life.

I used to sit at Hillary's piano recitals and every time I would think … this…my children, they are valuable. They are one concrete thing in my life that is good, precious, and of immense value and worth. It always came to mind, during those quiet times, as the daily grind rarely gives you enough quiet time to reflect, but in those small, still moments, I could see clearly and grasp it. I knew that no matter what kind of shambles we were in, I wouldn't change it and I could even forgive myself for any shortcomings I had as a mother. I could see that the children were thriving despite my foibles!

I am wondering if just the pressure of living in a small town is not weighing heavily on you. I am realizing that the longer I am away from Morehead, the more I see it as a pressure cooker environment. Everything seemed so open to display and criticism in such a tiny pool of humanity. Small town life is both good and bad, one negative, for sure, is that everybody does seem to know everything. When I read the local paper, that my mother "lovingly" paid to have sent to me, I can feel the narrow-mindedness and social snobbery and the rigid guidelines jump right off the page. It hangs like a cloud over the whole place. Sicily for me has been a breath of fresh air and an answer to prayer. I think you may be feeling that pressure and are expecting too much from yourself. You are a great mother, friend, counselor, person... so lighten up! Stop striving for perfection. I've been thinking lately that all the sane people are in institutions and only the crazy ones, like us, are out. Meaning that if we were completely sane, we could not stand this world of atomic bombs, hunger, war, prejudice, etc., and it would disturb us so much it would make us crazy and drive us into the institutions. The fact that we can function in the madness means we are the crazy ones. Am I crazy?

I don't know why I am writing all this, but I want you to be anything but depressed and I want you to marvel at your treasures. During Hailey's First Communion please look at what a marvelous miracle she is and take some credit for it. There was no guarantee we would get this far. Enjoy it, bask in it, celebrate it! I know you will.

All the good times are not over, even though we are getting older. I fully plan to enjoy their graduations, weddings, and much more, if I am given the opportunity. I need to get off this soapbox. I'm sure you are ready for me to do it...Not much news here anyway. We are going to try to hop on one of the flights next week to Tel Aviv. Wish us luck on getting a free flight to Israel. That should be exciting if it happens. Take care, write when you can, much love,

Susannah, *Baronessa di* Old Chums

Friday, March 2, 1990

Dear Sue,

I certainly enjoyed our conversation last weekend! It was great hearing your voice. Thanks, also, for sending the book. I have started it. There is a lot of tension between Mom and me. We haven't spoken beyond very superficial comments since I spoke my mind a while back. I am waiting for time to take care of it. I think this book may help.

Thank you so much for getting Hailey's dress! She is so excited! Your thoughtfulness has meant so much to her and me.

Today is a teachers' workday. Anne and I are the only ones here and this is her last day. She'll be starting at the middle school on Monday. I will really miss her.

I'm going to get this in the mail right away. Please let me know if I can do anything more about your certification. I'm sending you information about a new phone number in Raleigh for teacher certification information, but I know you really can't take advantage of it from Sicily. If you send me your SS number or a question, I'll call from here, or at least follow up on your written request. I'm guessing you're getting ready to work. Let me know what I can do from here. More later. I've been so enjoying your letters.

All my love, Anne

Saturday, March 17, 1990
St. Patrick's Day

Dear Sue,

I wish I had thought to have a tape recorder on when Hailey opened your package with her dress. We had talked so much about it and she was so excited that, quite frankly, I was beginning to worry if anything would live up to her expectations. I needn't have worried. She was just ecstatic when she saw it. She kept saying, "Oh Man. Oh Man. It's beautiful!" about every detail. And when she saw the crinoline petticoat and the shoulder pads, well, I just wish you had been here. You really did it. And it fits her like it was made for her, length and all! Thank you so much for this wonderful gift to all of us. It has meant so much to me. I don't think I can even begin to tell you how much. Charles keeps commenting on how thoughtful it was. The little floral headpiece is beautiful, too. Hailey has tried on the dress and the headpiece for everyone who has walked in the door. We got it on Thursday afternoon and when she wasn't modeling it, she had it hanging in her room to admire. Friday morning, she got excited all over again when she woke up and saw it. I can hardly wait to send you pictures. We will soon, I promise.

We also got Laura's birthday presents last week and she opened her Pinocchio right away. She loves it. I am impressed with the Italian toys. It looks so cute in her room and she has been playing with it. I'm saving the "Do not open till March 20th" presents until Tuesday. Didn't even show them to Laura since she is not one to wait. Hailey did open her books from Germany. What a good idea. She's just at the right age where drawing is now her favorite activity. It really must be fun seeing such a variety of toys and merchandise as you hop from country to country. We are planning a family party (with Melissa and probably the Herrings) for Laura on Tuesday. The girls each had someone spend last night since that was Laura's choice rather than having a class party. Charles and I are really tired, but it went quite well.

I have started two letters to you this week, but haven't been able to finish them. I feel my life is on fast forward. I hope it's just a phase, but I'm afraid that, realistically, it won't slow down without some real changes on my part.

There has been real drama at St. Andrews School, which I've managed to avoid. Since Charles is on the advisory board, he's been involved to a degree. Tiffany has been laying the groundwork for a confrontation with the principal for some time. It has been inevitable that two such dominant and opinionated personalities, working so closely together, would finally have it out. Well, they are! From what I've heard, Tiffany has been going to the priest for quite a while with complaints. He's been listening and probably thinking that the principal would go too far one day, giving him a chance to get rid of her. That's just my theory. I really think the parish priest and the principal have been at odds since day one. Again, two strong, opinionated personalities.

Well, the proverbial straw that finally did it, as far as the parent was concerned, was the notorious Science Fair!

I wish you could have seen her daughter's project. It was at least four feet tall, all enclosed, plywood and plexiglass with a hermetic pump to simulate a hurricane. I didn't study it up close, only from a distance, since I was trying to maneuver in that crowded space with Stephen, who wanted to reach out and touch everything, on my hip. Charles said it was obviously done by adults. Parents try so hard. Well, it received honorable mention and I'm sure the parents were counting on first place. Tiffany was convinced the judging was rigged. There were nine judges this year and, of course, no identifying information on the entries. First thing the next morning, she began calling the judges to see if they had been instructed to only rank her daughter's show-stopping entry as honorable mention. Apparently to Tiffany, the rigged Science Fair was the last straw and she decided it was either her or the principal...one of them had to go. I even heard that she had an attorney and the names of twenty-five parents who were prepared to demand the principal's resignation. Having watched their previous conflicts, I feel these two women are evenly matched.

Although I haven't had to, nor will I, openly choose sides, I'd have to say that I trust the motives of the parent a little more than those of the principal. It's the manner and approach to the whole thing that bothers me most. The latest word, however, is that after a tense back and forth, the principal's authority prevailed with the backing of the Diocese, and the family has been asked not to return to St. Andrews next year. I am writing you all this so when you have a wave of nostalgia, you can read this and thank your lucky stars you're living at another level above all this pettiness. It's a sad commentary for a Catholic school. I feel sorry for the kids. I wonder if one day they'll resent their mother for being too involved. I guess there may be a mass exodus of some other families from the school this year. The parent who has agreed to be home-school association president next year and Tiffany are close friends. Supposedly, the teachers were a hundred-percent behind the decision and want the family to actually leave this year, immediately. I heard that the idea of instant banishment was a little too drastic for the powers-that-be. I haven't talked to either woman. I think I'm chicken and probably too much of a hypocrite. If I came face-to-face with either one, I'd probably just nod and agree with whichever one I was talking to. Such is life in Carteret county!

Things are almost as bad at the high school with the rumor being that the principal's contract won't be renewed. I haven't had any big problems with him because I've accepted the fact that he's very moody, volatile, forgetful, and lacks follow through, just your typical male authority figure. Fortunately, I've learned that if I time it right, he'll go along with almost anything I ask. I like working with the new assistant principal and with Beth, so I pretty much avoid the principal. I have missed having Anne around. The other female counselor has gotten a little weirder. The token male counselor has started being very nice to me after pretty much ignoring me for the first half of the year. We've been told they won't be replacing Anne this year, although I think Renee would like to move into that position. The best part of this job has nothing to do with the school, except the fact that my commute is literally four minutes from home.

Guess you all have settled in for another year. Rachael came by today for a visit. She seems fine, still involved with Harry, just emotionally, not face-to-face. She's still going to Rose and is starting a flying/pilot course at CCC. Harry is also signed up for the same course, not to mention that he's a pilot. She asked about you all and said she was going to start writing to you.

Well, I'll close for now. Is there any chance you guys could come home for a visit this summer? You know our house is your house for as long as you could stay. And you could have a car to use as you pleased. It would make our summer! It would make my year! Please consider it.

Everyone's asleep here so I'll go hit the sack, too. Hope you are all well. We loved the pictures of Leonardo and the bird. Of course, my kids started clamoring for a pet, but I held my ground...we still have two birds!

Take care. Thank you again for Hailey's beautiful First Communion dress. She'll never forget this wonderful gift and neither will I.

Love, Anne

PS Charles and I, or should I say, Hailey, won 2nd place at the Science Fair with her entry "Hot Air Rises." We are already promising ourselves that next year we are not going to wait until the last minute. Ha!

Globe-Trotting Along

March 22, 1990

Dear Anne,

Well, we just returned from Israel. It was a short trip but high-powered. We just couldn't miss the opportunity because these flights are not offered very often. We just dropped everything and went for it. Tel Aviv is not a usual flight destination from here, but when there are ships to be serviced, they have flights for a week or two. We left Sunday morning at 4:00 AM and flew on a C130 plane, which is a cargo aircraft. We were in little net seats with cargo stacked over our heads and a military life jacket strapped around our waists, very Indiana Jones style. We left the kids with friends and jumped at the chance to go. The price was right; they charged only $10.00 for a round trip which included a boxed lunch. It was a four-hour flight and we landed at Tel Aviv airport around noon. We found a great hotel right on the beach for $48.00 a night. We were lucky as the tourist season begins April 1st, so we were just under the wire for reduced rates.

Monday morning, we decided that maybe the best way to see the most in a limited amount of time was to take a tour. We grabbed one that took us to Nazareth, Tiberius, the Jordan River, Sea of Galilee, and then took a boat ride over to the ancient city of Capernaum. The ruins there are massive. The whole city has been excavated and you can actually walk the ancient streets among the foundations of the houses. They even pointed out the house of the disciple Peter. We had a lunch of St. Peter's fish on the Galilean shore at a seaside restaurant before embarking on the boat ride. It was all impressive and the weather was perfect.

On Tuesday, we toured Jerusalem and visited the Church of the Holy Sepulcher, which claims to contain Golgotha, the site of the crucifixion. The tomb site is also in that church complex. We walked the Via Della Rosa, stopping to visit the site where Pilate sentenced Christ, visited the site where Solomon's Temple stood, now the site of the Dome of the Rock and the Wailing Wall. Our guide was Jewish so she refused to go on this part of the tour. Jews are not free to walk around the area because of their belief that it contains the actual location of the Holy of Holies, somewhere within that temple area. We also visited King David's Tomb and the room of the Last Supper. We saw the Mount of Olives, the Moslem quarter, the Jewish quarter, the Christian quarter, and the Armenian quarter.

After lunch, we visited Bethlehem where we saw Rachel's tomb and the Church of the Nativity and enjoyed some good views of Jerusalem from that vantage point. I got in a little shopping time, but we didn't get much leisure time to soak up the local culture. With only limited time, we chose to see the main sights. It was all impressive, but most impressive to me were the Jewish guides for our tours. Their enthusiasm about the scientific efforts to build a new Israel and establish their own state was quite remarkable. Sometimes I felt like I was listening to a modern-day Ben Franklin. We toured a farm in the desert using aquaponic greenhouse agriculture.

Everywhere they pointed out all the new innovative ideas they are using to be self-sufficient. Much of Israel is desert and they are learning to make the desert bloom. I guess you have to be inventive when you are a young, tiny country surrounded by enemies. The new Israel left a deeper impression on me than the old. I guess all the religious sites seemed like a lot of hype to me. (Not afraid of being struck dead.)

Almost everywhere we went there were army soldiers with machine guns on street corners and atop buildings. They are on guard for violence constantly and security is tight, especially at the airport. I have never seen anything like it. Guards came around about every ten minutes and asked if our bags were our bags. They emptied the trash every ten minutes and checked the bathrooms, even inside the toilets with mirrors. There were signs all over saying not to accept anything from anyone, not to make any jokes concerning bombs or security or you would run the risk of being prosecuted. I hope the Israelis don't evolve into a paranoid society, as I don't know how it would feel to live with so much pressure on a daily basis. We got back around 3:00 AM on Thursday. It was well worth our time and effort. I'm so glad we got the chance to go.

Got a letter today from Elizabeth saying Ray was planning to come in mid-April for a visit. That will be nice. As a father-in-law, he rates at the top of the chart for me. The kids will be ecstatic to see him and spend some time together. I am also glad he is coming now because the spring is so beautiful here. Everything is green and wildflowers are blooming. I just love the red poppies everywhere. The Italians do a bang-up job with Easter, too. Loving everything Spring!

Much love,
Susannah, *Baronessa di* Globe Trotters

March 25, 1990

Dear Sue,

I think I'm going to make it. You didn't know it was that critical, did you? Seriously though, I'm just getting back to my usual roll-with-the-punches self and can once again find things to smile about (even though I just "balanced" the checkbook and that isn't one of them).

I thought of you and M today as Hailey made her First Communion. It was very nice. She looked like a princess in that dress. She was so excited about wearing it. I can't wait to send you some pictures. She told me she plans to save the dress for her little girl. Thank you again for being so thoughtful and so generous.

I'll bring you up-to-date on the outcome of the war of personalities. The principal won. It was quite a week of drama and I was torn between the two of them as far as who had my sympathies. It wasn't a black-and-white issue. The principal has a lot of shortcomings, as far as I'm concerned, but the parent is just too pushy. Her drive for power intimidates me, even though I believe her heart is in the right place. The earlier issue between the two of them concerning fencing in the playground and raising the money really stepped on toes. I'm not surprised that the family, when asked not to return next year, decided to withdraw immediately. I think the whole thing was handled very poorly and I blame the school for that. It certainly detracts from the Christian spirit of a Catholic school to ask a family to leave because of personality/communication issues. The children pay the price and had nothing to do with the problem. Charles has been more involved than I since he is on the advisory board. At the Thursday night meeting, he felt compelled to state his feelings that doing all this in such a petty, underhanded manner was not the correct way to handle it. Typical, though, I'm afraid. I feel this whole conflict has had a sobering effect on the school's atmosphere. We will miss Tiffany's energy. Lookout public school!

In the meantime, Charles and I have been invited to the Gapners' big annual fling at the Civic Center. We'll probably go unless I chicken out. I can still picture you and M circling the parking lot last year and driving away. I'll probably feel like doing that, too. I just don't want to do anything that suggests we have any negative feelings against this family. Tiffany just saw a lot of room for improvement at the school and met her match when trying to act on it. I'm enclosing the letter that was sent home to families stating the school's version of the story. I think it's tacky. Cynthia Greenleaf was reading it to her daughter and the poor second-grader burst into tears thinking it was about their family! Cynthia called me because that was the first time she had heard about it. I haven't mentioned anything about it to Hailey. Oh well, enough of that. You better believe I won't be crossing anyone in power at the school!

It's exciting to hear about your travel itinerary for this spring and summer. Isreal. Israel. Wow! I can't even spell it! I still have a feeling I'll get to see Sicily while you are there but, right now, it's hard to make plans.

I'll close for now. The girls just came back from Melissa's house and Laura is bugging me. Time to fix supper. Take care.

Love to all, Anne

PS Please get a phone. The call I made to Jackie's house that Saturday afternoon when I talked to Hillary only cost $6.00. I couldn't believe it.

Days of Whine and Roses

March 28, 1990

Dear Anne,

Thought I would drop you a line while I babysit the washing machine. I have to bump it through all the cycles because of the difference between the 50/60 cycle electricity. It is plugged into a transformer, but if the dial is not bumped along, it will not automatically run through the cycles. It will just keep washing forever. And also, because it drains into a large sink that may run over, if not watched. The last thing we need is another flood. The Italians have a washing machine called a *lavasciuga* which washes and dries in the same machine, but like everything else here, it is tiny. Two pairs of jeans fill it completely up. Not practical for a family of five, but it is a creative idea.

I wanted to call yesterday, but all the AT&T lines were down and no one was able to get a call out. I was hoping Hailey's big day was a *grande* success. I kept imagining that the dress never showed up and that you were having to make one from scratch, at the last minute! I surely hope not!

Thanks for the resume sample as I might get busy and try to get a job. I also want to get some renewal credits done and get my teacher's certificate up to date. The extra money would come in handy and it would be a more constructive use of my time since I now spend most of my hours watching washing machines and gazing at the countryside.

I must say it is a feast for the eyes, the countryside, that is. Spring comes in here on a gentle breeze and brings a burst of color in wildflowers. Sicily really shows off in early April. The surrounding meadows are full of pink, purple, and yellow wildflowers, with blue flax, and bursts of red, red poppies. The almond trees are in bloom, and the scent of blossoms permeates the air. The very thing that was so shocking when we first arrived, the barren rural landscape, is the very thing that is looking so delightful now. I have had to stop the car several times along the road just to take it in. It's like a painting everywhere you look. I can't get enough of it. I wish you could see it. If you are thinking of visiting us, I suggest the spring, but the summer is nice too. I will warn you that summers can be hot and all of Italy practically shuts down during the month of August. Many businesses are closed and hotels are full as all of Italy goes on *vacanza*. You know I will take you anytime I can get you, and I probably won't stop asking you to come until the week before we leave.

Everyone here is fine. Drew is to be in a school play and needed a ladybug outfit which I just made. It turned out very cute and she is excited about her acting debut. Everyone else is good, except for You-Know-Who, who is still hating this place and pining to go home. I am campaigning to stay as long as we can now, so send me some happy pills for him if you have any. Several cases should do it!

I have a new favorite song, the Linda Ronstadt and Aaron Neville rendition of "I Don't Know Much, But I Know I Love You." Did you see the Grammy awards where they performed it? Did you see Meryl Streep give Paul McCartney the Lifetime Achievement Award? She did such a good job with that. Boy, Paul always acts so loony. It is disappointing to see him, no longer a heartthrob to me, as he looks like an utter goofball. I tried to find the record and realized there are no longer any albums, only CDs. We have outlived an invention...gone now are LPs. Does that mean we are getting genuinely old?

The children all went for a hike on Sunday with their father and they saw a baby goat being born in a field. They were fascinated and as I said previously, all the facts of life for them are now pretty firmly established.

Well, the clothes are done, so I better go hang them out. The balcony clothesline works great and things dry here so fast when it isn't raining and the volcanic ash isn't falling. Sometimes I have to shake the black sand-like ash out of them as I take them off the line.

My friend Jackie has returned to the States and she took Candice with her. She said she doesn't know if she will return. Boo Hoo! She has had enough of the foreign life and needed a dose of *Americana* conveniences. She does not like it here and the stress of all the recent terrorist threats have pushed her over the edge, I think. Life here is not the easiest, but the joys far outweigh the negatives to me. I hope she will change her mind and return. I miss her already.

Much love,
Susannah, *Baronessa di* Wild Blossoms

War and Peace

March 29, 1990

Dear Anne,

Received my birthday gift from you yesterday and have resisted the temptation to open it. I bought my own birthday gift this year, a watch in Tel Aviv, so yours will probably be the only gift to unwrap. I am savoring the anticipation.

I must say the letter you sent describing the battle royale at St. Andrews was funny and not funny. That Science Fair was bound to crash and burn eventually. I have my own horror stories on that one, but I can't believe it actually spilled out into the open and has resulted in a clash that might involve lawyers. Talk about a sore loser story! It was always interesting to see the parents anxiously awaiting the opening of the doors, and observe them rushing to see what prizes "they" had won. It was extremely obvious to me that the parents had done most of the work and student involvement was always minimal. But to be disqualified on that basis, and receive an honorable mention, was a blatant act of confrontation it seems to me. Someone really must have felt compelled to throw down the gauntlet on that one. I thought it was common knowledge that almost all the projects are done by the parents. It is too bad that it devolved into a war of words and actions and it can only mean harm for everyone involved, I am afraid. I can only imagine the look on their faces when they realized the situation. When you have all these projects that look like they were done by astrophysics majors from MIT, it is pretty obvious that the second-grader didn't do it. What will parents have to compete about in that school if they can't strive to win the Science Fair? Anyway, it was shocking that it became such a public fight. It sounds like a tale from the "Harper Valley PTA" more than a quiet, reserved little Catholic school. I am glad for once we aren't there to witness it. And I for one, am glad "I" didn't have to do any science projects this year! Put that in the plus column for being in Sicily.

Not much news here, Drew lost another tooth and her play was a great success. She was a delightful ladybug… perfect casting! Ray is definitely coming in mid-April for a visit. He has reported that Elizabeth wanted to come also, but was afraid of the flight and is now very mad that he is coming and she is not. So, it sounds like 1606 Evans Street is the same for sure!

I can't believe that I'm almost 38 years old...just a few heartbeats away from 40. Actually, I am glad to be here, in Sicily, as I think it would be more depressing to be back home and getting so old. I feel liberated from my mother, small-town life, and even less enslaved in this marriage now that I've seen a bit of the world from a different view. Whether this is good or bad, who knows? Don't be surprised to see our names in the "Can this Marriage be Saved" column, but if we go down, maybe I will be able to stand it. All in all, I feel pretty good, like a person in my own right. Am I growing up gracefully or am I just fooling myself? Who knows? Maybe that is all life is about anyway, managing to fool oneself enough of the time. Well, will close for now.

Love you,
Susannah, *Baronessa* at Peace

PS Whelp…it was bound to happen, and it did. Last night, as I was hustling everyone off to bed, I realized that Leonardo was absent. We all searched the house high and low, and he was not to be found. We knew his only fate could be that he had finally slipped on that railing and taken the three-story plunge. We were all beside ourselves, fearing the worst. Finally, Hubby took a flashlight and went downstairs to search around the outside of the building in the dark. Lo and behold, Leonardo was found clinging to the top of some tall bushes, unscathed, but minus one of his nine lives, I'm sure!

Buon Compleano

April 4, 1990

Dear Anne,

Buon Compleano (Happy Birthday) to me! It was a very happy birthday when I opened the gifts you sent and I loved them all, especially the hatbox. Now I have a place to store the hats I bought in London! How perfect, only you would have known what a splendid gift that was for me, lover of hats. I was so touched I felt like crying a river, not sadness, although I do miss you. It was just so touching the amount of thought behind the gifts. You are probably the only person in the world who would know how much I would love a hatbox! And I do! I also like the address book and planner, the one I have been using is falling apart and out of date, so I will definitely put it to good use. I may also use the planning section to jot down some thoughts about being here in Sicily. I haven't been very good about keeping a diary, but we will have our letters, maybe if we ever want to look back at this time. I am saving all of yours and you said you were saving mine. I sometimes think of our letters zipping across the Atlantic in cartoon fashion with little wings. I like to think of that image for some reason, my thoughts speeding their way to you and yours to me.

Well, Ray is supposed to fly into Rome on April 9th and that is coming up fast. We will meet him there and drive down to Pompeii first thing before heading back here. The children are so excited. They can't wait to see their grandfather. They are off from school all next week for spring break, so that works out perfectly. Sometimes I do live a charmed life!

Not much news here. All three kids have signed up to play softball, T-ball for Drew. They are looking forward to that, but it means lots of practices after school which will lengthen our days

A friend of mine went to Germany and brought me back a piece of the Berlin Wall. He said for $2.00, you could rent a sledgehammer and bang away for ten minutes. It is just a small piece, but he said it was incredibly hard to chip off anything.

Everything else here is fine… Better close for now. All of your recent letters seem to be reassuring me that you are in better spirits. Guess you don't want another lecture series, huh? I promise not to do that, but please don't gloss over the facts. I promise not to give too much advice if you promise not to send generic letters. I really can't imagine that happening on either end. Keeping it real, as you know by now, is my forte. Love you and thank you so much for the gifts…you made my birthday wonderful.

Love and kisses to all,
Susannah, *Baronessa di* Older and Wiser Women

PS More good news, Jackie is back!

Spring Fever
April 7, 1990

Dear Anne,

Hope you had a nice Easter. The good news is I've lost 10 lbs. That Nautilus program is paying off … Things here have been up and down. Down, as this marriage is hanging by a thread. More miserable than the usual. I am looking forward to seeing Ray and hoping his visit might improve the atmosphere around here. As of right now, I'm ready for a divorce and am fighting hard to shake this never-ending depression that comes from the lack of communication and the constant sulking. Where the hell is my magic wand so I can make all his dreams come true? Truthfully, I think that would mean I would have to make the kids and myself disappear while transporting him to a sailboat in the Bahamas. The second part of that sounds okay with me at this point. I am just so tired of living with someone who constantly makes me feel sad and inadequate in every way. I know I'm far from faultless but I have tried so hard to keep all the balls in the air and this family functioning smoothly and he just remains so unhappy. If I try to engage him, he just acts like he wants to be left alone. He hardly talks to me at all. I am running out of ideas and out of reasons to keep trying. Nothing I do seems to help things. I feel like a dying plant just withering on the vine, trapped in a day and nightmare. I am hoping that with Ray here, he will step up and act better in front of his father. At least a fake show of cooperation will be a relief at this point. Maybe he won't act so completely miserable and can bring himself to act as if he cares about someone besides himself. I'm worn out with it! How do you know when you have reached the breaking point? We meet Ray in Rome and then it will be 21 days of trying to present a good front, I guess. Say a prayer for me.

Love you,
Susannah, *Baronessa di* Out of Whack Wedlock

Tuesday, April 10, 1990

Dear Sue,

The kids are asleep. I just took a bath. Charles is in Monterey, California, this week and I walked out to the mailbox just now to get today's mail. It makes my day to get a letter from you. You've been great about writing. I really need your letters. They are like a fix! I'm so glad you liked the hatbox. I was so excited when I got it and knew it was just right. Then as time went by, I began doubting my judgment and by the time I was wrapping it up, I was sure it was the dumbest gift and wanted to rush out and look for something else. It's so funny how we start to doubt our judgment when usually it's pretty good, especially I think, when it comes to knowing each other. I know you understand. For example, your letter, or *lecture series* as you called it, was wonderful! I truly needed to read that. Everything you said meant so much, made me feel so much better, and gave me the reality fix I needed. And you knew that. It's just that as time goes by, it seems easier and easier to doubt my judgment and decisions. I remember that George Elliot quote you gave me way back about friendship being the comfort of never having to measure words or something to that effect. I have saved that card. I wonder where I've put it?

I finally broke down and made an appointment with my dermatologist in Greenville, Dr. Hendrix, and got whittled down a little. Charles went with me for the day and we went to the mall. It was the Friday of the big party so, of course, I was in a panic about something to wear. I thought of you and M buying clothes, hiring a babysitter, and changing your mind. Well, we went through with it. We sat with some other school parents who are very nice. Didn't mingle much, but all in all, enjoyed the evening. I just can't imagine being able to or wanting to give a party like that...for four hundred of our dearest friends! We couldn't come up with forty. Of course, the staff of the pediatrician's office, practically the entire congregation of the First Baptist Church, etc., does beef up the guest list a bit. Noticeably absent were the principal and faculty of St. Andrews School and also Kay. It's hard to believe she and Tiffany had a falling out over the school mess, but it's true. Kay told me she had written you about the whole thing. It will be interesting to read another point-of-view.

I know that Ray is there by now. I loved hearing your voice the other day and I want you to know as soon as we hung up, I went straight to Roses and bought the seat covers. Not a bit of trouble, actually fun. Please don't hesitate to ask me again if something comes up. It must be wonderful having Ray there. I'll bet the reunion at the airport was a sight to behold. Don't give up on our coming, just aren't sure when.

Well, I've managed to double the drop-out rate at the high school. That's right, not cut it in half, double it. Fifty students had dropped out at the end of six months last year and at the end of six months this year, it's exactly one hundred. Rather depressing. I'm going to a drop-out convention in Raleigh April 24 through 26 with the student services director, a school counselor, and Dick. I'm looking forward to it. Plan to spend one night with Susan in Chapel Hill. Hope I get a shot of optimism and enthusiasm.

I'm glad you wrote your mother. I had a session with Rose and my mother this week. Had a headache for three days straight before the therapy! It went alright. Mom did most of the talking, but it did clear the air some. Do you know what seems to help our relationship most? When Mom talks openly and emotionally about situations and experiences of her childhood and adolescence and the hang-ups and reactions of her parents. She rarely does that, she's ever the Pollyanna. She's a master at hiding and denying her feelings, probably to the point of hiding them from herself, so she never seems real to me. I want to keep that in mind with my kids. I do think I show them more of my true emotions. My kids see me sad, depressed, mad, hurt, embarrassed, oh yeah, and happy, too. I guess it's always hard to see your parents as real people who also had to deal with growing up and finding their way.

Susan and Sarah are coming tomorrow for four or five days. I can't believe it's already Easter. It's been a short winter-into-spring for me.

I better close for now and hit the sack. I am so impressed by your Nautilus commitment. Keep it up. My neighbor and I had been walking five mornings a week for thirty minutes for the past month. Though this week with Charles gone, I couldn't. I haven't noticed any big improvement, but at least I feel like I am doing something. I hope she and I start back again after Easter break. I sure miss walking with you. Tell M Happy Birthday! Hope your Easter is nice. Is there an Easter bunny in Sicily? I doubt it, probably something much better. Take care. Hugs all around.

Love, Anne

Friday, April 20, 1990

Dear Sue,

Thanks for the card. My sentiments exactly, but then you knew that. I've been thinking of you this week with Ray visiting. I know that has been fun. I've enjoyed this week at home for a change of pace. Susan and Sarah were here until Wednesday. I enjoyed seeing them, but it does get intense. Sarah is a typical 4-year-old, which is an older version of the terrible twos. Charles has worked this week so we've had nothing else planned. It's been a beautiful week weather-wise and the kids have enjoyed playing outside. Stephen does well in the backyard, too, and the girls are pretty good about watching him. I was dreading this summer with Stephen, but it may not be so bad. Although, when he realizes that the world goes on beyond his own backyard...

I am counting the days until school is out and, although I am planning to work this summer, I know it will be at a different pace. I'm hoping the extra money I make will bail us out from this year. It is amazing how much we can spend without seeming to do more than the bare essentials. We could easily spend twice what we make and still probably have trouble showing where it went. Oh well. *C'est la vie.*

Well, I'll let you know how the spring carnival goes next

weekend. So far, I'm keeping a low profile as far as volunteering to help. I have a hard time getting psyched up for it. Tell everyone hi. Miss you!

Love, Anne

Rambling to Roma

April 29, 1990

Dear Anne,

Well, Ray's visit is winding down. As a matter of fact, we are on the train to Rome to put him on his return flight as I write. Jackie, Ray, and I are headed up for a few days before he flies out on Wednesday. Jackie was game to go with me so I didn't have to return by myself, thank goodness. Guess it is back again to St. Peter's, the Forum, Colosseum, etc., I shouldn't complain but I'm a bit toured out at the moment. We have tried to take Ray someplace every day and I think he has gotten a good taste of life in *Sicilia* and we have enjoyed him immensely. Ray is easy to love, but I am looking forward to a few moments to myself after this week.

Everyone is fine; the kids got report cards and everyone did well. One bad thing that coincided with report card day was that Hillary was bitten by a German Shepard dog on base and ended up getting a tetanus shot. The dog belonged to an American and was up to date on its shots, but the bite has left a horrible bruise. The owner was very apologetic, but I could have shot the dog on the spot!

We just passed through Naples on this train ride and their soccer team is winning evidently because they have painted the town blue. Every balcony and street are hung with banners with anything blue in a show of support. They have literally painted the town. Italians love their soccer games and it takes over like a fever here. All bars are packed with people watching the games. Sicilians drag out their TVs and easy chairs onto the balconies and watch the games outside. The cheers can be heard all over town.

Well, will close for now. I hope Rome is eternally wonderful and I imagine it will be and we can send Ray off with many happy memories of this grand tour. Jackie and I will return to Sicily on Wednesday on this *rapido* train, which means it makes fewer stops at every little village, but it still takes a full twelve hours and makes stops at all major towns. The train cars are divided into individual compartments that seat 6 to 8 people and are attached to an aisle with opening windows. At each stop gypsies board and work the aisles begging and they are slick thieves. We were advised to avoid standing in the aisles with any valuables during the stops. They hop off before the train leaves the station and if you are unlucky, they possess your wallet, watch, or anything else they may have robbed from you.

Did I tell you that at the city of Messina, the jumping-off point to cross from Sicily to the mainland, the entire train is disassembled and rolled onto tracks which are built into the hull of the ferry? It takes several hours to make what is usually a twenty-minute ferry crossing to get all the train cars shipped across and lined back up before heading north or south. It is strange to be in a train car in the belly of a ferryboat making the crossing. Weird, huh? And every train every day that leaves or arrives to the island has to go through this arduous process. If you're a passenger it feels like hours of backing up and going forward inch-by-inch.

I have been told that everyone wants a bridge and train trestle built but the Mafia owns the ferries and they are not about to let that happen because they reap so much money with this monopoly. It's rather strange but Sicilians seem to silently suffer a lot of inconveniences due to this sort of graft and corruption. It just goes to show the power of the Mafia and extent of the fear of them that is pervasive here.

Well, hope things are fine with you. I will close for now. I am pretty tuckered out and better try to rest up for Rome.

Love for now and ever,
Susannah, *Baronessa di* Haggard Travelers

Riding the Rails, Again
May 2, 1990

Dear Anne,

I am sitting here trying desperately to understand the four Italians who are sharing our train compartment. Every now and then I pick up some words, but I still have a long way to go to be fluent. Jackie and I are headed home from Rome. Ray should be flying the friendly skies on his way home now, too. We said our goodbyes this morning at the hotel and he headed for the airport and Jackie and I for the train station. The train is not a bad way to travel, but the trip gets so long before we pull into Catania station. We left Rome Termini at 8:50 AM and should arrive in Catania around 7:30 PM but it is almost always late. The train is now picking up speed so this writing may get messy. We enjoyed Ray's visit so much and he really seemed to love every minute. I think he is better satisfied now that he has seen what our lives are like here. He said that the children seemed extremely well adjusted and before he left, he was already talking about coming back for another visit.

Rome was a nice ending for Ray's trip. I never get tired of the Eternal City. I think it is my favorite European capital. I love the bars, the people, the feel of just the right amount of energy on the street. Not to mention the history and the fact that it really is true that it would take a lifetime to see it all. Jackie and I have just had a very good laugh about the fact that I can never get enough of traveling and You-Know-Who is trying his best to finagle a way to get us back home. He keeps talking to his old boss back home and the two of them are trying to cook something up. Jackie and I were laughing that my time in Europe was running out before I get sent back to "Hooterville." I sure hope we can stay for the next year. Go figure...if I love it...he hates it. He announced just recently for the hundredth time that there was nothing to do here but shop and eat out. I guess he isn't interested in the customs, culture, and history that surround us. Jackie says we are like the couple on the TV show "Green Acres." I'm like Lisa, the wife who loves city life, and he is like Oliver and wants to go back home to small-town life. So, I might be saying, "Goodbye City Life" if he gets his way. It seems that time is going by so fast, one more month and we have been here a year.

We did the usual in Rome; ate a lot of very good food and walked and walked. We climbed to the top of St. Peter's cupola and that was a first for me. All in all, I had a nice time and think Ray did too and I'm thrilled to have Jackie along to keep me company.

Well, I just returned from the *banyo*, the restroom, and let me tell you, there is a real art to hovering over a toilet on a moving train. Anyone planning to visit Italy should work on that skill. Most of the time there is no seat and even if there is one, I wouldn't suggest using it. Italy is not the cleanest country but it is the most colorful, and that makes up for any inconvenience in my book. I am looking out the window now and the hillside and fields are so green. Farmers are out working in their fields and it is a lovely day.

I loved your letter about doubling the dropout rate at school. I don't think if that is the case, it could be your fault. It is a very knotty problem and most of the time the students need so much support in so many areas that making education their first priority is just about impossible. To meet all their needs, one would need a small crew with unlimited funds. All you can do is try to help them make good choices and I know you are doing all you can there.

Well, it's 1:00 PM and everyone in this compartment is fast asleep taking *reposo*, the afternoon nap, so I guess I will close and take one too while it is quiet. I sure do miss you and sometimes I just wish so much you could be here enjoying all the fun I am having. Well, maybe in another life.

Love you,
Susannah, *Baronessa di* Wayfarers

Friday, May 4, 1990

Dear Sue,

No, I haven't forgotten you! I can't believe I've been so remiss about writing. Well, Sue, it's been almost a year. It has been a year since you decided to move. I keep getting flashbacks of what we were doing this time last year. I was keeping Hillary, Matt, and Drew, and you had this job. I don't know how you orchestrated your move and did this job at the same time! It is a very hectic time of year. What I want to say is "It's been long enough!" I've handled it. I've managed, but I think this is my limit. I'm not going to do so well next year. You must come home! I've been able to put up a good front, but the real feelings are starting to come through. I miss you! Come home! (I told Charles the other night that I was going to run away to Sicily. I am the only one in the family with a current passport, so they couldn't follow me right away.)

Tonight was the kids' talent show at school. What a spectacle! The grand finale fifth-grade performance was a circus...somewhat better than in previous years. The second-grade was awful. They dressed as monsters and did the "Monster Mash." It was pitiful. Hailey and one of her classmates decided to do an act dressing as scarecrows and doing a jazz-type dance to the music of "Ease on Down the Road." It was okay. They had practiced enough, so they were pretty much together. These talent shows are just not my type of thing. Several people filmed it so I'll probably get a copy since it was Laura's first year. The kindergarten was cute. They acted out nursery rhymes.

I was surprised to see Tiffany and her children there. She asked about you. She said she wanted to write you but hated to mention all the trouble at the school. I didn't tell her you were kept up-to-date on the big news from more than one source. I guess she doesn't know what a gossip I am.

I signed a new contract for next school year for this job and don't know whether I am happy or sad. (I've heard that there are two openings in the history department!) The principal really lost control in my office the other day. He brought one of my students to me because she possessed a guidance pass on which she had forged my signature. It was a dead give-away because she spelled Ann without an "e." He began yelling, and I mean yelling, at her with the door to my office open and the guidance waiting area packed with students. The student got madder and madder. She told him that he had no right to yell at her and, after starting to cry, she got up to leave, yelling, "You can take this school and shove it up your ass!" To which the principal immediately yelled back, "You've already got it up yours!" I was speechless. I couldn't believe it and kept trying to decide whether or not I should have tried harder to de-escalate the conflict. I think part of me, clearly, the part that won out, wanted to see how far he'd go. I don't think that he will be with us next year. I hope she will.

I'm finally sending you some pictures of Hailey's First Communion and some of Easter. The pictures don't do the dress justice. It fit her just perfectly, as you can see, and she just loves it, as you can see. Sending the pictures of the rest of the gang, minus the Mama and the Papa (just picture Mama Cass with red hair. I avoid cameras like the plague!) Also, sending a few *action shots* because, as you well know, the little darlings are not always posing as nicely as I would like. The picture of Stephen in the navy-blue outfit even surprises me, he looks so grown up. I know you'll be shocked. He is still a baby, but not for long.

Hailey's birthday presents arrived in plenty of time for her birthday. (I am impressed with the mail service!) She was so excited! She loved the briefcase, headbands, party hat, little notebook, coloring book, and, of course, her own Pinocchio! I love seeing how neat and different toys are from your part of the world. Hailey took several of her gifts into school for show-and-tell. And, of course, Laura's crayons, *petit* coloring books, and puzzles were a big hit, too. That girl loves a present! Thanks a bunch! Hailey and Laura are really missing your family. Hailey had a dream the other night that Hillary came home.

Saturday morning

I'm going this morning to help administer the SAT at the high school, so I'll mail this on the way. Have a Happy Mother's Day if you receive this in time. We never get enough recognition for our Herculean effort, do we? I am anxious to hear if you have any plans for heading back across the Atlantic this summer. Take care.

Love you, Anne

Hailey in her First Communion dress

Laura, Stephen, and Hailey in our front yard, 1990

Splitsville

May 10, 1990

Dear Anne,

Well, I guess I will remain in the land of the living for a while longer but for the past two days, I was not completely sure. I came back from the Rome trip and woke up with fever, sore throat, chills, headache, and just about as sick as I have ever been. I went to the clinic and had severe strep throat and now am on penicillin and feeling some better. I could not eat, drink, or talk for two days and never want to feel that poorly again. So far, no one else has come down with it. I strongly suggest you go wash your hands after reading this letter. I think I caught it from the train.

Hillary's birthday is coming up and she has invited three friends for a sleepover this weekend and has organized a day-long list of activities for Saturday. I am hoping I am recovered by then. I suggested she and her friends make cupcakes as one of the activities and she agreed so I am off the hook for the cake this year. Things are looking up.

Well, the lights just went out so the rest will be written by lamplight. Just heard a big clap of thunder and down the lights went which is not unusual as we lose power a lot here. It doesn't take much for it to blow. I have learned to keep the oil lamps full. The kids loved the gifts you sent, especially Matthew. I think you may be the only living soul that understands the boy!

My big news is that we are moving! Don't know where just yet but we are definitely moving, not back to the States, but here in Sicily. We finally had it out completely with the landlord. Things have now deteriorated beyond belief, but the real crisis began on Friday when the landlord's wife, Signora Santanocito, went downstairs and grabbed and shook Hillary because she did not close the gate fast enough to suit her. Hillary arrived upstairs in tears and was very shaken up, to say the least. Then on Saturday, she accosted us as we were leaving the apartment and shook her finger in our face, saying God knows what.

On Monday morning, we went to housing to register our complaint and guess who was there registering a complaint against us…well, sure enough, Santanocito himself! It was wonderful because we had an Italian interpreter to speak for us. I unloaded, and told them that we had irreconcilable differences and no longer wanted to reside in his house. I stated that they had accosted my children and made life miserable for all of us. We agreed if the landlord would give us our deposit back, we would gladly leave. I am so glad I got to tell him how disappointed I was that he had been so cruel and unfriendly towards our whole family and that I was so glad to move away from the likes of them. I also suggested to housing that their apartment be blacklisted from the housing list and they should not be allowed to rent to Americans again. I don't think that will happen since everyone here says that the housing office is controlled by the Mafia and I wouldn't doubt it.

Speaking my piece through the interpreter and knowing

they were finally understanding how we felt about them, gave me such delight. I had watched the movie *Mask* and Cher inspired me to tell it like it is. (Try to see it, if you can. I really liked it.) So now, we are desperately looking for a new home. We will be moving as soon as we can find a place. Hopefully, we can find something soon as everyone is anxious to put this episode behind us. Maybe the next letter you get will be from a better place. I am not even hoping for better, just livable at this point. Life is tough enough without having a disgruntled landlord watching your every move.

I watched the movie *Beaches* this past weekend and cried. I thought of you the whole time and how lucky I am to have a best friend to share all my trials and troubles with. I shudder to think how I would have survived if I didn't have you to listen to all my little calamities. We will be glad to move as no one feels comfortable here now. Jackie has suggested we salt the landlady's rose garden upon our departure as the Romans did to Carthage so nothing will ever grow again, but I think that may be taking it a bit too far. We would just like to leave and find a bit of peace.

Well, the lights are still out so I guess I will stumble into the bathroom and bathe by candlelight. Wish me luck house hunting…at least that's an area that I have some experience with. I am interested in it being livable but mainly in sizing up the landlords!!!

Love you,
Susannah, *Baronessa di* Nomads

PS My Mother's Day was nice. I got candy, flowers, and wine and declared that hereinafter, they should be the official Mother's Day gifts forevermore.

May 17, 1990

Dear Sue,

Thank you so much for the wonderful picture of Hillary, Matthew, and Drew. I would recognize them anywhere, but they are growing up and have really changed this year. They look great! I miss them so much! I sure hope they know how much I love them.

I've also got your letter about your strep throat. Wow! It bothers me to hear that you were that sick. I just picture all of you in the best of health (which I know you usually are) safe from anything harmful. When you write me about Hillary's dog bite, Drew's nosebleed, your strep throat, or Matthew's stitches, I worry. I just want to picture you all frolicking in the hills with the shepherds, shopping at the markets, eating pasta, and swimming in the Med. Please take care!

I am counting the days until the end of school. It's getting very hectic. The Parallel High School is doing a booming business, really truly, more than I can handle. There is still no replacement for Anne and the other two counselors, who are sharing her load, are beginning to get bitter about it. I'm dealing with some very heavy-duty crises with these kids. Talked to three pregnant couples this week. It's hard to know what to say. These kids are so oblivious to what is really in store for them. Although I'm having a fairly good week, I've decided I do have a problem with PMS and it's getting worse as I get older. I couldn't stand anything about my life two weeks ago. Things are more tolerable now.

Hailey has her dance recital this weekend. I may try to film it. I have done very little filming this year. The NEC VCR finally died, not to be resurrected.

For goodness sake, please don't feel you omitted Stephen in any way with Hailey's birthday box. You know he's way too young to even know what's going on with opening gifts. His favorite playthings are the forbidden fruits he comes across in his daily ramblings, such as toothpaste, a toilet, telephones, anything that will plug into an electrical socket, the inside of the refrigerator, markers, various containers of shampoo, hand cream, Windex, and birdseed (we still have two parakeets!). I could go on and on. Anything age-appropriate would probably not keep his interest.

Well, I better go to bed. I am back to getting up at 5:15 and walking for thirty minutes. Are you skinny yet? Don't worry, I still love you, just send me all your too-big clothes.

Let me know if I can intervene with the certification office for you. I could start calling them every day. Just send me the info I need and your social security number and I'll get an answer for you.

Love to everyone and especially to you, Anne

May 22, 1990

Dear Sue,

Did I thank you for the uplifting Mother's Day Card? Well, thank you very much! I sure haven't felt like anyone's inspiration this year, but thank you for the vote of confidence. I needed it. Your Mother's Day sounded much better than mine, although Charles did go to the curb market for flowers on Saturday and, of course, I did get the school-made gifts from the girls. Made me think of Erma Bombeck. I will miss those gifts one day.

It sounds like Hillary's birthday was a big success, very smart to turn it over to her. I can remember her first birthday party. What a celebration! I can't believe she is eleven years old.

I hope all moves quickly with your move. Sounds to me like you really put up with a lot. I'm sure there was constant tension living so close to such a landlord. I hope that he gets what he deserves in his next tenant. Maybe you will get a place with a phone! That would be wonderful. By the way, how did you get a $700 power bill? You mentioned that in your card. Is it that much more expensive? Was that one month? Wow. Does the government pay it?

Charles and I went to apply for a home equity loan this week. I hate doing anything which involves disclosing our financial situation. As we were sitting in Wachovia

Bank waiting to talk to our personal banker who is now someone new (they never stay long enough for you to get to know them or use them more than once), anyway, as we were sitting there, I told Charles I'd rather be waiting for a pap smear! That's how much I dread admitting we have no assets, only debts. Try as we might, we have not been able to make a dent in our credit card balances. As a matter of fact, they've been creeping up. We now owe about $8500 total and are paying 18-percent interest with no tax break on the interest. I have never understood home equity loans, but they're not as bad as I feared; the interest rate is about 11 percent (prime plus one) and it's separate from a house payment. You can pay it off as fast as you like and only pay interest for the time you owe the money. The interest will be a tax deduction and, of course, we're planning to pay it off quickly. We've earmarked my summer school paycheck for this purpose, plus the extra we'll save from not having to pay for babysitting or school tuition. Charles and I are so much alike when it comes to money...there's not a thrifty bone between us. Maybe it's a reaction to our parents thriftiness. I would never borrow money from my mother. I was so angry this winter that I had decided not to ever take any money, not even inheritance. That may be a little extreme. Of course, I'm sure I won't have to deal with that for a while. My parents were so proud of being frugal that I hear that script in my head every time I face the fact that we have no savings and have bought things on credit.

To get this home equity loan, the bank had to appraise the house. Fortunately, it was fairly straightened up when they came to look at it, not that that has anything to do with value, just with my pride, I think. I'll be interested in finding out what they come up with. They have to find three houses in our area which have sold in the last three years in order to determine a fair market value. That may be hard to do. Charles and I told them we thought it would sell for $135,000. When we refinance next fall (1991) we will owe $73,000 on both the mortgage and home equity combined. I'm sure they will see fit to use the equity as collateral for another $8,500. I don't know why I'm rambling on like this... because it's on my mind and you'd be hearing all this if you were within earshot. As you can see, a trip to Italy is pretty much a dream. I am sure thankful I met you in London before I knew any better! Maybe we will win the lottery. Charles has been spearheading a big project at work (and driving me nuts talking incessantly about it). He thinks it might mean a promotion to a GS13, but that seems a little too optimistic to me. Oh well. We'll just have to tighten our belts a little this summer. (Mine's already tight in more ways than one.)

The CCC staff called a meeting today about the Parallel High School. I knew it was coming. The students this year, especially the seniors, have real attitude problems and are being rude to the college staff. I have to be there almost every time they attend. The college has hired a new night-time person. I like her, but she doesn't have the bounce or enthusiasm that Gale and Gilda have and she goes exactly by the rules as she interprets them. Some of the adult CCC students have been complaining about the high school students and she's afraid they'll stop coming, which would put her position in jeopardy. I think I am ready to move the program back to the high school.

The superintendent just presented the budget to the county teachers. It allows for a new high school history position, plus there also will be another vacancy in the history department. And they are planning to add an at-risk position at the other high school. This may be a pie-in-the-sky budget request. They're also asking for a six-percent teacher supplement. We'll see.

Well, good luck with the house hunting. I'm still looking for you here! I have seen the movie *Mask* with Cher. I liked it, too. The kid was so neat!

I better go to bed. Am getting a cold. At first, I thought I was getting strep throat in sympathy, but I think it is less serious. Take care.

All my love, Anne

Sunday, June 10, 1990

Dear Sue,

I am completely in awe of your ability last spring to juggle three kids, a husband, this at-risk PHS job, and a move to Sicily! I don't know how you did it. No wonder you felt a little crazy some of the time. I'm feeling very crazy most of the time. The end-of-the-year festivities at the kids' school, plus the frantic high school end-of-year stuff, have been almost too much.

I have frequently thought about what you said concerning this job. You were right. The hardest part is dealing with the CCC staff. It has gotten really bad. They do not want the program and have done everything they can to push us out. During the last two weeks of school, I was at the high school nearly every day, all day, and at CCC every night. Otherwise, several seniors would not have made it to graduation. We had no hours during the Easter break, which was a big make-up time last year. There will be some big changes next year, actually this summer. I'm pushing to operate out of the middle school during the summer, using the library. The assistant superintendent didn't want us pulling out. He wants CCC to say they could not handle it, i.e., they were unable to keep their end of the bargain.

We had the meeting with CCC personnel last week. The top dog present for CCC was the guy in charge of the curriculum. (I'll always remember him as the one who offered Charles a part-time teaching position, but made it clear he did not think Charles' little wife, with the master's degree who was teaching a psych class there, should earn more than the man-of-the-house, with the bachelor's degree, so said he would make up the difference for Charles's pay. Oh, these male egos! So fragile. We women certainly get the message loud and clear.) Anyway, the assistant superintendent represented the Board of Education. CCC ended up saying they could no longer handle the program, so on Thursday, we (school personnel) will meet to make final plans for this summer. My days at school are unbelievably busy. It is quite a hectic job.

A new male guidance counselor has been hired at the high school for next year. We haven't met him yet. I feel sure Nancy will retire next year. She will be eligible in January. They are a funny group and now with Anne gone, we are each keeping to ourselves. The new assistant principal used to be a guidance counselor and the two remaining counselors seem to find him very threatening. I like him. His wife is a guidance counselor at one of the elementary schools. They are about our age, maybe a few years older, no kids. What a life!

I am anxious to hear from you. Hope the apartment hunting and moving are progressing as they should. I can imagine you're very busy with all that. I hope it is easier now with your knowledge of Italian and your experience with landlords. Is a trip home this summer out of the question? Or even this fall? As I finalize plans for the year, I realize it will be gone before we know it. Since we are not *going on vacation* this summer, I have talked Charles into taking Fridays and Mondays off for most of the time that we are all out of school. A trip to Chapel Hill or the beach is enough of a trip for me with three kids. And actually, Jungleland is enough for them to feel like they have really arrived!

Monday morning

I'm up and ready for work, everyone else is staying home. What a snap! Only having to get myself ready. I have so much left to do at school and I know I'll be getting calls from desperate parents today.

Charles and I went to the Excellence in Teaching awards banquet. Remember that new incentive thing? Of course, Carol was there and we talked about what we'd heard from Sicily. She sounded like she was planning to go. I think that she really wants to. She seemed fine.

We've had a beautiful spring here. It is very cool for this time of year. We've had our air conditioner on one day so far. Had a leak in the upstairs unit this weekend and the more Charles messed with it, the worse things got. (Don't ever get a water-to-air system). I kept saying, "Call a plumber. Call a plumber." I'm wonderful support, aren't I? He did fix it, but we haven't needed it. It is nice to have a low electric bill for a while.

Charles' nephew is getting married in August and asked if "Great Performances" would video it. I said no. Mainly, because I don't want to, but I used the uncertainty about the equipment as the primary reason. Of course, they countered by saying they would borrow a camera for me. It will have been two years this August since you and I have filmed a wedding. Our video company, "Great Performances", created to justify buying all the equipment to film our own kids, was successful only because you and I were a team. I felt invincible then or, at least, only partly to blame, when we took on filming jobs. Weddings, birthdays, anniversaries, whatever, just seemed very manageable together. Even our fiascos were funny, weren't they? I don't feel confident on my own, plus it's awful doing it alone with a strange camera in front of all those people that I know. I just think that it is asking a lot. I'll call Dennis and see if he will do it instead. Then Charles and I can give the newlyweds a check for part of his price (I'm guessing he'll charge at least $200) as a wedding gift. I don't think I am being mean or selfish. The only advantage I can see to filming the wedding is that I would not be in the video!

Well, it's time to head to work (by way of McDonald's). I may use my supplement check to start at the Diet Center, but that's next week. Take care. I think about you all the time and *really, really* miss you all!

Love, Anne

Night at the Opera
June 12, 1990

Dear Anne,

Today marks the year anniversary of our arrival. I think now that it has been a fast year although it seemed long in places. Tomorrow is the last day of school and the children are looking forward to the summer. We are already having some hot summer weather with several sirocco winds, the ones that blow in off the north coast of Africa with the super-heated air. They are miserable. One would think you are in an oven and any breeze is little relief. The breeze just feels like super-heated air. We have fans but sleeping at night can be a sweat fest.

The teachers had the kids clean out their desks today and Matt brought home a book bag full of comic books, *Mad* magazines, and half a tube of glue. That was it! Guess we can chalk up this year to his international experience but not heavy on the academics. Anyway, he has loved it! His father thinks it is criminal to have had a year of leisure, I'm not so sure.

Yesterday, I went to the town of Giarre, about forty-five minutes north of Catania, still on the coast. It is known for its ironworks and everyone buys baker's racks and iron beds and all kinds of ironworks there. I shopped and bought a few things, but no major purchases.

Our real excitement came on Sunday night when we went to Catania to the Bellini Theatre to see the opera *Norma.* Catania is about 30 minutes from our house and we had hired a babysitter for an evening out on the town. The theatre was built in the grand baroque style in the 1880s and named for the local *Catanese (*from Catania) composer Vincenzo Bellini who wrote *Norma*, his most celebrated opera. It is a very grand theatre with painted ceilings, a marble foyer, magnificent chandeliers, and ornate stucco. The interior is strikingly gorgeous with a red-plush interior that includes seating on the main floor and four tiers of box seats. We had tickets for the box seats on the third level, perfect seating for a breathtaking performance. I was told it is supposed to be the third best opera house in the world.

Italy has 72 opera houses, proof positive that Italians love their opera. It is the only country that I have visited where the guy who pumps your gas at the gas station might entertain you with an aria. I find that refreshing and, no doubt, these people have art in their bloodstream. No matter what they do from stacking fruit to selling fish, they add that little tasteful flair that sets them apart with a dash of artistry. I just love it. We had box seats and got all dressed up and felt for a while like the upper crust. It was my first opera experience and it overwhelmed me with elegance and fascination.

I left the theatre transformed on a cloud of wonder and amazement that lasted all of the ten minutes that it took for us to walk to our car. The car started but lurched a few feet and stopped. We tried again and it repeated the same shuck-and-jive through several intersections where we were nearly broadsided. It finally died and we were able to coast to a curb. At that point, we decided we would have to leave it since we were already late to return to release the babysitter. We thought that we could get a taxi at the train station for the thirty-minute ride home so we started walking the approximately ten blocks in that direction down dark streets. I was peeling off my jewelry with every step.

Once we got to the train station, we saw a group of men standing around. When we said, "Taxi," a young man quickly escorted us to his car and off we sped. The keyword is sped! My God, he drove like a mad man and I was yelling, "Please slow down!" Clearly, he was enjoying my obvious fright and sped up. I think I smelled liquor on his breath and he drove like a drunk, crazy man the rest of the way. We paid him his £35.00 and I have never been so glad to see our apartment. We explained the delay to the babysitter and said we had to leave the car in Catania and she said, "Oh you shouldn't have done that. Thieves will probably strip it and set it on fire." Seems that is a common practice to hide any fingerprints, etc.

Our riches-to-rags story ended well as the next morning we found our car intact and we were able to have it towed and repaired. *Norma* is a tragedy that culminates with lovers joined on a funeral pyre but luckily our car escaped a similar fate. One thing I think most Americans who have lived or traveled in Sicily would agree upon is that everything in Sicily is an adventure. Sicilians expect this, even revel in it perhaps, and that is part of their charming spontaneity. We Americans are either appalled or amazed by it, at times, maybe both. I am learning to expect the unexpected.

Anyway, I lived to tell the tale. Hope all is well with you and that you are looking forward to summer.

Much Love,
Susannah, *Baronessa di* Coincidental Amazement

Midsummer Motta

June 28, 1990

Dear Anne,

Just a short note to say Happy Birthday again. I will be thinking of you tomorrow as you celebrate your birthday and hope you have a great day. Hope you are racking up more wisdom with your years than I seem to be doing. Our family discussions are still going on about returning home. There is a job waiting in the States but I am campaigning hard to stay. Everyone voted and it is five to one, me as the dissenting vote. Leonardo went with the majority as he has heard that there are no dogs in America and the streets are paved with kitty treats. No seriously, I am trying to convince everyone to stay, while appearing to let the boss do the decision-making. Ha! Pretty sure we will be staying as making a decision is not his forte.

All here is good, still scrambling to find a house to move into but the weather is nice. It is in the hot 90s in the day but cooler at night. These concrete houses absorb the heat during the day and give it off like an oven at night. Guess that is why the Sicilians spend so much time on their balconies in the evening. During the evenings, many ladies sit out in their chairs in small groups on the street, some turned with their backs to the street, to sew and gossip. Tradition is that respectable ladies aren't to be seen in public and many of the older set keep a very low profile. Older Sicilian widows wear all black every day for the rest of their lives, so they are easy to spot and Motta is full of ladies in black.

We went to Catania to the antique street market on Sunday morning and picked up a few interesting items. This antique market is held downtown every Sunday morning and it is not crowded like the regular market so it is a pleasurable stroll around that area of town. The bars are open so we can get coffee and pastries and check out various *trattorias* for lunch. There are many family-owned, tiny *trattorias,* small restaurants, tucked away on the side streets that offer daily luncheon specials. We have tried a few and the food is awe-inspiring and very reasonable. This weekend is the big Fourth of July festival on base so the kids are primed and ready for that. No other news at the moment.

Love you,
Susannah, *Baronessa di* Nothing Much Noteworthy

July 7, 1990

Dear Sue,

Thought about all of you on the Fourth remembering your letters from last year about the festivities on base. Hope it was as fun this year. Susan and Sarah were here through the holiday. They stayed for about a week. We had been looking forward to their visit for months. We had fun, but as you can imagine with four (were there only four?) children, it stayed hectic. Sarah is very much the only child and Susan is very much the parent of an only child...and I felt like the "Old Woman in the Shoe" ready to whip them all soundly and send them to bed! Stephen decided that he could bully Sarah, who is two years older, and get away with it. So, he did. I wonder if he already has testosterone poisoning. He loves to hit, grab, pinch, push, pull hair, typical male tendencies. So now, we're back to normal...for us, that is, which is pretty crazy by anyone else's standards.

Charles' mother called to offer us some butterbeans, which I politely refused. She then made a feeble attempt at an apology for our earlier disagreement, which I feebly acknowledged, but then we ended up disagreeing again and she hung up on me. I composed a letter that I'm trying to muster up the courage to send, asking them to stop calling so much, dropping in unannounced, and bringing food. Charles' sister calls regularly to check up on things and it drives me nuts. I don't know how this will be resolved. I'm beginning to resent Charles' mother. If she tells me one more time my children are undisciplined, I think I'll go for her throat!

Thank you for the great birthday card. It sums it all up. It has been depressing. My last year as "thirty-something." I'm not going to give up without a fight. Went to Diet Center Friday and am going to be on what they call the "last diet I'll ever need." Whew. Say a little prayer for me. I think it's going to be a lot harder at my age.

I wish I could talk to you. I can only imagine what you are deciding. It sure is going to be hard for me to wait another year to see you all. Everyone keeps asking about your plans and I just continue to say you are having a perfectly marvelous time and want to stay but M's boss at Cherry Point has just been pressuring him to come back. I'm not the only one who misses you all. Take care.

Love, Anne

July 9, 1990

Dear Sue,

Got up this morning to walk, was dressed, and at the door before I realized we were rained out, so now a perfectly quiet time to write you. I was so sorry I missed your call last week and have been trying to imagine if there was some big news, like when to meet you at the airport. As always, I'm anxious to hear what's new with you. Please don't hesitate to call me in the middle of the night. Really! I'm always home then and the phone will not wake up anyone else. I wake up right away, will have no trouble getting back to sleep, and will be fairly confident of no interruptions for our conversation. I'm serious. I want you to know that a call from you is always a welcomed treat any time.

I am beginning to feel back to normal after a week of what I think was strep throat. I finally, after much suffering, went to the doctor and, because by then I had an ear infection, was prescribed penicillin with no throat culture. It's such a relief to feel well again. I could not take any time off and last week seemed really hectic. It was awful.

The strep throat did, however, give me a bit of an excuse to skip some of the 1970 class reunion festivities. Charles seemed to have a very good time. It is funny how it brings up so many past feelings. I think he started acting like an 18-year-old again. He began celebrating on Thursday night with some of his old neighborhood buddies, Mike and Doug. They drank too much, so Charles just drank water the rest of the weekend. It seemed to be a good turnout. Everyone asked about you guys and I loved being the authority on what you've been up to. Although I enjoyed seeing several people on Saturday night, I wasn't that interested. When it is not your class, you are kind of on the fringe. I left early Saturday night (it was held at the Morehead City Country Club). Charles was out until about 2:00 a.m. I enjoyed talking to Judy, recently a first-time mother, totally unplanned, who has a 5-month-old little girl. She was hilarious. She wants another kid right away but says her husband runs when she mentions it. He seemed like a neat guy, although has one big flaw. He's a staunch Republican and Judy is a very outspoken Democrat. She's funny talking about it. Quite a few of your classmates attended from out-of-state. I thought everyone looked really good after twenty years.

The big news of the week, though, comes from none other than my sister Christine, who announced her engagement and upcoming marriage, not really at the reunion, but during the week. The guy (class of 1972) has been doing odd jobs for my mother and that is how Chris met him. They've set the date for early September. She has her dress and got a ring this weekend. Whew! Quite a surprise. I had talked to Chris about it but had not seen her new fiance until Saturday night at the class reunion. My mother is thrilled, in a weird kind of way. I'm glad for them, but it is taking me a while to absorb the whole thing and, at this point in my life, I want to ask why would anybody choose to get married. So, it's hard to get bubbly happy. He seems nice enough and seems to be a better match for Chris than some of her other boyfriends. She wanted to call and tell you. I told her I was almost as fast as a phone call.

No other big news. I went to yard sales on Saturday with Stephen Herring. It just wasn't the same talking to him! Had good luck. Bought some clothes, a small black and white TV for the kitchen, and a 6x8 oriental type rug ($75) for the newly furnished music room. Did I tell you we bought a piano from Carolyn's parents for $500? We put it in the computer room which no longer has a computer. I had been looking for a rug ever since Mr. Nelson, who came to tune the piano, said, "Well, it's going to be too loud in here because of this bare room." Well, that hurt my feelings. I thought the room's furnishings were fine. Anyway, I especially missed you on Saturday. I still have the yard sale bug, but it's not the same without you.

The Kramers bought Sarah's house in East Shore Estate for $197,000. I can't believe it! Then, they went on vacation to Disneyworld. I'm going to push my kids to sell insurance! I haven't been inside, but heard it's a knockout. Amy then hired an interior decorator and had custom drapes made, chairs reupholstered, and pillows made, the whole nine yards, for her daughter's room. And I get excited about a $75 yard sale rug!

Hope all is well with all of you. We will be thinking of Matthew on the 20th. Can't believe he's nine!

Looking forward to hearing what's new. Sue, I haven't forgotten about the certification office but, ashamedly, must admit I have not called. I'm sorry. I will do it this week, I promise. Take care.

Love, Anne

Looking for the Godfather

July 16, 1990

Dear Anne,

Well, decision made…as I knew it would be…we are staying. Once I backed away from the process, it fell apart. No one had the fortitude to make it happen. I suspected that if I ignored the situation, it would all come to naught and I was right. So, we are going to move from this apartment as soon as we can find a place. As far as leaving Sicily anytime soon, we are not, we are staying! Yeah, I am so glad. All that angst has melted away and we can continue to make the most of this experience.

We went to Forza d'Agro, a gorgeous ancient town, this past weekend. It is high up in the mountains and people have been living there since the 5th century BC. It is a charming place seemingly caught in the past. There were donkeys in the street and if you lived on the upper end of town, you would definitely need one. The streets are too narrow for cars and the climb is steep. The Santissima Annunziata Cathedral, located in the lower part of town, is famous for being used in a *Godfather* movie. It appears in the *Godfather Part II* as the backdrop for the scene where Michael Corleone marries the Sicilian girl after being struck by the thunderbolt. We took some pictures and I will send them. We are visiting a few places where scenes from those movies were filmed. There is a bar scene filmed in the town of Savoca that we plan to see, too.

We climbed all the way to the top of the town and met an English couple who are remodeling an ancient house built right into the mountainside. They took us inside their house and one wall is the actual stone of the mountain. They plan to use it as a holiday home. The town is so quiet that except for the cathedral bells and the occasional donkey braying, there is a total hush over the village. It is a place where you could soak in the quiet and hear only the sweep of brooms and the click of knitting needles. I would love to live there. The views are amazing and one can see broad vistas of the Sicilian coastline. We could even see the mainland of Italy across the Strait of Messina. There was one bar and very few other amenities. A perfect example of a place trapped in time. There are so many hillside towns and villages and I want to visit all of them. This is one that we will visit if you come? Ahem...hope you start planning soon.

We plan to go to Switzerland in August camping for a couple of weeks. We will drive the Volvo fully stocked up with food and supplies and tour the whole peninsula of Italy, stopping where we want. Thank goodness for a station wagon...we are going to need it. We plan to stop somewhere in the Naples/Pompeii region and also plan to stop and see the town of Collodi, the home of the author of *Pinocchio.* It is in the Tuscan region and the travel guidebook says the whole town is dedicated to Pinocchio. I think the kids will enjoy that. Italy is roughly the size of California so it should take us at least three days to get to Switzerland, depending on our stops.

In Switzerland, we will camp near Zermatt for two weeks. We have packed two tents and a carload of supplies. We will need to find hotels along the way and maybe for a few days in Switzerland if the camping is too rough. It should be cooler there and a fun trip. Hope all is good with you. I know you must be looking forward to your summer break. Well, will close for now and get this in the post.

Love you,
Susannah, *Baronessa di* Mountain Villages

PS I am so glad we are staying. There is so much to discover here so I need to get busy if I am going to make a dent in it all in this next year.

July 27, 1990

Dear Sue,

It came! My birthday present arrived safe and sound! What a fun present! It rattled like crazy when I picked it up so I was a little nervous, however, it was just the noodle pasta that had escaped from its bag. I love the ceramic sun! I am so envious of the wonderful things you must be seeing. Of course, you know my taste so well. There are a couple of places I have in mind for the ceramic piece but I haven't decided for sure. I'm doing great on the Diet Center program (15 pounds in three weeks) so the wine will be saved for my *I've reached my goal* celebration. The program now allows pasta, so I will enjoy that soon. Thank you so much! If it weren't for you and Susan, birthdays and Christmas would be a complete bust for me. You both always give me gifts I love. Was it last Christmas (or maybe the year before) you two gave me the same thing, ceramic soap dispensers? I loved them both.

I have one more week of summer school. It has gone fairly well. I've read *The News and Observer* every morning, as well as the magazines the library takes. I don't really teach, so there is no preparation. My biggest problem has been feeling guilty about my own kids. I think they've been enjoying themselves this summer and I know I'm not that much fun to stay home with, but in my mind, I know I should probably be home with them. I'll only have from August 4 until August 14 as a summer break, then it will be back to school. I am planning to approach my job differently next year. I was so naive when I started this job. It looks to be a very interesting year. The rumors are flying.

Chris' engagement has been called off. They had set the date but then I think Chris started getting nervous about the commitment. I really can't picture her ever getting married.

Well, it's 2:15 Friday afternoon and all my students have left. I'm going to leave, too. Charles just got back from a trip to Monterey. I'm glad he's home for the weekend. He is so ready for a different job. It makes me nervous.

Take care. Give everyone a hug and a kiss. Thank you again for my wonderful birthday presents!

Love, Anne

Tuesday, August 14, 1990

Dear Sue,

Thanks so much for the great pictures of you and the kids. Everyone looks so healthy and happy. I must admit it is a shock to see the kids looking so much older. It's amazing how much they have changed in just one (*long*) year. Sometimes I still can't believe you're there. What wonderful places you have seen!

I've been thinking about you constantly since this Iraq problem has developed. So many troops are leaving from here. I hope it hasn't meant a big change for Sigonella, however, I'm sure everything is on alert just because of all the activity. We're praying it is over quickly and quietly. Would the government even consider sending civilians home? I'm glad that you got your trip to Switzerland in before all this. It probably feels good to stay put now.

Can you believe I go back to work tomorrow? I can't. My ten-day vacation is over today. Quite honestly though, it is not a picnic staying home with three kids. Can you remember having a two-year-old (or two)? I can't take my eyes off him for one minute. He is much more active and physical than the girls ever were. He loves to push a chair over to the kitchen counter and climb up. Once up there, he walks around, talks on the phone, picks up knives, pencils, etc. It's wild! We keep the doors locked when we are home because if they are unlocked, he will go right outside. And to top it all, he can easily go all day without a nap! I do hope Beverly (Melissa's mom) can handle him. I worry she will let her guard down and he'll get hurt. I'm relying heavily on his Guardian Angel!

Hailey started piano lessons last week and I am wondering if I've made a mistake. I don't want to have to police her and nag her about practicing but it's just as frustrating to see money go down the drain. I'm afraid Hailey may have taken after her mother, hence not very musically inclined and rather impatient about results. Oh well, we'll see. All I need is another thing to worry about. At least she can get to her lesson without me.

Did I tell you that Hailey and Laura are sharing a bedroom again? After spending time and money moving Hailey into the smaller bedroom upstairs, wouldn't you know she and Laura just had to be together? Actually, it seems to be working out. It's a better arrangement for Stephen. Sylvia painted a five-foot white flying horse on the wall in the girls' room. It was copied from a picture in a fairytale book and includes a child on Pegasus' back with billowing clouds in a night sky. The colors in the picture, lavender and pink, are perfect with the comforters and sheets that I bought for the girls' twin beds. Sylvia did a wonderful job! She is very talented. I'll have to send you a picture.

I guess that's about all I've accomplished around here. Keeping Stephen safe and losing twenty pounds. Well, eighteen and three-fourths pounds to be exact. It has made a difference, but I'm still over twenty-five pounds from my goal. And it is getting harder and harder.

I'm enjoying my sun face ceramic. Hung it over the

stove. Looks great! My kitchen is beginning to reflect a very Italian flavor.

Think about us as we gear up for school and our life as *involved parents.* Charles has to organize painting the two student bathrooms at school. The health inspector said the brick walls had to be sealed so they could be washed easily. So that's what we will be doing on Saturday. I've gotten so I resent projects like that when our lives are so full of things to do at home. And, of course, getting volunteers is a job in itself.

Here's a human-interest story...The Bertrams returned from vacation this summer to find their house completely flooded from a broken pipe in the water-to-air heat pump which was in the attic. So, two floors down, three inches of water were standing in the house when they opened the door. I heard there was a cascading waterfall coming down the grand staircase. The whole house has to be gutted and redone. Furniture, rugs, floors are ruined. I wonder if Maryanne's extensive designer wardrobe escaped the deluge. They are staying in a motel and looking for a furnished house to rent. I bet she is freaking out. I would be. And with school about to start. Charles and I have made a mental note to turn our water-to-air heat pumps off anytime we leave, even for a weekend...turn that water off! I guess you had a taste of flooding yourself this year, I just remembered. Was anything ruined?

Well, I'm going to close. Charles' mother has the kids at her house and I said I'd pick them up at 2:00. I had a physical this morning with bloodwork, mammogram, pap smear, the works! I'd been dreading it, but I do feel better with someone looking me over once a year.

When do your kids start school? The 27th of August is the big day here. Hi to everyone. We sure miss you all. Let me hear from you so I'll know how the Iraq thing is affecting you. Take care!

Love, Anne

Hostilities

August 17, 1990

Dear Anne,

We got back from our two-week vacation in Switzerland and it was good to be home until we turned on the TV and heard the news. What a paradoxical situation. Switzerland was so tranquil and beautiful. We camped up high in the mountains near Zermatt and had a wonderful campsite. We had packed the Volvo with all our gear and groceries and we spent our days hiking and just enjoying the serene meadows all around us. The beauty of Switzerland cannot be overstated; it almost doesn't look real, with the wildflowers blooming and cows grazing. Every view was a photograph. We were able to fully relax and let go of the pressure we have felt trying to iron out all the complications of living here.

Our escape from reality lasted all of 20 minutes after arriving home. When we turned on the TV, we were shocked to learn that while we were basking in tranquility, America was planning a war! Everything here has heightened as far as security…troops are coming in...there are cots all over the gym floor and we have been told to be prepared to evacuate, if necessary. Now we are told to "maintain readiness," whatever that means. So, I guess I can stop worrying about earthquakes, volcanoes, bad landlords, and now just concentrate on war. What the heck is this insanity about? I plan to tune it out and see if it will just go away. Anyway, for the moment, life does go on.

School registration is tomorrow and Hillary has an orthodontist appointment coming up. We got Leonardo fixed and he was doing fine but then started with an eye infection. The vet said to use this cream on his eyes three times a day and we have wrestled him down and managed to get the cream everywhere else but his eyes so far.

I will close for now. I must say that as an old hippie-peacenik, I sure could have done without these new hostilities. I don't support any war and it is extremely hard to support an America that always seems so militaristic. Wonder if I wear my black armband on base I will get hassled by the MPs. Interesting times to say the least. Why can't America mind its own business and take some of the military's budget to support education and healthcare? I think it is a big mistake. America should take a clue from Switzerland and simmer down. Switzerland, now that's my kind of place, fully focused on maintaining their perfect environment and leaving all else alone. Can't we learn anything? Well, will close for now.

Love to you all,
Susannah, *Baronessa di* Peaceniks

PS I found a wonderful antique shop in Switzerland and got some incredible bargains. My favorite is a huge straw suitcase with leather straps that I am now using to save all of your letters.

Everything Comes at a Price
August 23, 1990

Dear Anne,

Got your letter and your dose of normal life was a treat and a tonic to me. Nothing much normal here at the moment. Many people here are nervous about all the march-to-war words being thrown around. I think we are safe but if things continue to deteriorate, we might just show up on your doorstep. Today all the military are being instructed on using a gas mask and we are getting a steady diet of anti-terrorist tactics that keeps everyone on edge. The threat level on base has been raised to BRAVO which makes getting on base a bit more difficult. We are the closest base to Iraq with dependents. They have flown all the dependents out of the base in Jordan already. They say, of course, they will do the same for us, if necessary. This base is a fueling depot for the Mediterranean fleet so it is important. The influx of troops has caused our shelves in the commissary to be emptied, but other than that life seems normal.

School starts Monday and I guess things will go on as usual. The kids are not immune to all this angst as everyone is talking about it nonstop. I would like for them to feel safe and am doing my best to remain calm and as normal as possible. It is strange to be an anti-war American in a foreign country and yet so intertwined with military life as we are. I am struggling with protesting against the hand that feeds us. I am hoping beyond hope that the whole conflict will blow over and hostilities will be resolved. I am keeping a weather eye out on the situation and will try to make a wise decision if I think it is unsafe for us to stay here. I must say it is really undermining my grand European vacation plans at the moment. Life here seems full of surprises. Never a dull moment, it seems.

We recently had a run-in with the prickly pear bush. Sicily is covered with huge prickly pear bushes and the Sicilians love the fruit. The *fichidindia*, the fig of India, is eaten peeled and chilled. The small oval fruit grows on the top of the cactus pear pads. The cactus bushes are everywhere and grow wild along the roads. The fruit is covered in fixed spines and small hairlike prickles that stick to everything. I am not a fan of the taste but the health nut I am married to is crazy about them. Recently, he decided to harvest his own as we were driving along the roadside. He pulled over and used several paper napkins we had in the car to pick a couple. He wrapped them in the napkins and put them in the glove compartment. Later that day as we were driving, Drew suddenly had a gushing nose bleed so I quickly looked in the glove box for tissues and grabbed the ones I saw, forgetting that the prickly pears were in the napkins. They fell out into my lap and I was covered in the clinging, hairlike prickles.

I went home, bathed, changed clothes, and removed all the prickles I could. I thought that was the end of it but later that week, the guy who catches a ride to work with Hubby sat in that seat and he was itching all day. He had unfortunately finished cleaning up the seat, poor fellow. So now for extra precaution, I am using a towel to sit on when I ride in that car. We have since learned that Sicilians use a special funnel-shaped tool on a long wooden handle to gather the fruit, not a paper napkin. They soak and scrap them to remove the prickles before they try to peel them. I now have an aversion to them and still itch every now and then. To me, they are tasteless and full of seeds to boot. The Sicilians love them, but that is understandable as they are plentiful and free for the taking everywhere. For me, they were literally a pain-in-the-ass and way too bland for my palate and certainly not worth the effort.

Anyway, life goes on, bittersweet and full of thorns sometimes, but all in all, we are doing well. I'll keep you posted as to how we fare in all this world turmoil. I told you they call this base "The Tip of the Spear" for the Middle East, not sure I care for that analogy. I am more chicken than patriot, but aren't all mothers? If only women ruled the world...

Love you,
Susannah, *Baronessa di* Calculated Risks

September 7, 1990

Dear Sue,

I know you probably fainted when M brought this letter home. I think about you all the time. I've been trying to visualize what "sorry I haven't written" card I should buy. Whether it should say I've broken both arms or been in a coma or been kidnapped by a UFO. Then, it dawned on me that the real reason would probably stand as a real excuse and bring tears of empathy. The reason I haven't written is that I've had to deal with three children, one husband, the responsibility of all the housework and finances, the beginning of a new school year, in-laws, a mother, and a full-time job *outside the home.* It's enough to bring a grown woman to her knees. I don't know exactly what has made this year seem so overwhelming, whether it's dealing with a 2-year-old or my diminishing tolerance level. Anyway, I have appreciated your letters. I truly miss you!

The girls are fairly well adjusted into school. No real complaints. Everything pretty much as we expected. Enrollment is up at the school and the overall morale seems pretty high. We took a four-day Labor Day weekend and went to Chapel Hill, stayed with Susan and Sarah, and then went camping, all seven of us, at a lake nearby. We had a lot of fun and lucked out on a huge, secluded campsite. We heard raccoons and a bear in the night. We only camped one night which is my limit with these kids. Then back to Chapel Hill for some shopping. That has been our only vacation this summer. And although it went well and pretty much as anticipated, it is not at all fun to spend any length of time with three kids in a car. We even had a little TV and VCR which ran off the cigarette lighter so the kids watched movies there and back. Got home Tuesday evening, so had a short work week.

We received the gifts for Stephen's birthday today and they couldn't have come at a better time. The girls had been fighting and pouting and the sight of a box from you turned it all around. They were ecstatic about their gifts. They love the way the belly pouches fit. They are nice ones! And the diaries are a great idea. The coin purses and candy were well received, too! Stephen looks so cute in his *lederhosen*. He was excited about his gift. We couldn't wait until his birthday to open the box. This way he can wear them to his party. We certainly are getting a sample of Europe with all your gifts. Thank you so much!

Stephen is certainly growing up. It's been hard this fall trying to decide what type of babysitting situation to use and then, of course, implementing it. Beverly helped me out this summer but has since indicated to me that a full-time all-winter commitment might be too much for her. So, I began the job of trying to find something else. There was space for him at My School daycare, but I wanted to find a mother babysitting in her own home. I went to two houses which were listed in the paper and was so depressed. Very nice women, but substandard surroundings and problems involving separations, money, and what felt like desperation. I stayed depressed for a week over that experience.

All this transpired the week before school started. Kay and other mothers would give me names of wonderful people they recommended, who, of course, were already full. Finally, Barbara gave me the name of her neighbor who was taking care of a 7-month-old and a 4-year-old. The neighbor had more or less decided that was enough for this year, but I was able to charm her into taking Stephen. Really, Sue, I felt I was applying for an Ivy League college, holding my breath to see if we'd be accepted...before I even met her! Well, I like her. She has a nice, clean, comfortable home, in-tact family, and lives close by. Stephen has had some trouble adjusting. This is a big step for him, having always been left with a relative or, at least, having Hailey and Laura with him. Louise, his new babysitter, says he asks for the girls as much, if not more, than he asks for me. Just as he was showing some acceptance of the situation, we took that long weekend trip. So then on Monday, it was back to square one with Louise prying him out of my arms. I can hardly wait for the day when he walks in by himself or doesn't want to leave her house in the afternoon. I know it would have been much worse at My School.

Work has taken a backseat this fall. Maybe because I worked so much this summer, I had trouble gearing up for another school year. The new male guidance counselor is very nice, extremely conscientious, but a little on the idealistic side. We still have our departmental issues and tensions so I have decided to try to distance myself from the *regular* counselors. I was asked by the principal if I would monitor after-school detention on Monday through Thursday afternoons from about 3:10 until about 4:15. I saw it as a way to earn some comp time, so I jumped at the chance. At first, I thought I'd come in an hour late in the mornings and therefore, have time to get everyone else off to school but now I think I'll save the time up each week and only work a half-day on Fridays. That way, I'd have some time without the kids to shop, just relax, do errands, or even clean the house. I don't think after-school detention is really a big deal and I am usually still at school until nearly 4:00 anyway.

After the school year started, another half-time teacher was added to the history department, but that would hardly have been a reason for you to rush home. I would begin applying early next spring, if I were you, and appeal directly to the principal. I'll help in any way that I can. I know there will be a position next year. The new half-time teacher lives in Cedar Island so would much rather teach at the closer high school.

I hope things have gotten a little more routine at Sigonella. I have quit watching the news so often, although I know nothing much has changed. Does M get overtime if his hours increase or is that just part of the job? Charles and everyone at the Lab received formal notification of possible furloughs if Congress doesn't settle on a budget. I think it involves most civil service employees, EPA, etc. It could be a day or a week that Charles would not go in and would not get paid, which could be a 20-percent salary cut. They have discussed this in other years but had never notified employees in writing.

Thank you again for the birthday package. I am working on Drew's package. I can't believe how old the kids are getting. Anything stateside that Drew has been wanting? You get such neat things there, but I figured there might be some tacky, made-only-in-America item that she has her heart set on that I could send. Let me know. Please take care. I really can hardly wait to see you. I haven't poured out my heart to anyone in person since our trip last Thanksgiving.

Love to everyone and especially you, Anne

Saturday, September 15, 1990

Dear Sue,

Is it true that this Iraq situation means that you might be home in less than month? I am so excited! I have been feeling down thinking about another year and knowing I couldn't afford another rendezvous trip. It will be wonderful, I promise. Leave everything to me. The good news is there will be plenty of room at St. Andrews for both Drew and Matthew. About five or so kids in Matt's class are gone and, of course, Drew's class has always been small. I think second and fourth are the only grades with openings. Isn't that a sign? Also, I have plenty of uniforms for Hailey, Laura, and Drew to use until we decide if we need to order more. I don't think Matt's uniforms will be too hard to get. I'll order some from Sears for him if you send me the size.

Charles talked to the Chapmans today and Steve is really ready to sell that house. He sounded fed-up and disgusted with the whole project. So, it is a good time if…number one, they are reasonable about the price and number two, you really want it after you see it. I know living in Motta may have altered your views on what is really necessary, etc., but it is a buyer's market around here and there may be a much better deal waiting for you. (Charles suggested that we sell our house and build two houses side-by-side somewhere. He has missed you guys.) Carole talked to me back around the time I wrote you about this house and said she wanted to find you guys a house. She asked me to please let you know she thinks she could find you just what you want. Meanwhile, we are counting on you all living here until a house is ready. We've already mapped out the sleeping arrangements and keep in mind, you would be here all day by yourself (from 7:30 until 3:00). Charles can take the kids to school and you can take Stephen (who gets dropped off at Miss Louise) and me (who gets dropped off at the high school) and have a car for the day to go house hunting or whatever. It will work out great. Of course, I do understand about your mother, but maybe after she's adjusted to having you back, etc., she won't mind your staying in Morehead since school and everything will be closer.

It really is all going to work out great! It's a good time of year to come home. School will have just started but you will have missed the cookie sale. Lucky duck. You'll have time to get settled before Christmas and if you do need to rent for a while, more properties will be available. You have all year to make connections for a job for the next school year. You could start by signing up for summer school if nothing else comes up. It's good money, five-sixths of your salary for five hours a day and you'll have your foot in the door. And really, Sue, you don't need to walk right back into a job before you even get settled. This year will go fast and next year is plenty soon enough for a job. Your other full-time job, plus its mandatory overtime, will keep you busy. I'm sure there will be a job for you available then.

I can't think of anything more to write. I'm glad the kids are ready to come home. Even if you are forced sell a lot of your household stuff, you still do have quite a bunch that you left in storage here and I am ready to make up for having to endure more than a year without yard sales.

Call or write if I can do anything at this end. Take care. And I'll see you soon!

Love, Anne

PS Hailey wants me to let you know that she has been stung by a bee twice this week. Just wants a little sympathy, I guess. Well, I'll mail this tomorrow. I can hardly wait!

Via Terre Nere

September 21, 1990

Dear Anne,

Well, false alarm, we are not coming home but we are certainly moving. The *Rawhide* refrain is bouncing around in my brain as we are finally moving and into a much better home on the range, I hope. We have found an A-frame house about a mile out of our town and the top portion is for rent. The address is *Via Terre Nere* which means black earth road. Two American families live downstairs but the top portion is available. It only has two bedrooms but a large living area and kitchen. It is brand new and has a fully furnished kitchen with cabinets and appliances. It has a long, wide, paved driveway, acres of yard, and is surrounded by meadows and orange groves with plenty of space for the kids to play outside and roam. The house is set apart with no neighbors nearby. The wide-open landscape and olive trees surely give it a very peaceful feeling. A cow herder brings his cows down to graze occasionally as does the shepherd with his flock of sheep and goats. I couldn't ask for a more serene place.

The house is new and we will be the first inhabitants to live upstairs. It is small but nicely laid out and there is space where we most need it. All the floors are done in Gianni Versace tile. There are two nice bathrooms and outside balconies both front and back. The front balcony is more like a large, square-shaped terrace than a balcony. It is large enough for a big table and chairs with room to spare. I am so ready for the peace and quiet of the country even if I have to sleep in the living room on a futon, which is the plan for us.

The views are spectacular from every direction. There is a beautiful view of Mt. Etna from the back and the plains of Catania stretch out in front of the house for miles, ringed by hills and mountains. The back gate is covered in trailing plants of deep purple clematis and blooming passion fruit vines. There is a large orange grove that belongs to the landlords' family directly behind the house, as well as almond and mulberry trees. I could not ask for a prettier place in the countryside. Best of all, the landlords seem divine. I'm utterly bowled over with this whole family. The house was built by two brothers whose last name is Bruno. Gaetano Bruno, the younger brother, lives here with his family in Motta Sant' Anastasia, and Salvatore, the older brother, and his family live in Palermo. Both families have children about the ages of our children. Gaetano and his wife, Santina, have two boys, and Salvatore and his wife, Maria, have two girls. They seem to be lovely people and could not have treated us more graciously. They all exude a warm and friendly personality, so different from our previous landlords. I think we are going to like the house and our landlords very much.

They all speak just a little English. Salvatore kept calling the kitchen "the chicken" which was funny but we managed to communicate a great deal without language. It was like we knew each other immediately and we were kindred spirits. Uncanny likability all around in every way. They were so kind to us and welcoming. It was such a contrast to our past experience and unbelievable to meet them and have an opportunity to rent the house. We were pretty badly shaken from the prior experience and it felt quite miraculous to be treated so well. We will have to scale down some, but at this point, I am ready to sacrifice any or all of our worldly belongings to just have a place we can enjoy. I am so excited about moving and starting over. I surely hope we don't get settled in and then get evacuated due to this crisis in the Middle East. I, for one, vote that we let this whole thing just blow over and stop trying to police the world. Too bad G.H.W. Bush is not listening to my advice. The world would be a more peaceful place, I think.

Anyway, it's time to break camp here, roll up the rugs and move on to our own green acres. Yeah! I'm so happy and so relieved to be moving away from our present situation and towards one that portends to be a land of milk and honey. That should cheer everyone up. It has lifted my spirits, for sure. I'm already over the moon happy about it. The gypsy in me is ready to roll.

Love you,
Susannah, *Baronessa di* Greener Pastures

The house the Halls rented from the Brunos at Via Terre Nere

Outfoxing the Incoming
October 1, 1990

Dear Anne,

Just as we have decided to move into the house in the country, we get news of an offer to return home to a job vacancy. I am over living in this limbo and no longer want to even discuss it. I swear I might jump off the balcony if this bottomless pit of indecision doesn't end. I want to stay for many reasons. I love Sicily and feel I have barely scratched the surface and am not looking forward to returning to life as I knew it back home. This experience has been a wonderful gift and I have soaked up as much as I can, but I know there is so much more to uncover. I realize that my feelings are selfish, but for the first time in all these months everything seems to be working out. The kids are doing great and we have a marvelous house to move into just waiting for us. A house that is in the country away from the noise and neighbors here which offers a place for the children to play and comes with great landlords, to boot! I actually think all our adjustments have been good for this family and each of us has grown and learned so much. Unfortunately, one of us doesn't seem to know how to enjoy anything! If I am forced to return now, I am afraid I will not go with a sunny attitude.

I hope I am being responsible and not just selfish. I know there may be a war and I don't trust George Bush but at the same time, I don't want to give up this beautiful life without a fight. Where else can you see a herd of sheep out your window or a volcano smoking? There are no bars back home where strangers pay for your bill without even letting you know. There are no corner *panificio*s with fresh bread baked every hour or wood-fired pizza ovens or wildflowers blooming or almond trees or ancient Greek ruins or street markets or charming hillside towns or shepherds in the fields or orange blossoms or panoramic views or beaches where you can get a massage! Not to mention the *gelato* and *cappuccino* and *espresso*! As you can tell I am hopelessly smitten with this place. Each season has brought such rare gifts, I am really hard-pressed to describe it all. Maybe it is just me, but I am in love.

My friend Jackie, on the other hand, agrees with Hubby that Sicily is second-rate and, in her view, down-right repugnant. She did not want to come in the first place. Jackie doesn't like her landlord either and since she is a military spouse, she went straight down to housing to complain and demand they move her to better quarters. She was told that she could get on a list, but the waiting list was six months long. She says she is going to put up a tent in front of the housing office with a sign that reads "Six more months til housing." She says she will sleep there in protest until they find her a new house. She is just crazy enough to do that. She is really a hoot. She is so smart and funny and full of life and, except for her views on Sicily, we agree on most everything. Her description of this place is hysterical even if I don't see it the same way. She attributes my infatuation with Sicily to my lack of exposure and she is right. But for me, Sicily seems a return to sanity without all the commercialism and competition found in the States. I can do without the air-conditioning, fast food, and other conveniences. I came here for less of that and more of the simple beauty and that I have found in spades. Now if we can just avoid war, I think I can be perfectly happy. I even think I could live here forever.

I have been packing and sorting things to move somewhere, either the house in the country or back home. Either direction means I have to down-size; I am getting rid of a great many things. I met some missionaries who live around the corner and they are moving to Germany and accepting donations so I have given them some things. I wanted you to know that as they left here this afternoon on their way north, the wife went off wearing your old denim maternity dress! I thought you would like to know that your generosity was blessing others on another continent.

I'll close for now. Drew's birthday is in a few days and I haven't planned anything yet. I think I will try to talk her into a shopping trip to Catania and dinner and *gelato*. She is a shopper, for sure.

Security at the base is still ultra-tight here and the general feeling is so pro-war. Seems the military is simply designed to kill people...the Pentagon doesn't really seem to care who or how many. We talked to Ray last week and his health is good which was a relief. He expressed the same feelings about this troop build-up and tension between Saudi Arabia and Iraq. I was glad to hear it since I was beginning to think I was the only one alive who opposed it. Well, take care and we will see you sooner or later.

Susannah, *Baronessa di* Sicilia
(claiming it as my own)

PS I mailed you a box with my girls' two black velvet dresses and Hillary's fur coat. Maybe your girls can use them, if not just hang on to them if you can until we come back. If we all come back...ha! I might try to become a permanent resident. Hope you don't mind hanging on... to the dresses that is...

Monday, October 8, 1990

Dear Sue,

This is the third letter I've started since I received your last letter. Things have changed around here so fast and rumors are flying about your plans that I don't know quite what to say. Then again, I never have been at a loss for words, just time to write them down. First of all, of course, I'm not mad. I have no way of knowing what you are going through and all that you have to weigh and consider when making a decision. I can certainly understand not wanting to leave M but if he can come too, then that's a different story. Steve Chapman told me M had called him and that you want pictures of the house in our neighborhood that they are renovating. I'll try to get some to you as soon as I can. It is a good location and a very nice yard. There's room for improvement, but good potential. The house is livable now, but I can picture how much renovations would improve it. I have not been in it since the Chapmans have worked on it. I know furnishing it would make a world of difference. The remodeling could be done gradually.

Sue, I feel like a rat about the phone call. It must have made you feel like nothing would work out with all the bad news I was giving you. The coach who was doing ISS, a real creep, resigned so I talked to the principal today about you possibly taking that position. He's trying to find a wrestling coach, but I wonder if that is going to work out. I may mention it again since it would be a good job with no preparation or work to take home. This high school is such a mess though, I wonder how long I can stand it. I do feel good about what I accomplish, but also feel there are so many people who are undermining the program from the top down.

I heard through Kay who heard from your mother that your sister saw your request to come home November 15 with M. That would be wonderful! I'll be glad to do what I can about measuring the house, etc. Steve Chapman told me tonight they'd give you and M a "special deal" but I'd be afraid for you to buy it sight unseen. Talk about buyer's remorse! I would feel awful. Would you remodel extensively? It only has three small bedrooms. If I videoed it, could you watch it there? Of course, there is nothing cute about it now. It is very dated. I have no idea what it would take to expand and modernize it. Now it sounds like I am trying to talk you out of it. I wish you could have gotten it for $54,000. That would have been worth it. I think Steve and Lori want $89,000. That's too much. Can you come home and look at it? I will video it this weekend. Remodeling can be fun. All in all, our final results with our house were very gratifying and there is something about redoing an older house that appeals to me. I was fantasizing today about winning $8 million on the new McDonald's game and how I'd spend the money and I couldn't imagine moving out of this house. Now, I could imagine putting another $100,000 into it...deck, fireplace, built-in furniture, expensive landscaping, paved driveway, etc., etc., but I would not change the location or neighborhood. The location and lot (with the golf course right behind it) of the Chapman's house are better than ours. Well, enough of that. I am dying to talk to you, but I don't blame you if you don't ever call again; that last call was awful, I know. I'm going to enclose a check so you'll be obligated to call or give me a date, time, and number and let me call you.

Sue, I am so sorry about neglecting to send Drew's birthday present. I don't know why I didn't even send a card. I had her gifts ready to send but knew you didn't need more to pack. Can you explain it to her? I will plan to write her. My life has gotten so incredibly hectic that I sometimes wonder if I'm going to make it. Charles and I both get involved in too much and it really is a full-time job managing the household, not to mention dealing with an 8-year-old, 6-year-old, and 2-year-old. Charles spent all weekend at the Seafood Festival. Susan and Sarah came for the weekend. Whew! By the way, Catherine and Mike my friends from London are coming for a couple of days. I'll see them Wednesday. It's almost been a year!

Wednesday, October 10

I got your October 1st letter today. I was hoping something was definite about coming home. I'm glad that you feel safer, though unsettled. Your kids are troopers! It would be great if the government paid for you to come home early. Could it be November 15?

I just realized that it is nearly 11:00 p.m. so I better close. I'll mail this tomorrow and promise to do better about writing. Give my love to everyone. I miss all of you. You would not believe how much we talk about all of you. The kids are hoping you'll be home soon, me too. Take care.

Love, Anne

PS Went by Susan's house Saturday walking to the Seafood Festival. Wanted my sister to see it. Susan has a new boyfriend who looked to be in his late forties, though hard to tell. He seemed nice. Sort of reminded me of Susan... enthusiastic, friendly, sweet. She seemed good.

PPS Got the rabbit coat and velvet dresses. Thank you. Hailey was thrilled about the coat. Looks cute on her. Haven't tried the dresses on yet, but am sure that Hillary's will fit one of them.

Paradise Found

October 12, 1990

Dear Anne,

We have finally moved! I can't tell you how much we love our new place. Finally, a good move on our part and good decision and our new place is lovely inside and out. I'm sitting here looking out the glass double doors and the light is filtering down on the hills in the distance and there is so much beauty and peace. We have the top of this A-frame house with two American families living down below. The A-frame has such high ceilings that although it is like a little studio, it feels spacious and our furniture looks good. Our large pine table fits perfectly in front of the glass double doors and it is our place for eating, doing homework, and for me to write letters. Off to the side is the small kitchen with all new appliances which is open to the living room. The living area has plenty of space for the futon and our living room furniture and serves as our make-shift bedroom/living room. The overall look is tasteful and attractive. It looks very contemporary and I like the arrangement better than the old apartment.

Matt has his own room and the girls have bunk beds in the other larger bedroom. There are two full bathrooms and even if it is small, the house is altogether charming in a way that just makes for serenity, contentment, and a feeling of home. That feeling is amplified by the surrounding olive trees, beautiful views, and the knowledge that we can just live here, breathe fresh air, and be happy with no irritable landlords looming large. I could not be more excited to be here and finally just concentrate on enjoying the beauty of Sicily. The house has huge knee walls that have been perfect to store boxes of stuff we don't have room for. There is a grand hallway that accommodates the piano and yes, I am still the owner of the piano. We hired professional movers to move it for us.

One of the American families who live downstairs has three children aged seven, five, and one. The seven-year-old is named Jennifer and is the perfect playmate for Drew. They have quickly become fast friends. The five-year-old is Jessica and reminds me so much of Hailey. The little one-year-old boy is Andy and all the kids just love him. He is adorable and the children play with him like a doll, dragging him along with their games. His mother doesn't seem to mind the extra babysitters.

I am enchanted with our new landlords and their families, too. Salvatore Bruno, the brother who lives in Palermo, said it was destiny for us to move in and I must agree. His beautiful wife, Maria, is a school teacher and they have two daughters aged thirteen and eleven, Grazia and Titti, short for Santina. Gaetano Bruno is the younger brother who lives here in Motta with his wife, Santina. Santina is charming and funny and about our age. Gaetano and Santina have two boys aged ten and twelve, Antonio and Filippo. The boys come over to our house often to play around and help with their orange grove that is behind our house, so we see them almost every day. My children are becoming fast friends with them, too.

The Bruno family also owns a t*abacchi* shop located on the first floor of their large three story house on *Via Roma* in the center of Motta. Grandma Bruno, who is clearly the head of the family, and her sister-in-law *Zia* Angela (Aunt Angela) both in their eighties, run the shop. They are so cute sitting in the shop behind the counter, all dressed in black, and make quite a pair with their little gray heads together sewing between customers. I want to photograph them as they make a classic picture.

Tobacco products are only sold in *tabachi* shops and you have to have a special license to operate one. They sell other things, like magazines, candy, and small sundry items. The t*abacchi* shops also sell Lotto tickets and bus tickets. Lotto tickets are a big business and very popular here. Everyone likes to gamble and come up with lucky numbers sometimes based on their dreams or favorite soccer team scores. Sicilians seem to be very superstitious. The magazines on the shelves are what shocked me. Most of them would be X-rated in the States but Grandma Bruno acts like it is the most normal thing in the world to have them there staring her in the face. Italians are so unruffled by the facts of life and certainly aren't hypocritical puritans about nudity. I must say while it shocks me at times, it is actually refreshing to be so upfront about it all. It doesn't seem so false and sanctimonious. A beautiful body is a beautiful body, enough said. Pay it homage, give it credit, leave off the pious criticism.

We sure were glad to leave Santancito's house and we couldn't have found more different Sicilians to be our landlords. All the Bruno family members seem to like us. The connection was instant and they are treating us like family already. It literally brings me to tears just to think of their kindness. I hope I don't sound too besotted, but I really have fallen in love with this whole family. I feel so lucky to live in their new house in the country that they built themselves. Salvatore and Gaetano told me they did most of the work themselves as construction is very costly in Sicily They said the materials alone for this house were over a half-million dollars. As bad as the other place was with the constantly complaining, pinch-faced landlords, this place is all the more sublime and the landlords and their families have been sensational. They have made me feel like a real adopted Sicilian and not just an outsider anymore. I can't tell you how good that feels. It was my dream to find that feeling when we came here and meet some Italians and get to know them. I guess we took a circuitous route, but we finally have the whole shooting match, and I can tell you it is *bellissima*. I really can't stop smiling about our good fortune. Pinch me.

All else is good and school is in full swing. The open house was last night and all of their teachers were impressive. Hillary's teacher, Ms. Cooley, could be straight out of St. Andrews, very organized, very fair, and gives Hillary all the praise that she flourishes under. All is good except this looming war situation. The whole base is under super strict security. They still have the armed guards on the school buses. That is unsettling to say the least, and we are told to avoid eating out and to take alternate routes to work. Mainly, just keep a low profile all the time. There are hundreds of military troops sleeping on the gym floor on cots and all the temporary living places are full. Everyone is on edge and if war isn't imminent, then they are putting on a very convincing drill. This level of concern really does take some of the fun out of being here and adds another level of stress, but if there was ever a peaceful place to weather this storm, we are in it. It all seems so political and trumped up. We recently supported Saddam Hussein against Iran and now he is the monster. I sometimes wonder if we aren't just fueling the military complex economy and have to make a nice little war just to keep the economy pumped. If that is true, we Americans are really despicable. Do you think the powers that be care about the people who are now at risk? Some of us are not in agreement with their war games. We can only pray for peace.

Hope you are having an easier time at work and I'll bet your children are getting excited about Halloween. We may have to skip it this year as security is so tight, they may cancel all festivities. Italians don't celebrate it so that may be our stance this year. Thanks, George Bush!! To tell the truth my heart is really not in it this year with all this war talk. Well, much love and happy Halloween if I don't write before.

Ciao for now,
Susannah, *Baronessa di* Nuanced Paradise

Living in a Paradox
October 25, 1990

Dear Anne,

Got your check, but am returning it to you and hoping we can get a better deal. I know I am starting to nag, but I want you to visit… but I do realize it is complicated. More so, by this never-ending drumbeat for war. It depresses me to no end. I guess with Thanksgiving coming up I can't help but think about last year. Can you believe it's been a whole year since our trip to London? It was wonderful, wasn't it? I am figuring that this year will be a real letdown after that.

We may try to go to London or somewhere as we are allowed another free flight for all of us that we have to use before January 1991. The only thing holding up our travel plans really is the possibility of war starting. One day the news sounds good then the next it sounds dire. I think the consensus around here is we are going to war for sure. Now with war looming, I am concerned we will be dealing with even more danger. I do not know how that will affect us.

We still have armed guards on the school buses. It is amazing how one adjusts to the unthinkable. Was coming here the smart thing and must I adjust to even more danger?

There is not much news here. I have been pretty stagnant lately. I spend all day waiting for everyone to come home so I can wait (as in waitress) on them some more. I should try to substitute teach at the school, but I am so fired up about this war business I am not sure I am suitable for public consumption. I've written the President, the Governor, and both of my Senators. Gov. Terry Sanders sounds like he is not beating the war drum. I like him very much. I read that Elizabeth Dole has resigned to take over the Red Cross and that everyone expects her to run against Sanders for Governor. I will campaign for Terry, the non-war hawk. It really appeared back in August that the whole country would rush to war, so it is good to see some people pushing back on that idea. I feel sure with all this military build-up we are going to find a good excuse to use it, unfortunately. You would not believe how the military is reacting here to this situation ...they love it. Everyone wants to go and be a hero and try out their new weapons. It is really sickening to me. One letter in the *Stars and Stripes,* our daily newspaper for Europe, was from a woman whose husband was there and she said she was so proud of her husband and that at long last, he could do what he has trained for 14 years to do! Kill people? Yikes. I am like an Abby Hoffman surrounded by war hawks. The platitudes of making the world safe for democracy are wearing thin on me and if George Bush is the embodiment of that, I think I'll pass.

Well, how is your life going? Better than mine, I hope. Drew's birthday was a fairly cheerless event, unfortunately, but our one bright spot is this house. I love it. It is the most wonderful place to live and at this particular time, I sure need it. All I can hear all day are sheep bells and birds singing. I wish I could take it home with me. There is something special about this countryside. I can't imagine recreating anything like this back home even if we owned plenty of land.

I got another haircut from Monika, my German hairdresser. She is a wealth of information about everything from German educational systems to the Mafia here in Sicily. She said as soon as she opened up her salon, the Mafia came calling and demanded their *pizzo* money. They explain it as protection you are paying for. I asked her if she paid it and she said, of course, otherwise I wouldn't have a shop, they would have burned it down. Sometimes I think I'm living in the wild west. I thought the haircut would give me a pick-me-up but it hasn't worked. I am not motivated to do anything and I guess it may be due to stress. I can't seem to get anything done. I am reading a great deal and that is my escapism. I am wearing the library shelves out.

We also quit our marriage counseling, although God knows we need it. The counselor seemed unqualified and I really did not like her at all. It is disappointing as we do need some help. Maybe we can find a therapist when we get back home, if we last that long. The real deal-breaker for me was she made us sign an agreement that if we talked about suicide or anything harmful, she would have to report it to someone. I was fearful to say anything after that, as I was nervous that I might wake up in a straitjacket in a padded cell with all the negative thoughts I have had lately. I understand that is fairly common practice for reporting suicidal thoughts, but being under the thumb of the military makes it more severe. They take rules and regulations seriously and I was afraid between them and Hubby I might find myself with a one-way ticket home in short order. Past that point, it just felt futile to me. Besides I was tired of listening to the counselor go on and on about her own issues! Ha!

I'll close for now. Hope things are good with you. I appreciated your letter. Don't apologize for that phone call… I'm a woman on the edge. Please don't hold me responsible for my words or actions as of late. I guess we are all relatively fine and in good shape and I shouldn't complain. My main problem is that I just miss you.

All my love,
Susannah *Baronessa di* Eastern Front

PS Now I can't find your check. I think I was using it as a book mark. I will find it and send it on in the next letter. Just void it in your records for now.

Monday, October 29, 1990

Dear Sue,

I almost feel too guilty to write. I can't believe I've let so much time lapse since I have written. This year is going to be so much harder having you so far away. I don't feel like I am doing too well. I'm falling behind both at home and work. Enough of trying to get sympathy; the point is I haven't written and feel awful about it.

Basically, everything is fine here. Hailey and Laura are enjoying school. Third-grade homework adds another task each evening. Hailey is fairly good about doing it herself but likes having me close enough to be involved. Laura has soccer practice twice a week and a game on Saturday mornings. As I know you can imagine, I'm the one who keeps on top of where she needs to be and when. I keep asking myself if her childhood would have suffered if we hadn't done soccer this year? I doubt that I will have any energy left for Stephen. It is a good thing that he is a boy because I am hoping Charles will step in at some point with some father-son activities. But really, Sue, my life just isn't fun since you left. I have trouble getting excited about things that used to be so much fun, like the kids' Halloween costumes and doing things in the house and going to yard sales. I can hardly wait until you and I can go to yard sales again. I went Saturday with Cynthia and missed you the entire time. I am having a yard sale with a neighbor this fall if I can get it together.

I took pictures of the Chapman's house which I am sending. Their asking price is too high. At that price, I know they are going to have trouble selling it so when you get here in June, they will be desperate and more realistic and you'll have a chance to talk to a contractor and see if it's worth it. Meanwhile, who knows, there might be something better. Anyway, here are the pictures. It looks better in the pictures than in person. I didn't get shots of the bathrooms which are so dated. I think that the fixtures and mirrors they added are extremely tacky. Oh well, maybe they will accept $65,000 in June.

This isn't going to be a very newsy letter. I am so tired I can't think. Beth asks about you often. Dick is writing a grant ($60,000) for a new dropout prevention program that would add a couple of new positions like a social worker and regular teacher. It is still in the planning stages, but Beth did ask when you were coming back. I am working on having a job for you...with me! You could then move into the history department in a couple of years. I can hardly wait until June!

I am going to close for now with a promise to write again soon. I am going to do better...and I'll try to cheer up. Take care.

Love to all, Anne

PS I'm including a batch of pictures Hailey took with her camera. Note Stephen's birthday celebration and his *lederhosen.*

Grazie Molto
October 29, 1990

Dear Anne,

Just a note to say Drew got her birthday box and everyone was thrilled with their gifts. Drew is in love with "Snowball" and everyone loves the clackers. Great gift idea as we had heard about them but had no way to purchase them. Matt is overjoyed with his spider and shackles! Everyone loved everything and it made their day.... maybe their week. Thank you so much for the time and effort you put into making my children feel special. You are the best. Enclosed are some photos of our new charming country chalet. It is beautiful and I think it is the best place in all of Sicily for us. We couldn't be happier on that front.

The news is really bad and everyone here is basically just waiting for the bombs to start dropping. I can't guess what war will mean for us here. Hopefully, we will not feel the effects too much. The biggest handicap right now is there are so many troops here that the base is overrun and the shelves in the commissary are stripped clean. Not a real problem because I can shop in town for anything I need. Oh well, as my great Aunt Mae would always say,

"That's a deep subject." But, oh well, we are safe for the moment and hope you are too. Will write soon when there is more news.

Much love,
Susannah, *Baronessa* di Deep Subjects

It's Midlife Crisis, I hope

November 5, 1990

Dear Anne,

We have been in this house for a whole month. Time is flying. In another month we will be gearing up for the holidays... I suppose. Quite frankly, I'm pretty sick of this family and the idea of an intimate holiday of togetherness really doesn't sound appealing. All I can think of is how far short this Thanksgiving will be compared to last year in London. Anyway, every holiday means time is marching on. I am glad for that because this nuclear family is about to self-destruct if we don't get back to the rat race pretty soon. The lack of diversion is highlighted here without it. I need to talk to a friend. I never realized how much my sanity and ability to put up with this ungrateful family hinged on my having someone to complain to...someone like you...poor thing. I've hardly let you off the hook on that by coming here...I write all the time and out of desperation, unloading on you, but I think otherwise I would really lose it. Do you think we could just trade families for a while? I don't think my kids would be so unappreciative living with you. Let's trade husbands too. I will warn you that this one is a dud. It is hard to watch him struggling like Sisyphus pushing his stone every day, making us all aware that he is not doing what he wants.

Everything here is somewhat okay; it's just a bad combination of needy children and a husband who appears to be from another planet. I have been reading John Updike, who describes marriage a bit too painfully honest and a bit too true to really be funny. I guess I am having a mid-life crisis of some sort. My hair is turning gray, my skin is aging, and it generally looks like all the good years are behind me. I keep working out at Nautilus, then come home and eat six donuts…what can that mean? I wish someone would shoot Jane Fonda. No one should look that good after forty. Here I am…no career, no figure left, three bratty kids who treat me like the refrigerator, meaning they tolerate me as long as I am handing out goodies. My marriage is cheerless…I have too much time on my hands and I am struggling with a sense of unreality all the time. Living here is like being on vacation for too long and it starts to grate on your nerves. Nothing permanent…always treading water.

We spoke on the phone with Elizabeth Friday night and that smacked of reality, for sure. It was good to hear that they were fine, but then she said my mother is still upset about our leaving. Lord, I want to tell her to please give it up or we are never coming back! Being here really is not so bad compared to dealing with her. This house has made a world of difference for us. I thought today that I am glad we came and I am glad for this experience, uncomfortable at times, but definitely worth it. It is not our immediate surroundings that present a problem, it is just that each member of the family is struggling with their own private circumstances and I am a bit lonely. Where is the love? Do I expect too much?

There is not much other news. Hillary starts piano lessons tomorrow finally; I doubt she can still find middle C anymore. All three kids have soccer games on Saturday morning that they enjoy and I resent. We get their first report cards on Wednesday and I have conferences with all their teachers. Halloween was pretty much of a bust. I was not in the mood to be much help with their costumes but they managed on their own fairly well. Matthew was a werewolf cowboy if that's any clue. What is to become of me? I've lost my enthusiasm for life. Maybe it's middle age. I am afraid it is burnout. I like the bumper sticker you sent but I thought it should have said "I can't handle anything…I've had children" instead of "I can handle anything… I've had children." I guess I had better dig my heels in and prepare for another ten years. The fact that I have no job or life of my own bothers me most. That will be my number one objective when I get home. Keep your ears tuned for any openings.

Hope all is well with you. I haven't started Christmas shopping yet. Last year this time I was almost finished. Don't be surprised if nothing materializes this year…I am holding out for your coming for a visit here. I do believe in miracles as I have lost faith in myself so that is all I've got left. How are you holding up?

Today was the first really cool fall day we have had. The sky was unbelievable, so blue with clouds ranging from bright white to gray-blue and fifteen shades in between. Absolutely lovely and the sunset took my breath away, all pinks, blues, and purples. The oranges and tangerines are almost ripe and they are picking the olives. They spread nets out under the trees and take sticks and beat the limbs and the olives fall to the ground and then are gathered up. I've decided I love Sicily: that it's just this rotten family that stinks.

Jackie, her husband, and Candice got into an automobile wreck in downtown Catania, which is not surprising given the driving situation here, but is unfortunate. Italian insurance is really unbelievable; their system is decidedly comical. I drove them to the town of Lentini, an hour away, to meet with their insurance agent. They came out of the building with glazed looks on their faces and all Jackie would mutter was, "This is where the horror begins." She thinks she may have to give the agent her Lazyboy recliner to get the claim processed. The agent kept hemming and hawing about so much paperwork and that these things take time, so Jackie asked if there was something they could do to hasten the process. He remarked that he had been wanting one of those big American chairs that recline. Italians do not have big comfortable recliners and they are just crazy about them. No kidding! Greasing the palm is so typical here.

Well, take care, keep the faith, and don't forget me.

Your friend,
Susannah, *Baronessa di* Loose Ends

PS Do you remember the name of the Bed and Breakfast we stayed in outside Gatwick or the name of the village? I can't for the life of me remember it. If we go back, I want to stay there and eat at The Crown one more time. Also, in London what was the name of the Bed and Breakfast on Belgrave Road? It is times like these I wish I kept a diary.

Pluck and Circumstances

November 9, 1990

Dear Anne,

I had to laugh yesterday when I got your letter because the last one I had just mailed contained the same sort of message. Only I think mine was more depressing. I am feeling some better as I have decided that I must pull myself together and try to keep this three-ring circus operational. I can tell you that it does take a toll. I only wish that I did not feel so alone in the journey.

Thank you so much for the pictures of your next-door neighbor's house that is for sale. The price does seem high for such a dated house but the neighborhood is marvelous. Do you think living right next door would be too much togetherness? If they come down in the price maybe we could think about it, but I doubt I could maneuver that one. Building seems to be our best option now. Anyway, thanks for the pictures. It really helps to get a mental image and thanks for including a few of your house and the children as well. Stephen is really changing and Laura's hair is even blonder now. They are growing up way too fast for me. The photos made me so homesick for you.

Please give Beth my love and tell her to get busy and write that grant! That would be wonderful to be working with you in the drop-out prevention program. That would be my dream job. I can't think of anything better than that. I plan to contact the Board of Education in January and ask them to pull my old application for any openings that might come up after June. I am certified until 1992 and they approved the certification courses that I can take here. I surely have the time so I might as well knock them out. The classes are available on videotapes and each has three objective tests which I think I can breeze through. They cost $150.00 each, but it's the easiest way I think to get the credit.

I got a letter from Kay Jones and she said Laura was a star soccer player! Glad she is having a chance to shine.

Never apologize for not writing me again. You have been so faithful to write so often. I have a large straw antique suitcase that I bought in Switzerland now filled with all the letters I have received. It is amazing how many you have written. I have so much more time than you and I can't believe how much you have written. I've loved each and every one. They are the high points of any week. Don't apologize. You have outdone all my expectations. Also, don't cheer up…miss me…miss me…I miss you, too. I am looking forward to getting home so we can just spend time together. I think we are due a whole weekend shopping trip to Raleigh or to Williamsburg. How about it?

I have finally decided which photo to use for the Christmas card. I had some good choices but the one I am using is sweet and unique. It's a lovely shot of the kids feeding the pigeons in Rome at St. Peter's Square. It captures the kids in Italy, for sure. I love it.

Well, better close, we may go to London around Thanksgiving although guess who is not too keen on it. But then he doesn't seem to want to do anything lately but suffer in silence. It is maddening. I am at a loss to help him out of his despair. As a matter of fact, I am pretty sure I am the main cause of it. He has always been withdrawn but he has taken it to another level for the past year and a half. Our relationship is almost non-existent and I don't know what to change or how to fix it. I wish I had a clue how to improve things. I guess you expect better the second time around, but life is full of surprises, isn't it? I am in this for the long haul and I sure would like the journey to be worth living. Carrying this yoke alone is both too heavy and too lonely. It feels like standing on a tight wire with no net and not knowing where the safe base is located.

I think George H.W. Bush has completely lost his mind… sending more troops. Recently, they moved nuclear missiles from a US Air Force base called Comiso, about an hour south from here, to Sigonella at 3 AM in the morning. I think they are expecting something big…at least, they are planning for it. Bush appears to me to just be a big bully or maybe the American military are just like lemmings and every now and then they have to go off the cliff! It is a sin!

Well, peace to you, my friend, take care and thanks for the photos.

Susannah, *Baronessa di* Trapeze Artists

The Halls Christmas card 1990

Sunday, November 18, 1990

Dear Sue,

Isn't it amazing how our lives/thoughts/moods run parallel? I got your letter and wanted to write you immediately; it made me feel like someone understands me. I started a letter the other day at the end of a great day. I didn't get to finish it and am now writing during one of my low swings. Yes, my self-diagnosis is now manic/depressive.

I have to pick Laura up at a birthday party in twenty minutes, meanwhile, all the kids are gone and Charles is upstairs watching TV. I just paid bills and that activity has contributed greatly to my depressive state. It would help me out a lot this year if we exchanged Christmas cards only. Charles and I have just been living beyond our means. We do not watch how we spend our money and with expenses going up, we are barely managing the commitments we have. That damn jeep is a big part of the problem, but I can't escape being part of the blame myself. Charles had another job offer and I just laughed at him. There's no way we could scrape up enough money to move. I hope when you get back, it's not this hard for you. I can guarantee you will have a job. A new at-risk program is being proposed for the school which will add positions for some part-time nontraditional nurturing classes. If you want to work, that's in the bag. Wouldn't it be a treat to be working together?

I am glad Hillary is starting piano. Hailey is begging to quit. I know she is not musically talented, but I do feel it is the training and discipline that's important, not to mention the fact that I bought a piano! She wants me in the room when she practices, which doesn't usually occur until the night before her lesson. I am really frightened that I am raising kids who want instant gratification, something for nothing, and have no self-discipline. I have told her she will take lessons for at least six months, but I don't know if I can stand it. It makes me want to throw in the towel and let these kids raise themselves. Dealing with the behavior and poor decision-making strategies of at-risk students at school has made me uptight about the futures of my own.

Charles and I are going away for one night on the Friday after Thanksgiving. I think we will spend the night in Wilmington. We're not eating Thanksgiving dinner with either his family or mine. We just decided to do it alone, just our family. I am losing interest in staging these family get-togethers that make me feel worse when they are over. It sure won't be a Norman Rockwell picture at our house.

I'll sure be glad when you're back, but I wonder if you'll find me the same person you left. I feel like I've gotten so bitter. I am going to try to write you on an upbeat day...if I have another one.

I love getting your letters. They really keep me going. It was so sweet of Hillary to write. We miss you all. Take care. Love, Anne

Thursday, November 20, 1990

Dear Sue,

After I wrote you about just sending cards this year, I had an overwhelming desire to send you guys a Christmas box. So here it is, not much. These are things that I would have brought over to your house if I could have gotten to your house. The *Homes and Gardens* magazine is one that I bought last year at Gatwick Airport after you left and while I was waiting for my flight. Maybe it will remind you of our trip. Isn't England a wonderful country!? Maybe you are all there right now!

The book I'm sending was a gift my mother gave us last Christmas. I remember my parents laughing at George Price cartoons from *The New Yorker* magazine when I was little. I would look at the cartoons, but never understood what was so funny. Well, now I am old enough to identify with the characters and I think you and M would enjoy them. I turned down a few pages because I would have shown you those cartoons first. Hope you have a good laugh or, at least, a few chuckles. Keep the book. I'm giving it to you, so don't worry about returning it.

The third gift is one you'll probably hate me for. I just saw this jar of Now-and-Laters and thought of your kids. (I obviously didn't think about the dentist or orthodontist.) Sorry if it was a terrible idea. Tell Hillary to suck them. No chewing if she has her wires and bands on.

Please don't send us anything. We have gotten so many wonderful gifts from you that you can just rest on your laurels. I'm already feeling the pressure of Christmas, wondering if I should drag the decorations out on Thanksgiving weekend. My time is so limited, as well as my motivation. Remember how much energy we used to have? Remember our baking day before Christmas? What a wonderful memory, tunnels of fudge!

To change the subject... I was in court with a student on Friday and saw Henry Wilton get his divorce from Deidre. She wasn't there. I suspected they were separated. I felt certain about it when I noticed she had lost so much weight. The sign of a life released from the confines of marriage! I haven't seen her in ages. I hope that she is happy. It was probably a good move.

Charles and I are going to Wilmington tomorrow for one night. I don't know if it will help our relationship or make it worse. He's been in a terrible mood lately, seems like he is always getting mad at the kids. He talks incessantly about how much he hates his job. I'm convinced that he doesn't want to change any of his behavior to improve the situation, he just wants to complain. If he hates work so much, why does he spend so much extra time there? That's my question. I won't have to listen to him yell at the kids in Wilmington, but I'm expecting to listen, again, to every detail about his problems at work. Oh well. Next year let's you and I do something. I'll start saving my pennies.

I'm going to stop now and search for a box so I can get your Christmas gifts in the mail tomorrow. I started this letter on Tuesday, but it's now Thanksgiving. I know I'll write you again before Christmas. Maybe I can scrape up some Christmas spirit. Take care and keep me posted on your activities. I get vicarious pleasure hearing about your adventures and fun. Drive carefully. That sounds like the biggest hazard you face. I sure miss you all. I'm counting the days!

Love, Anne

Yuletides

December 2, 1990

Dear Anne,

It is 11:00 PM and all are nestled snug in their beds and I have just finished a ton of dishes. Jackie and her family came over for dinner. She has moved into a new apartment and doesn't have a stove yet. I cooked spaghetti and have finally learned how to make a good tomato sauce from scratch. I can go home now and not be ashamed to show my face.

We got your Christmas package already and having learned my lesson last year, I let the children open the presents right away. Last year I insisted that they save their gifts until Christmas morning thinking it would be more traditional, but it was a big miscalculation. Each gift, when it was unwrapped, threw me into deeper homesickness and by the end, I was fighting back tears. Lesson learned…this year we opened on the spot and enjoyed them. I wish you could have seen their faces when your gift was unwrapped. You would have thought they had inherited a candy store. They were so excited and delighted. We cannot get the Now and Later candy here, so they were a huge grand slam hit. It has been a monumental candy weekend! Drew counted them tonight and there are 65 packs left of the original 144 if that gives you any clue as to what a smash hit your gift was.

Also, I loved the magazine, cartoon book, and the special mug. I've already had several great cups of coffee in it and you know how some cups are just right...well this is one of them. I choked back big tears as I read your letter which was the most special gift of all. We do have some great memories and I am ready to make some more. I am looking forward to starting soon after June 12, 1991. Unwrapping your gifts reaffirmed my good judgment of unwrapping them as soon as we get them. If I had read your letter Christmas morning, I probably would have just died of homesickness. As it was, I enjoyed it in the most sweet and sentimental way. Thank you, thank you for everything.

We are all fine. Life sure has been busy lately. Last Sunday, our whole family was invited over to Gaetano and Santina's home in Motta for a traditional Sunday dinner. Salvatore and Maria and their two daughters were there as well as Gaetano and Santina's two sons. Grandmother Bruno and *Zia* Angela were also there, so we were a group of fifteen. They made it look easy to serve a five-course meal which took the better part of the afternoon. The food was lovely and the homemade wine even better. The children were all seated in the kitchen and several beverages were put out for them. The adults ate in the dining room around a huge table with a lovely, handmade, cut-work, linen tablecloth, I might add. By the time I checked on the children in the kitchen, Matt had selected and downed his first entire beer. Italian living agrees with him for sure.

The Bruno family are such gracious hosts and we were made to feel at home. The language barrier is both challenging and fun and makes body language and facial expressions really come alive. *Zia* Angela is very old and suffers from partial dementia. When I was introduced to her, she said, "*Brute Americani*" which translates to "Ugly Americans." Everyone laughed at that. I didn't try to explain that I did moderately agree with her and see her point, dementia or not.

Life here is so hard and expensive for Sicilians. Americans come moving in here, buying up everything, renting all the expensive houses, and the young Navy guys get drunk and pee off the balconies, making a general nuisance of themselves. I am determined to muster all my Southern hospitality to show them we are not all like that. I am quite taken with this family, both sets, the Motta ones and the Palermo ones. I can't stop thinking about how renting their house has changed our lives. They have extended every courtesy to us imaginable. It means so much when you are a stranger. Every little kindness is magnified because it is so freely given without any requirement and I am basking in the kindness.

Did I tell you about our Thanksgiving? We had a turkey... that's about it. How was yours? How was your weekend getaway in Wilmington? Glad you were able to get away, but doesn't it just kill you how the grandparents act when you get one night away, as if you have been to the French Riviera? Guess we take what we get for sure.

I have about finished Christmas shopping. We took a few days off and went on a whirlwind spree to Caltigerone for ceramics, Taormina and Catania, and then the Catania street market. I think I am *finito*! Thank God! I have had a hard time concentrating on it this year. I guess we will get a tree soon. The Italian ones are so tiny and pitiful, about four feet tall with three limbs. They all look like Charlie Brown trees. Even the few artificial ones I've seen are scrawny. The Italians would keel over to see our trees. I suppose they would think they could build a house with all that wood or heat a house for the winter. I am sure whatever they think, they would not waste it. One thing I have noticed is that they take great care to not be wasteful with anything.

The kids are fine, Drew stepped on a nail on Thanksgiving Day and had to take antibiotics, but it has healed up nicely. Everything here is pretty sane for a change. I guess we have a cease-fire reprieve until January 15, according to the news. I am keeping my fingers crossed. We have a mandatory meeting to attend on Wednesday about evacuation procedures and I might know more after that. The general feeling is that if things get bad, they will send the dependents home and keep the sponsors. My first choice, of course, would be for the whole mess to blow over and let us all stay until June. One thing I can testify to is that this adventure has not been dull!

Well, better close for now and get some sleep. Thanks again for everything and let me be one of the first to wish you a very Merry Christmas.

All my love,
Susannah, *Baronessa di* Good Cheer

Monday, December 3, 1990

Dear Sue,

Well, life goes on with all its interesting twists and turns. Today all five of us are home with the flu, complete with fevers, vomiting, and diarrhea. Not a pretty sight. Stephen came down with it Friday so he isn't sick today. The rest of us are lying around arguing about who feels the worst. I pray this is a 24-hour version.

Granny died on November 26. Gretchen was home with her and Granny had a little stroke, went into a coma, and died peacefully in her bed seven hours later. Dr. Brady came to their house. Sister Gretchen had no intention of using the hospital. It was sad to see the end of a wonderful life. Of course, it made us all think about Dad's death two years ago. But it was also a natural end and a beginning. Granny had so much faith. She was ready for heaven. The funeral mass was on Wednesday, then Granny's body was flown to Minnesota where another funeral mass was held, and her burial next to my grandfather. Gretchen went to Minnesota, too. There will be big changes for her, too, because the Order of St. Joseph supported her while she was taking care of her mother. She is planning to look for a job around here so she can justify staying in North Carolina. It would be hard to lose her, too, if she had to return to Minnesota. I am sure that she will find something. She has so many contacts here. My mother has gotten so dependent on her since Dad's death. Granny was 95 years old on October 23.

I was glad to hear Hillary was starting piano lessons. Is that on base? Hailey has done well this fall, but has not enjoyed it. I have to sit down with her for every practice session. The real struggle, however, began this month with Hailey begging to quit. What a dilemma. I think this parenting job is too much. I don't want her to quit everything that is challenging, but I also don't want to make her too neurotic. She keeps insisting that the piano is not her thing. I know the feeling. I talked to Susan, who feels that she and Hailey are a lot alike, and she reassured me that Hailey has more than her share of stick-to-it-ness and it may be more detrimental to force her to keep taking lessons. But oh, my pride. I hated like anything to call her piano teacher and break the news that we were done. The teacher said she had no idea because Hailey was one of her best beginners. It was so embarrassing. So anyway, that's the end of that, for this year at least.

I thought of you this weekend as I was sitting up late one night making Christmas dresses for the girls. I was hoping to use Hillary and Drew's black velvet dresses but the girls are just in the middle, as far as the sizes are concerned. Drew's is too small for either one and Hillary's is a little too large. I had all intentions of buying dresses, but was so disappointed in what was available in their sizes. The styles look like miniature teenagers instead of little girls. I bought dark green velvet fabric, got the very simplest jumper pattern, no zipper even, and bought white cotton blouses with lace collars. I am almost finished and I haven't screwed up yet. I think that they look pretty good. Stephen can still wear his Christmas outfit from last year.

It is now Tuesday, another day at home. Everyone is on the mend and getting cabin fever. I just re-read the letter I wrote you yesterday and can tell I was feverish. I hope that you can read it.

Charles leaves tomorrow for four days in the Florida Keys so he has been zipping around today making arrangements and buying a new bathing suit. It makes me so mad that he can completely lose himself in his job and make it such a priority without giving the home front a second thought. We are on such different wavelengths.

I'll close for now. Hope you are all well and happy. We're going to hear Handel's *Messiah* on Monday, December 10, in New Bern. I will think about you. We haven't gone to hear it since you and M got tickets for us and babysat so we could go. I am looking forward to it. We are taking Gretchen, Mother, Chris, and Hailey. Whew! Gretchen's birthday is on December 10. Let's go together next year.

Take care. Maybe the Christmas bug will bite me and I'll be soon sending you a more chipper letter...then again.

As always love, Anne

Unplanned Parenthood

December 6, 1990

Dear Anne,

This letter is written by a woman who is afraid…not of war, earthquakes, or volcanoes...just the future. I've glimpsed the life to come and I am pretty sure my children are going to lay waste to me. We have just experienced an episode with Matthew who has really been testing all the limits lately.

About a week ago at Matt's last soccer game, he asked me for the car keys as he said he wanted to put his fanny pack in the car. Being suspicious by nature as is every good mother, I offered to hold it for him instead since the car was some distance away. He reluctantly agreed, but with enough hesitation to get my radar up. So as his game was going on, I looked inside his fanny pack to see what kind of contraband he might be hoarding. What should I see but two boxes of condoms! After I regained my breath and balance, I put the fanny pack in the car. After the game, I let him carry it into the house without alerting him. I waited until his father came home and told him he needed to have a talk with his son, as I thought this should be handled as a Dad issue. He did and the story was that Matt got an older boy to buy them for him from the Seven Day Store on base. So, we chalked it up to curiosity and tried to explain some facts and thought that was the end of the story. He had two boxes but one was completely empty. When we questioned him about why one box was empty, he said he had just found that empty box. Both boxes were placed in a basket on top of the refrigerator and we thought that was the end of the story.

Oh, no.... On Wednesday, I asked all three kids to meet me at the laundromat after school. Hillary and Drew showed up first with very sad faces and Hillary said, "Is it true?" I took a deep breath and asked, "Is what true?" She answered, "That Matt had condoms at school." Needless to say, I was floored, again. I asked her how she heard that news, while mentally killing Matthew if he was bragging about it. Well... it seems the vice principal had called Matthew into the office to discuss the issue because Matthew had brought some condoms to school and given one of them to a fellow student. That student's mother had found it and called the school to report Matthew. Well, the vice principal and Matt discussed the situation and the use of the said contraband. According to Matt, when questioned by the vice principal as to the use of the alleged items, he told her that they were to prevent disease and used for sex and that everything had sex, even trees do it. She told him they were not appropriate for school and that she was going to inform his parents. Matt quickly assured her that we already knew! Can't imagine what she is thinking now. So far, we haven't been contacted. I think I should apologize but I really want to just crawl in a hole and die. I'm keeping a low profile in the hopes it will slip her mind. I may never show my face there again, at least not anytime soon.

Anyway, having Matthew around keeps you humble. I don't think he will return to St. Andrews next year. His newly gained Italian *savoir-faire* probably puts him out of that league, I am afraid. I can chalk most of it up to curiosity but it is never a dull moment with him. I am amazed at how drawn he seems to anything forbidden. I'm sure that does not bode well for the future. Hillary and Drew were mortified beyond belief. I told them to forget it and not worry about it too much. All men have their minds in the gutter! Needless to say, I could have done without this experience…I'm thinking now a nice boarding school might be the answer. Can you get a scholarship to Boys Town or something?

Otherwise, we are surviving. I am thrilled today with the news that Hussein is going to release all the hostages. That should minimize the American interest and maybe avoid a war. Fingers crossed.

Hope you are well and starting to be in good holiday cheer. I finally got my packages mailed and hope they all arrive intact. I put a gift for Chris in with your box, hope you don't mind. Altogether the gifts are not much, but they are sent with a tremendous amount of love.

I had better close for now. Telling this sordid saga has worn me out. I guess I should look on the bright side, at least it did not happen at St. Andrews where, being the good Catholic school, Matthew probably would have been expelled …can you imagine Maryanne's face if she had to address that situation? I am trying to be open-minded and also wondering if some better sex education would have prevented this. Seems we parents are not always ahead of the curve, are we? I'm not ready for these issues, but I don't like learning things the hard way either. With Matt in the family, I suppose I better up my game and start expecting the unexpected if I plan to get ahead of this curveball.

Love to you all,
Susannah, *Baronessa di* Juvenile Delinquents

PS Tell your sister Susan her prediction of Mt. Etna erupting was spot on. It started last week and has been spilling lava down ever since. The top is all snow-covered with red lava glowing at night. It is quite a delight.

Let the Holiday Begin
December 15, 1990

Dear Anne,

I read with sympathy the news about your grandmother. I am glad she was able to stay at home until the end, but I know it is always hard to say goodbye. I read somewhere that when an elderly person dies, it is equivalent to a library burnt to the ground. It is so true that so much history is lost when we lose our ancient elderly. I am so glad that Sister Gretchen might stay on in Morehead. Losing her, too, would be very hard.

Also, sorry to learn that all of you had the flu. I have a slight cold but everyone else is fit. Well, did you hear about our recent earthquake? Yes, another one! It was exciting. It woke us up in the early daylight and I got up and walked to the kitchen window. It only lasted about thirty seconds, but it was awesome. I actually saw the earth move. Everything in the kitchen was clinking together but seeing the earth undulate was awe-inspiring. It did not frighten me at all because I was just too awestruck by the magnitude of the sight. No one can feel and see the earth move like that and not be impressed by such power. This house felt so put together I had no fear of anything falling on me.

Although this earthquake was more powerful than the one we experienced in the other house, that one felt much more threatening. Sadly, nineteen people died in this one and there was damage to some houses and buildings in Catania. Fortunately, we had no damage. Now that I have experienced two quakes, I firmly attest that is fully enough for me. I have had the experience and lived to tell the story, but need no further investigation on the subject.

Ray and Elizabeth called and so did my mother. It was good to talk to them. They are concerned about us with all the war talk but they could tell we were in good spirits which hopefully alleviated some of their fears. We are really lucky that our downstairs neighbors are willing to take calls for us and then run up to alert us. It is rather comical as we run as fast as we can so our callers aren't paying to be on hold. The number is 011 39 95 307903 if you feel like talking. I can be down in a jiffy. I call it an earthquake drill to see how fast we can be out of the house. Both calls from home resulted in my ending up down there in my bathrobe. When my mother called, I was in the tub! Naturally!

I am almost finished, as if we ever really finish, with the Christmas preparations. Most of the shopping is done and I've got the tree up and house decorated. I am glad I did not bring the sentimental Christmas decorations from home. It has forced me to be creative and everything on the tree is homemade. It has given me some projects to do with the children. We made cinnamon dough ornaments, among other things, and we really look the perfect picture of a cozy, homespun Christmas. It should be a good Christmas. The children are excited; they get out of school Wednesday, which is a blessing that they don't get out too far in advance of the holiday since the waiting can be miserable for them.

Hope all is well with you. As for me, I could hardly be happier. Meeting and getting to know the Bruno family and having Jackie to pal around with and our wonderful neighbors and their children as playmates has really made things ideal. I am at total peace and things are going very well. I am already dreading having to leave here in six months. It has taken some radical ups and downs, but I really do love Sicily and the life we have made here. This house has changed our lives. I never thought I would be so attached to a place, but I am totally in love with it. I really could stay like this forever. I am enclosing a photo of the children playing with the neighbor children in the field next to our house. I hope you see what a fine pack of young sprouts they all are. The weather is ideal and for once in my life, I will admit things are pretty much perfect for this family.

Well, I had better close for now. Tell Charles happy birthday for me and give the kids our love. I probably won't write again until after Christmas so I will wish you, again, my friend, a very Merry Christmas!

Much love,
Susannah, *Baronessa di* Good Vibes

PS Just FYI, Jackie's Italian insurance agent just picked up the Lazyboy. That should expedite the claim! Ha!

Hillary, Matt, and Drew with neighborhood friends at Via Terre Nere

Sunday, December 16, 1990

Dear Sue,

I hit the jackpot yesterday. Two letters and a Christmas card from you! I loved it! You have no idea how great I feel getting a letter from you. I hang on every written word! We also received the big Christmas box from you this week. We're saving it for Christmas, but the kids are so excited I don't know if the packages will stay wrapped until December 25th. Thank you so much. You are always so generous. I'm glad you liked the box I sent (although I still feel guilty about all that candy).

I am so anxious to hear news from you after the earthquake this week. I didn't hear about it on the news, but Gretchen did and told me it was on the eastern coast of Sicily (Yikes!) and that eight people were killed. I kept watching the news, but it was not mentioned again. That's probably a good sign, however, it didn't reassure me. Our news is so focused on the Gulf crisis and the threat of war that I am sure disasters in other parts of the world aren't rating much coverage. I hope you didn't have any damage or too much of a scare. I can't imagine going through an experience like that. I hope you were all together so you weren't worried about each other. I'm anxious to hear. Have you got access to a phone yet? Please let me know the minute you get a number!

Monday evening

I'm right dab in the middle of a Christmas, this-is-supposed-to-be-fun, panic. I'm becoming quite a Scrooge, I'm afraid. The school Christmas pageant is tomorrow night. No reception following because of bingo, which is somewhat of a relief. School is out on Wednesday. Charles is planning to take Wednesday through Christmas off. Susan, Sarah, and Susan's new beau may come after Christmas. Now I face the dilemma of whether to let them bed down together and face the kids' questions, or tell Susan and company that they will have separate beds because I am raising my kids with guilt and hypocrisy. After your letter about Matthew, I think maybe I should face the fact that the kids probably know more than I think they do about premarital sex. Hailey was talking the other day about two lizards "mating" on the front porch and Laura asked, "What's mating?" to which Hailey replied, "Having sex." I asked Laura if she knew what that was and she said, "Sure! Something people do before they are married!" I didn't know what to say! She's right, of course. I'm just not prepared emotionally to deal with this. Help! Matthew is really something! He's such an independent spirit. You'll have to write a book!

I'll write more later after my so-called vacation starts. Take care and, of course, Merry Christmas!

Love, Anne

PS My Harrods' bear is in place on the tree. I'm ready to go back. Of course, right now, I'd settle for a trip to New Bern if you were going with me! Miss you.

PPS Loved the Christmas card! Give the kids each a kiss or two from me.

Laura, Stephen, and Hailey, Christmas 1990

Sicilian Christmas Musings

December 20, 1990

Dear Anne,

Well, we are all wrapped and ready for the big day and hope you are too. Christmas this year in Sicily has really been a treat for us so far. Being in our country home has made us relaxed, happy, and able to enjoy our surroundings. We are just outside the town, within walking distance, so we are perfectly placed to enjoy both the town and country lifestyle. The Christmas decorations here vary from our small town, which are quite simple and homemade, to the big city of Catania, which really decks out the streets with elaborate lights strung over all the large avenues. In both places, shop owners put live trees out in large pots on the sidewalk in front of their stores. Here in Motta, there are homemade arrangements made from oranges, citrus fruit, cotton balls, and greenery placed in the niches of many buildings. There is one of these on the building that is the Brunos' house. It is so simple but so charming.

There are three magnificent forty-foot-tall artificial trees in the piazza in downtown Motta that are decorated with lights. Storefront windows are sprinkled with a few Christmas items, but Italians really don't go in for all the commercialism that you see in the States. The emphasis is on food and family, not gift-giving. I haven't seen any wrapped presents under anyone's tree. The holiday period starts around December 8th, the Feast of the Immaculate Conception, and goes through January 6th, Epiphany. Almost everyone has a large nativity scene called a *presepi* in their homes. I've seen Santina and Gaetano's and it covers about two square yards and is a mixture of animals and buildings, forests and streams. A great deal of care is given to the design and scenes created, which can be added to every year. I've been told that St. Francis started the tradition of the creche. It has definitely caught on in Italy. All the churches have their altars made into miniature Bethlehem creche scenes. I went into a church in Nicolosi, a town up towards Mt. Etna, and the *presepi* was so elaborate, a miniaturist dream, that it must have taken days to create. It depicted towns and forests and streams, complete with tiny lights and hundreds of figures. Beautiful. I think it was a collection of about forty different scenes put together stretching the size of a basketball court. Quite amazing.

Every food store and bar has towering walls of *panetone*, the Christmas cakes, stacked to the ceiling. These are eaten by the truckload and exchanged as gifts. It is a fluffy bread-style cake, sometimes with raisins and powdered sugar. It is not too sweet and does go well with *espresso*.

The meat market here in Motta has hung a full deer carcass, whole rabbits, and pheasants, as well as the whole head of cows and pigs, outside with strings of lights over them. It would be really funny as decoration if it weren't so provincial and earthy. After all, Italians are all about the freshness of their food and aren't afraid to proudly own up to it. Jackie came barreling around the corner and came face to face with a wild boar hanging up and was mortified. Another example of what she sees as grotesque, I see as delightfully colorful.

There are a few small booths set up in the squares selling Christmas decorations, nuts, and candy, and there are vendors roasting and selling chestnuts in paper cones. It is all just charming in my opinion, not overdone, but full of good cheer without the hectic shopping. I certainly get the feeling that these are the holiday traditions that they have been celebrating for many years. One thing about Italians, they love tradition and they don't hunger for the new and different or want to change things up. They seem to get great pleasure in doing things the way they have always done them and I can appreciate that. The bars and bakeries are full of special treats. Italians undoubtedly put the focus on food during this and every holiday, which is fine with me. Food, family, and fun seem to be the things most emphasized. Traditionally, they play cards for the entire season and I've seen many old men sitting and playing them on the street and in the piazza. I really get the feeling that Italians are not concentrating on the almighty dollar and are just much more attuned to the daily joys to be found in life. I guess that is *la dolce vita.*

Mt. Etna today looks like a big baked Alaska out our back door, all covered in snow. All these sights of the season are certainly putting me in the holiday spirit and I am thoroughly enjoying learning all the Italian customs. We are having the Bruno family, both sets (the Palermo set and the Motta set), along with Grandma and our neighbors for dinner on the 30th. There will be nineteen people and I am doing the unabridged, full *Southern Living* version with a ham, a turkey, and all the southern trimmings that

I think they might like. I plan to introduce them to jello salads and pecan pie. I thought I should try to show them a bit of how we do Christmas *Americano* style. I am looking forward to it. They have been so generous with us, I want to do something for them in return.

I am enjoying everything about Christmas this year. One of the most endearing customs I've seen are the *Zampognari*, the bag pipers. They are shepherds who come down from the mountain for the Christmas season and play their bagpipes all over town. They stop in your doorway and play for you, like carolers, and expect a small tip. They are dressed in traditional outfits and the bagpipes are made of bright white sheep bladders. I was at Grandma Bruno's house when they came by, played a few carols for us and I was just thrilled. It actually felt like I had gone back in time and was experiencing life as it may have been years ago, standing in the doorway with her. I guess if you maintain the traditions then the thread of continuity can feel like that for everyone. It brings tears to my eyes now just thinking of that sweet experience.

Well, will close for now, hope you have a good Christmas and a wonderful New Year. I know it sounds like mine is pretty idyllic, and it is. I don't want to rub it in, but I am overjoyed with all the new experiences of the Christmas season that I am learning to understand and want so much to share all of it with you. It's the next best thing to having you here with me. I am not wasting a single minute of all this *amore* that I am getting from my new friends. Making friends with the Bruno family has enhanced our lives so much. They include us like family. It is wonderful to feel like I have real friends and am not just a semi-permanent American tourist in this little town. It couldn't feel more different from last Christmas with our Grinch landlords. I am really so happy and loving all of it. I think I may have found my tribe. I might just have to stay here if I can find someone to adopt me and I really think Grandma Bruno might be up for it. She has taken a real liking to me. I think she knows I am curious to learn and experience all I can and she is eager to teach me. We are becoming very good friends and she doesn't speak a word of English. Much of our communication is in pantomime and just pure love and affection shared together through our demeanor. When she greets me now, she kisses me right on the mouth! I often think, wow, my own mother has never done that. It is just so wonderful to be loved. And maybe the fact that we can't talk is a good thing…I am learning as much Italian as I can and now speak like a cheeky four-year old. But we get by. I think Grandma was needing a little love too and we just fit together. She lost a daughter when the child was three and maybe she thinks I can substitute in some way. Or maybe she just can see that I need some love, too. Either way, we are fast becoming bosom friends, to my utter delight. I always wanted an Italian grandmother. Anyway, for the time being, all is calm and very merry and bright. Wish the same for you and that you have a wonderful holiday.

Love you all. I miss you bunches and hope you have a very Merry Christmas.

Susannah, *Baronessa di*
Christmas Cheer

Grandma Bruno and Sue at Grandma Bruno's house

January 1, 1991

Dear Sue,

It was wonderful to have that nice, long conversation with you today and to hear the kids' voices. It was such a lift to start 1991 out that way...a good sign! I'm so glad everything has turned out so great. Don't you think it takes about a year to adjust to such a dramatic cultural change? I think you have done amazing! I don't blame you one bit for wanting to stay. I hope Bush doesn't mess it up. Of course, I will go off the deep end if you stay, but don't feel guilty; I have been moving toward the edge for a while.

As I said on the phone, Christmas had become a bit of a chore for me and I am rather relieved to see it behind us, although, I have enjoyed staying home. Charles took off the same time that the kids and I were off so our relaxed schedule, coming and going as we wanted, has been wonderful. I am dreading going back on the work/school schedule tomorrow. Stephen's babysitter's little girl has chickenpox so he can't go to her house tomorrow, Thursday, or Friday. I may be staying home, after all. I'll probably break down and ask the grandmothers to pull some duty. It's always something.

We saw Simon and Linda Newberg at Kay and Chuck Jones' house. I enjoyed talking to them; of course, we spent a lot of time talking about you guys. We were over there for Kay's birthday, which also happened to be the evening before Charles was scheduled to have a vasectomy. We had discussed his having the procedure immediately after Stephen was born, but Charles chickened out because he didn't think he could stand the pain. Well, needless to say, that isn't a very sound excuse to give the mother of your three children. Stephen was a wonderful surprise but a surprise, nevertheless. I didn't bring it up again. Last month I mentioned that I felt pregnant. I think it was PMS. Anyway, that comment made an impression, so he scheduled the surgery right away to take advantage of our 1990 insurance deductible. I babied him. It hurt. It's taken a little longer than expected to heal. I think it bothered him much more psychologically than physically. Oh well. I'll breathe easier.

I'm going to start sending you information on this new system that is going to be implemented at the high school. It's a wonderful program; very different and has been tried in other high schools with dramatic results. There will be openings for part-time, as well as flex-time, positions. Don't worry, if you want a teaching job, I guarantee you'll have one.

Our electricity just went off. It's about 5:00 p.m. I better see if we can scrounge around and get some supper.

We have all enjoyed the Christmas presents. The box arrived early, so your presents were the first ones wrapped under our tree. They were fondled and shaken and moved. The little tops were taken off and put back on. Everyone loved their gifts when Christmas morning finally rolled around. The calendar is beautiful and so is the holy water font. The jump ropes are neat and the kids are crazy about the bike bells which were ringing repeatedly throughout the entire day. All those angels getting their wings! The socks, Stephen's blocks, everything was great. Thank you so much.

I promise I will be checking into a visit to Sicily. I know everything you said is true and it is the best way to spend time and money. A trip like that would never be regretted. Shoot, we are already in debt, so what's another little splurge? I'll let you know.

Hope things continue to go well. Send some pictures so I can see the Brunos. Take care. I hope 1991 is the best yet!

Love, Anne

We'll Take A Cup O' Kindness Yet

January 3, 1991

Dear Anne,

The number is 011 39 95 30 7903… Give me a call any old time. Even though that's my neighbor's number, I can be there in a flash. They don't mind coming to get me. We could have a phone put in here, but we've given up on that idea and to tell the truth, I really don't want one. I would rather pour my thoughts out to you in these letters and pretend the rest of the world doesn't exist. I think it would interfere with this fairy tale existence that I've stumbled into.

It was great talking to you, hearing your voice and I probably sounded a bit crazy, but I have been on such a high roll this entire holiday season and must say, it has been wonderful. I told you most of the news on the phone but will retell it to you again as I am reinforcing the notion to myself that it is actually real.

The *famiglia* Bruno has proven to be the most wonderful group of people alive…at least that I have ever met here. First, they had us over to their house before Christmas for an evening of card playing. They played Baccarat, which is played with a dealer who deals from a wooden box containing several decks of cards. The game involves betting against the dealer and any number of people can play. Anyone, including spectators, can place bets on any hand. Twenty-five people were standing around the crowded table playing, shouting, betting, screaming *Aie Madonna*...I never did get the complete hang of it but it was great fun. Salvatore, from Palermo, hereinafter referred to as Turi, (roll the "r") is such a gracious gentleman, as is his brother Gaetano, but Turi takes the lead as the older brother and steals the show. He helped me bet and insisted I take all his winnings at times. He has stolen my heart, which was up for grabs, and I am totally enamored with him and the entire lovely family. They served *panettone* cake and wine and soft drinks and espresso, of course. They drink very little alcohol but are plenty animated without it, for sure.

We were invited to their house to begin playing around 10:00 PM and stayed until 4:00 AM and left them going strong. That is not unusual for Italians who take an afternoon *reposo* and eat dinner as late as 10:00 PM. Most restaurants don't even start serving dinner until 9:00 PM and pizza places do not have the ovens heated properly until then. It is hard on Americans who aren't accustomed to this late schedule, especially with children who are hungry at our usual dinner hour.

The *reposo* is universal; all stores, schools, and everything closes at 1:00 PM and reopens at 4:00 PM. It is frustrating until you adjust to it. It took me several times of running up to the stores only to find them closed to get used to it. Italians still enjoy a big family lunch and really do take, probably need, a nap after that. I think part of the custom comes from avoiding the heat of the day and waiting for the much cooler temperatures in the evening to be out and about. I am sure there is some good reason for it besides the family meal as if that isn't reason enough, which it is.

Then on December 30th, they all came here, Turi and Maria and two daughters, Grazia and Titti, Gaetano and Santina and two sons, Antonio and Filippo, Grandma Bruno, of course, and her eighty-five-year-old sister-in-law, *Zia* Angela, and our downstairs neighbors. Including us, that made 20 people for dinner. I cooked for two solid days straight, non-stop. I had a 20-pound ham studded with pineapple and cherries, a 20-pound turkey with dressing and gravy, potato salad (which was not a big hit), cranberry Jello salad (which was a huge hit), sweet potatoes stuffed in orange halves, roasted vegetables (broccoli, zucchini, and Brussel sprouts) with cheese sauce, green beans with almonds, and baked apples (which is a wonderful recipe that I'll send.) Oh well, here it is: 1/2 cup of brown sugar, 1T cinnamon, 1 box instant vanilla pudding, 1/2 cup dark Karo syrup, 1 1/2 cups orange juice, 1 T lemon juice. Core and place about 9 apples in a buttered pan and pour the mixture over the apples. Bake at 350 degrees for 45-minutes depending on size of the apples. The baked apples were also a big hit with everyone.

Everyone was impressed, including me, and luckily everything turned out great. The table was so pretty it reminded me of our October Fest party at 15th Street when our table was suitable for *Southern Living* photos. Do you remember what a lovely table that was?

For dessert we had pecan pie, individual cheese cakes, and Turi brought his special *panettone amaretto* cake made with heavy cream and 15 egg yolks! It was amazing but they went nuts, literally, for the pecan pie and I have promised to teach them how to make it.

During the evening, we had a loud knock on the door and when we opened it, there stood *La Befana*, the Christmas Witch, carrying a large sack of gifts. Actually, it was Antonio, Gaetano's son, who had slipped away and dressed in costume and gathered a sack of presents for all of us. How amazing is that? I was given a beautiful leather wallet and a bottle of Gianni Versace perfume which, hereinafter, will be my signature fragrance. It is heavenly. Each of the children got gifts that were specially selected for them. This was so unexpected and so gracious. Each gift was thoughtfully chosen. I was so touched at all the trouble they went through to dress up Antonio and orchestrate the event. Getting a thirteen-year-old boy to dress in costume and cooperate in the ruse seemed exceptional to me. No matter what you do for these people, it will be dwarfed by their response which is overwhelmingly kind. I don't think I can keep up with them and that comes from a person who thought they knew a thing or two about southern hospitality and graciousness. I am really not used to being on the receiving end of so much affection, but I think I can get used to it. It really does bowl me over.

Then on New Year's Eve, it was back over to the Brunos' house for a wonderful dinner that put mine to shame. After dinner, there was a huge black-tie affair at their house with about 50 guests. I squeezed myself into my neighbor's size eight, silk party dress which was lovely, but tight as a tick and hard to sit down in. I borrowed it with no idea what a lengthy, orchestrated event it would be. At midnight, we popped Dom Perignon champagne corks and every person there went around the room kissing everyone on both cheeks and wishing everyone a *Felice Anno Nuova,* Happy New Year. I was kissed and greeted by about thirty total strangers. Not a person was left without kisses and acknowledgment, even the children were expected to participate. My children played along but it was obvious to me that kissing strangers in the wee hours might be their limit on these new customs. Funny how we Americans are uncomfortable with outward signs of affection and we really do like our space.

Then we were all given sparklers and went out on the terrace and lit them as the fireworks of Motta exploded overhead, along with my heart. The town put on a big fireworks display that sparkled in the night sky. Once again, I felt transported into a magical movie scene of my dreams.

After the fireworks, we all gathered back inside and we were treated to a sample of a twenty-year-old bottle of wine and served lentils and sausage (a tradition similar to our black-eyed peas). Everyone brought out their wallets so they could be filled with dry lentils to ensure money all year long. The trick, they said, is to manage to keep the lentils in your wallet all year. If you can manage this, you will always have a supply of money. To finish the evening, we were served cannolis and a wonderful, stacked Christmas cake. Whew!!! I barely made it home in that size eight dress without splitting the seams. As we left, we were given special matches to keep in reserve throughout the year so that we would always have light.

We took lots of pictures so I'll send you some. I can't tell you how wonderful each member of this family is. They are such loving, kind human beings who treat you like royalty and just radiate goodwill. I really am struggling to take it all in. I guess the fact that it is so unexpected makes it even more special to me.

Well, I came out of my utopian Christmas fog yesterday when I read the paper and saw Saddam Hussein's promise to attack American military interests worldwide if hostilities break out. Yikes!!! Everyone on base is buckling in for the storm. The feeling here is that war is imminent and if so, things here could be bad. Jackie is leaving with her daughter, Candice, for the States. She may already be gone and she has urged me to go. We are working to get our EML papers in order so we can leave quickly if we have to leave on a military flight. I plan to stay as long as possible as I do not want to go home, but I sure don't want to stay here if it means putting the children in jeopardy in any way. There is some talk that all Americans would be confined to the base…put us on cots in various buildings, etc. YUK! I would like to avoid that at all costs. Besides, I don't think this black arm band I have been wearing will go over very well on base with the military wives. I will not take it off no matter what. I'm praying for a miracle. Right now, eight guards are surrounding the base commander at all times. I surely don't want to die here, especially since I see two sides to this issue. I am against all aggression, his and ours! So, you may see us sooner than you think, but I hope not. If we get confined on base then we would just be stuck there until they could move us somewhere else, like Germany or to the States. Guess time will tell where this thing is going. I hate Bush's January 15th line in the sand deadline.

Wouldn't you just know it…we have a great Christmas and New Year and finally are so happy here and then all hell breaks loose on the international scene. I tried to keep Santa simple and if I hadn't drunk so much wine on Christmas Eve, it would have been perfect. As it was, Hillary ended up with Matt's model Italian airplane, Drew with a book on ancient Rome meant for Hillary, and Matt got all twenty boxes of fireworks which were meant for everyone. Giving Matthew that amount of fire power could prove to be dangerous. Hopefully, this Santa has learned her lesson on that front.

We ordered a microscope and lots of little stuff which did not come in until after Christmas, so I am saving those gifts for *La Befana*, January 6th. Anyway, my kids will get to double-dip in the gift-receiving this year again, thanks to *La Befana*. That is about all the news here for now. I hope you all are fine and that 1991 will be a good year for all of us. I especially hope that 1991 will bring us closer together. I miss you guys so much, especially you, of course. I called my mother on New Year's Day and, of course, she cried the whole time and said she hoped my children did not grow up and break my heart as hers had done. Boy, Anne, I don't miss that! How do you fix that? No wonder I don't want a phone, huh?

Take care, pray for peace, and keep the homes fires burning. I'll see you in June, if not before.

Love you,
Susannah, *Baronessa di* Auld Lang Syne

All the Bruno family with
La Bafana at our house Christmas 1990

Christmas at the Brunos, Sue and Zia Angela

Drew and Salvatore share a cannoli at the Brunos

New Years Eve at the Brunos,
Milena (Santina's sister), Gaetano, and Santina

Give Peace a Chance?

January 7.1991

Dear Anne,

Got your letter today and can't tell you how much I enjoyed hearing from you. I am trying hard to remain sane, but the insanity of the world situation is genuinely getting to me. Where the hell are the children of the sixties? Is there no opposition to this march to war? Must we always pretend that bombing others is done in the name of peace? It is full-on madness in the extreme and to see polls saying the GHW Bush is rising in popularity because of it, it is just bewildering. I am trying to remain calm but the closer to the January 15 deadline, the more nervous I am getting. I still have my lovely Christmas tree up and when I plug it in, I can almost fool myself that it is still Christmas and January 15th will never come. This deadline for Saddam to remove troops from Kuwait seems futile and I think the US is more than ready to pounce. The news is simply awful with Saddam saying this will be the "Mother of all Wars" and he will attack any and all Americans everywhere. Are you guys worried about it or are we just getting caught up in the nightly news hype? Can't someone have GHWB committed? I know Hussein is a nut, too, but my God, Bush is pretending sanity! I must change the subject as I cannot keep harping on the inevitable. My tiny voice means nothing. The war machines must be fed, I suppose, but seems insane to me. Thank God, I don't have a son or daughter committed to the slaughter.

Well, I do have some big news and it is related somewhat to this whole mess. Today I went to the children's school on base and met with Dr. Antrobus, the school principal. I talked to him about the possibility of enrolling the children in Italian schools here in town. After hearing all my high sounding reasons, like total immersion in Sicilian culture and language fluency, as well as my opposition to the military situation, he agreed with me and said that he highly recommended it for us. Because of the children's ages, he thought it was a good idea and promised to do everything he could to assist us. He was so nice and helpful and said that at the end of the term we could bring the Italian record to him and he would see that the children got a full school year of credit. He also agreed that we could re-enroll later if it did not work out.

So, with that in mind, I am going to enroll the kids in the Italian schools here in town, if it is possible. I think this might be a first for an American family. I feel such a burden lifted off me by limiting the exposure of the kids to the base during this war-time period. I am elated about the idea and Hillary and Drew want to do it, too. It will be a grand experiment, to say the least. Matthew is reluctant, which leads me to believe that it might be a good thing. I feel pretty sure they may miss some academics but should gain a wealth in culture and language and they won't be on that armed school bus anymore or the base. You don't know how happy that makes me. I was having nightmares about it. Now tomorrow, I will see the Italian principals and enroll them as soon as possible. I need to take an Italian translator with me, but luckily, I have one.

Also, I have started private Italian lessons to help bridge the gap and I am making good progress. Besides, if I am going to run away with some hot, handsome Sicilian stud, I'd like to be able to communicate. (I never again want a relationship with a non-communicative male.) I am excited about the new school plan, and as they say, "It is an ill wind that blows nobody any good." I've managed to come up with a plan that will keep the kids safe and also take advantage of our cultural situation. This precaution may not be needed, but at least I will have done what I can. I sure hope it isn't a disaster. I think I would do anything to keep from going home right now. I am not ready. Jackie and Candice have gone back to the US and she preached me quite a sermon about going myself with the kids. It is a judgment call and I hope I still have some!

Drew got Laura's letter and was thrilled. I am sending you a whole stack of photos to look at and then please pass them on to Ray and Lib and they can pass them to my mother. It is so much easier than sending three sets. Thank you. Also, tell Charles that I am so impressed that he got a vasectomy and not to worry, I'm sure there's plenty of pop left in the old pickle! I had to say that. He has taken a giant step towards true manhood in my eyes.

I am thrilled at the prospect of a job back at the high school. Working with you is really the only thing that could lure me home at this point. It will surely soften the blow and I know I am going to miss this life. I am already dreading the thought of leaving.

I do have a big favor to ask. Would you please mail me the video camera? I am enclosing a check for fifty dollars to cover the cost. You-Know-Who has been bugging me about it and insists that we need to film Sicily. I want to do that, too. It will be great to make some footage of our life here. Hope you don't mind. Let me know your thoughts on it. Or you could just bring it to me, ha, ha, once this Persian Gulf mess blows over. I know you've said you can't afford it, but Charles' vasectomy has maybe saved you thousands so you should celebrate with a vacation. Besides, I am going to be so broke when I get back, I need someone to be poor with. No pressure, but hope that you will think about it. I will close for now, it's 1:30 AM and I had better call it a night. Take care, keep the faith, pray for peace and kiss the kids.

Love you,
Susannah, *Baronessa di* Chicken Hawks

The Calm Amid the Storm

January 14, 1991

Cara Mia Anne,

I have to practice my Italian. There is a terrible thunderstorm going on outside right now. Very sharp lightning cracking all around and now it's hailing huge ice balls. It is 11:30 AM and the kids are all in school. I have to pick them up at 12:30. Sure hope this storm passes before then. We have been having very nice weather up until today. The power is off but that's not unusual. It doesn't take much to knock that off here. I just got back from my Italian lesson. That is working out well, and my Italian is improving. I should be almost fluent about the time I leave, which is about par for my timing. Ha.

Well, I suppose everyone is poised and ready for war. I guess it is inevitable now. Tomorrow is the 15th, so I guess it won't be long now before we know how serious it will all be. One of the latest stupid statements I heard George Bush say was that all we could do now is pray and that he and Barbara are praying for peace. Would someone please tell that idiot that as Commander-in-Chief, he has the authority to not fire the first shot? The lies and stupid rhetoric I've heard lately are so bad, it is embarrassing.

Typical American mentality… start a war and then pray for peace. I'm beyond praying. I've done what I can to try to keep us safe here in our little house in Sicily. I have bought tons of groceries and have cash on hand so I won't have to go to the base at all. Workers there will continue to have to show up unless they go to security level D; we are at C right now. If we go to D, then all non-essential personnel will be asked to leave the base. This whole thing has really tested my sanity. I am furious with Bush, the Congress, and the Pentagon. We are so warlike and it is shameful to be part of such a bully nation. I just hope all those young American soldiers now in Saudi Arabia know what they might be dying for. Do you know? I've heard that the rich Kuwaitis have all left the country and haven't done one thing to contribute to this war effort. I guess you don't need to if you have a war machine like America to do it for you.

On the brighter side, we are pleased as punch with ourselves for putting the kids in the Italian schools. It is wonderful. The kids seem to like it and didn't even complain about having to go on Saturday. School is 8:30 to 12:30 for Hillary and 8:30 to 1:00 for Matt and Drew. They are at separate schools; Matt and Drew's elementary school is located near the *piazza* and Hillary's middle school is located down lower in town nearer to our house. It works out beautifully to pick them up and something tells me that is no accident. Drew wears a black cotton knee-length smock over her clothes with a little white collar and Matt has to wear a little black zip-up jacket. Seems perfect to me as it protects their clothes and makes all appear uniform. Hillary's class wears jogging suits with the school's name on them and I have to order her some.

So far, the schools are impressive and the adjustment has been a dream considering the magnitude of this decision. We are the first non-Italian-speaking family to ever enroll in the local schools. On the first day, Drew reported that all the teachers and students hugged and kissed her and were extraordinarily friendly. Seems the Italians are crazy for all things American and our pop culture, so the kids all got treated like rock stars. I knew it would be different when I went to enroll them and the teacher who came out of the principal's office, and turned out to be Matt's teacher, was wearing a mink coat, four-inch heels, and was smoking a cigarette. I just did not know if it would be good different or bad different. Drew says her teacher knits in class!

The teaching methods are very interesting. All of their work is done in ink in bound composition books. Nothing is ever turned in separately and nothing is thrown away. So, at the end of the year, you have a record of all the work done that year. We buy the books called *quaderni scholastici* at the newsstand or stationery shop. They are small, stapled, paperback books that have about twenty pages of lined paper in them. Hillary said that on her first day all the students competed to see who could do the most for her, get her coat, show her things, etc. That is so Italian, to see who could be the most gracious, but I really did not expect to see it demonstrated so plainly in the schools. Matthew has made a best friend already with the one boy who speaks English in his class so that has been a godsend for him. Hillary said the other day, "You know something else different about this school? When the bell rings the teacher is the first person out of the classroom." I have seen her also, walk straight to her car without a glance backward. No bus duty for her; students and parents are on their own outside the classroom.

I am totally enchanted with what I have seen so far. School is dismissed before lunch, and I haven't seen any support staff in the schools but they do have a lady called a *bidella*, who works in a little side room making espresso and selling cigarettes to the teachers all day long. The students all have snack time at mid-morning called *merenda* so the children and I stop at the bar each morning before school and they get a fresh-baked pastry. After school we go over to the little shop called *La Sicilia,* also the name of the newspaper, and the kids pick out a treat. They are a feeling very Italian now. All three are learning Italian rapidly and I expect they will surpass me with their fluency soon. They knew a tiny bit before they started which made the transition a bit easier and now have a four-hour language lesson every day.

One thing I have noticed is that the Italian school children do not even get to the bottom steps before their mothers, who are waiting for them, have scooped them up in their arms and are kissing them like they haven't seen them in six months. It is really remarkable and is a stark contrast to my demeanor, which I think is pretty typical of American mothers. My children would die of embarrassment if I kissed them in public like that.

Well, I'm back from the school pick-up run and everyone had a great day again. I am amazed at how well they seem to have adjusted; I don't think I would have adjusted so well. Seems the different way of doing things agrees with them. Italians do seem more relaxed about rules. Their school takes in around 8:30 and usually there are lots of students who are still arriving at 9:00. There are no late passes, no questions asked, they just start whatever… whenever and if you miss something, you miss it, no repeat for you.

No one seems to be in a hurry. The teacher usually starts her lessons around 9:00 AM. I've visited all three of their classrooms and the students are all talking non-stop, even when the teacher is instructing. There does not seem to be a rule about that! How very Italian is that, but I must say it is unusual from my teacher's perspective.

Drew's class has twenty-five students and three teachers. Matt's fourth-grade class has about twenty-five students and one teacher, the one I saw on the first day in the mink coat and high heels. Hillary has one teacher Signora Bombieche and she looks fairly young and reminds me of an Italian Audrey Hepburn. All the teachers are fashion plates. Good looks and presentation, *la belle figura,* are very important to Italians. To not look your best is a sign of disrespect. Actually, this focus on appearance doesn't come across as crass or hollow or even competitive. Italians cannot comprehend why anyone would go around in public wearing shorts and tennis shoes. Short pants are for children and grown men are not seen in them. I was warned that if I went shopping in Catania and did not dress up, clerks would ignore me, not even take my money, and I have seen this happen. Italians are sure to let you know that your appearance offends their idea of *la bella figura*. The opposite is the *brutte figura*. To be sloppy or under-dressed says you did not care enough to put your best foot forward. That is interpreted as insulting and rude. Italians go to the trouble of dressing up to see and be seen. They like to stare and I think they like to be stared at. After all, they have gone to the trouble to dress up...others should enjoy.

The storm did let up enough for me to pick up the children from school but now it is raining cats and dogs and lightning. We are all sitting around the living room with our feet off the floor. The power is still off. God, I hope if there is a war that it is confined to Saudi Arabia and Iraq. I look around this room and can't imagine putting these children in harm's way. Oh well, we should know soon, then no more suspense. Today one of the mothers expressed her concern that the base will be bombed. I don't really think that will happen, but I am not going on base regardless and I hope if it does happen the enemy is accurate. I am only about five miles as the crow flies from the base. Too close. If I die over here, I sure am going to be mad as hell at George Bush. Please put that on my tombstone.

Ray and Lib called Friday night and begged us to come home. My mother called Saturday and insisted on the same thing. I told her to name a place on planet earth that was safe and I would go there. Maybe I should have gone home… time will tell. By the time you read this we should have some idea of what it is going to be like. If I bite the dust here, I went down with my tribe, so *c'est la vie*. Carol wrote that a lot of her kindergarten students had fathers in Saudi Arabia involved in the effort and that she had to deal with their worries daily. What madness! I suppose we should all take Jackie's advice and stay low to the ground these days. Well, take care and say a prayer.

Love you,
Susannah, *Baronessa di* Steady Onward

Life Goes On

January 20, 1991

Dear Anne,

Well so far, I've experienced two volcanic eruptions, two earthquakes, and now, one war. I wonder how much more my nerves can take. Evidently, some more as I'm still here and living on the edge. I'm in the car outside the laundromat waiting for the clothes to wash. I did not want to come on this base but duty calls and we were buried in dirty clothes so I decided to bite the bullet (wow, poor choice of words) and come and do it. Security on and around the base is extremely tight. They checked under my hood, inside my car, under the car with mirrors, in the trunk, and I thought they might go digging in the dirty laundry before it was all over. All the roads leading to the base have Italian *polizia* parked all along the roadside with machine guns, and when you get nearer to the base, you are stopped, must show your ID, and explain why you need to go on base. So, I passed the gauntlet and am just trying to get these clothes done and get home. Terrorism is the biggest concern as we are so close to Libya, Algeria, and Tunisia. They say there are known terrorists living here in Sicily. Guess they aren't taking any chances. Never thought I would wash clothes under armed guard, but here I am. I have to adopt the philosophy of Jackie and say you really haven't fully lived until you do it. Ha!

Actually, our lives are pretty normal considering the state of the world. On January 15, the "Line in the Sand Deadline Day," I kept the children home from school, just as a precaution, and we were all huddled around the TV watching the news, on pins and needles. Around noon, a huge explosion went off and I almost jumped out of my skin. It scared the bejesus out of me. Thought for sure the war had started and I was just before telling the children to get under furniture when I went out on the terrace to see what the hell was going on. I could see the smoke coming from the castle as those crazy Italians were firing the cannon to celebrate some saint's day. Really, it almost scared me to death. I thought Jesus, Mary, and Joseph, don't they know this is the "Line in the Sand Day?" A bit of culture clash that was funny later but, at the time, I was cussing that saint! Ha!

I really feel for the people of Iraq and Israel and what they must be feeling as the bombs start dropping. As for the flavor of the US military here, they are all in and, to use their own words, "Pumped Up!" At this point, I think that if Bush told them to bomb their grandmother's house, they would do it.

I just finished reading *A Voice to Sing With,* an autobiography of Joan Baez, and she describes being trapped in Hanoi for ten days during the 1974 bombing campaign. Her description is so horrible. She talks about walking down a road and seeing a teeny, tiny human hand...nothing else, in the rubble. How can humans justify this constant warfare and destruction? I do not get it...I think it is evil, and think we are just living in a barbaric world, not much different from cavemen tribes who adopt the philosophy of kill or be killed.

Well enough of that, how are you? We are fine. The kids continue to like Italian school (God, that is a relief… can't tell you how I sweated over that gamble) and they are learning heaps. I am impressed with the school system and what seems to be occurring there. I am just glad the kids are insulated from all the anxiety on base.

We talked to Ray and Lib last night. We reassured them that we were fine and told them to try not to worry because next month we would probably be concerned about something different. All things pass. Thank God for that.

My Italian lessons are helping tremendously and I am enjoying them. The clothes are in the dryer now. The laundry facilities are inadequate in normal times and when you add the 20,000 per month extra troops passing through, you can't imagine how crowded it is. You practically have to fight for a washer or dryer.

There really isn't much news here to tell. I've been labeling photos to send home. There is a new meat and cheese store in Motta and it is so modern and fancy. Very unlike anything else here. We went last night and bought some great prosciutto, cheese, bread, and peaches and had a picnic dinner. It was perfect.

We've made a good friend, an American from New York, who is assigned here temporarily. He likes to play Trivial Pursuit with me and we sit around and bash George Bush and try to decide what is just punishment for him. So far, we think that he needs to be stripped naked on the White House lawn, have his mouth stuffed with broccoli, and driven out of town with a horsewhip. Then we say, "Naaah… that is way too good for him." Ha!

The economy back home sounds horrible which may work to our advantage if we are going to buy a house when we get back. We still have our building lot, so I guess we are still in the market to build one also. Right now, I am trying not to worry about anything that far down the road. Well, I had better go check the clothes and get off this base. Take care.

All my love,
Susannah, *Baronessa di* Resistance

PS Don't you just love this "Kinder, Gentler America?"

Wednesday, February 6, 1991

Dear Sue,

I finally figured out how to write you a letter. I'm staying home sick today so I have all day to write you. Yippee! And I know it needs to be a super-duper letter to make up for the serious lag in correspondence on my part, so here goes.

First, the good news/bad news about the video camera. I found a guy who analyzed the whole system and said he could fix the base unit for $85. He said the big battery is fine but needs a connection to use it with the camera. The good news is everything can be fixed. I told him to go ahead. The bad news is that he said it would take four to five weeks, which means the first week of March before it's completed. Maybe it will go faster. I told him that I needed it sooner and asked if he could work on the base unit and let me mail the camera and VCR to you, but he said that he needed both to work on it. I am sorry. I should have done this eighteen months ago. I just put it off. I have everything ready to mail it immediately as soon as it is ready. I'm getting a new little battery, too, which the guy says will run for two hours, so you will have a big and little battery. I hope this guy knows what he's doing. Don't send any more money. What you sent will certainly cover postage and insurance and I have been planning to fix the camera, have been wanting to, just needed a push. Here's hoping you'll have it by St. Patrick's Day!

I am betting big on our working together next year! I am hoping you won't recognize the program you left as far as at-risk students are concerned. We are completely revamping the organizational system. Boy, does it need it! I am sold on the program. It is a package deal and then on top of that, we got that $150,000 grant to dovetail another program into it. As a matter of fact, a group of us may be going to Massachusetts to visit a similar program. There will be several new positions so I am optimistic you can walk into a job. We also have a part-time social studies teacher now who lives in Cedar Island and would rather be teaching in Beaufort, so that may be a possibility. Plus, ISS will no longer exist, but the position will be there for a dropout prevention counselor charged with teaching small (ten students) nurturing classes which at-risk students can take for credit. I see several possibilities that you would be perfect for. Let me know when you write the personnel officer who, in my opinion, is a certified nut.

The superintendent's contract has been extended for four more years, but nobody knows our principal's fate. He's been job hunting with no success. He's been out sick a lot this year. I've gotten so I feel sorry for him. He lets me do anything I ask, so for those reasons I kind of hate to see him leave. I don't think that he is a very good principal and all the vice principals have had it with him and his inconsistencies. It is an interesting place. I have enjoyed it. My problem has been not enough time or energy to do it all...home, kids, work, self.

I have had so much fun telling people that you put the kids in an Italian school. Everyone is so impressed. It was such a good idea and I am so in awe of your kids for being so adventuresome. What a great experience. Back at our school, we have made it through another science fair. They moved it up to Catholic School Week, which is the end of January, and they wisely limited individual projects to grades 3, 4, and 5. Students in the lower grades cannot submit an individual project, only class projects. What a Godsend! Hailey (and her mother!) received second place, so I consider it a success. Now, if we can just get through the talent show which is this month. It has been a quiet year, especially compared to last year. The girls have seemed to enjoy school, although I am a little afraid that Laura is bored. She has a very immature class and she's able to master the work without much effort. I sometimes wonder if she would be pushed a little more in public school. Oh well.

I guess I'll close for now and take a little nap. I really do feel lousy. I am promising to do better about writing, as a matter of fact, I am promising myself a lot of big improvements this spring. I am already keeping my eyes peeled for a house for you guys. Interest rates should be in your favor. I'll write again soon.

Love, Anne

Blossoms in the Snow

February 28, 1991

Dear Anne,

Sorry I haven't written lately. I've been consumed with the news and trying to foresee where this war was going to take us. So far, we are not impacted and our lives have gone on in fairly normal progression. Basically, I am maintaining the philosophy that if I just ignore it, maybe it will go away. And in that vein, we have managed to have some fun and make the most of our days.

The whole family went skiing on Mt. Etna last weekend. It is so strange to leave home in 70-degree weather and drive for an hour and be in the snow. We went to *Etna Sud*, the south side, and while everyone skied, I spent the afternoon perusing the little chalet shops that carry souvenirs, lots of things made out of lava, and hanging out in the bar there drinking cappuccinos. Should I have bought you a Madonna made out of lava? Ha. Most of the ashtrays and doodads are very tacky, just souvenir-style junk. There are three to six ski runs open depending on the amount of snow on the mountain. From the terrace of the bar, the view is amazing. You can see all the way down to the blue Ionian Sea and all the little towns dotting the mountainside and coast. Sicilians love this volcano and consider it friendly. It truly is an amazing natural phenomenon. While it may cause some trouble with lava flows on occasion, it also spews out natural chemicals that fertilize the farmland and make the area very fertile. At 10,000 feet in height, we can usually count on snow here from October to March. The kids love it and I won't get tired of the view anytime soon.

Our other big excursion was a lovely weekend in Palermo. Salvatore and Maria invited us to come for the last weekend in January. They were such gracious hosts. They wined and dined us and even insisted on paying for our hotel. They took us all over Palermo and showed us the sights. Palermo is very interesting and quite different from Catania. The Arabic influence can be seen in the food and culture and buildings. Funny, remember my saying I felt like I was in outer Mongolia or the Middle East when we first arrived? Seems parts of Sicily actually do bear the marks of being ruled by many different cultures; the Arabic influence predominates in Palermo. I read that Sicily is called the "Cradle of Invasion" because they have been invaded and ruled by the Greeks, the Arabs, the Normans, the Romans, just to mention a few, and they have all left their mark. We visited the Palatine Chapel of King Roger II dating back to 1130 and the Monreale Cathedral built in 1170, which has a gold mosaic nave with the typical depiction of Christ. The depiction that is found there is similar to the one in Cefalu which claims to be from an actual memory drawing of people who knew Christ himself. We went to the Archaeological Museum on Sunday and there was so much more to see. Salvatore is an enthusiastic guide and he truly loves the city. Did I tell you he is the chief engineer for all the streets of Palermo? At least that is what I have surmised. It is funny we never can fully converse so we get about half of the information right and I suppose we make up the rest. Ha!

It was a wonderful weekend and we spent most of our time in their home which is artfully decorated with antiques. Both of them are so gracious and kind and go overboard to make sure we are all having a great time. Italians on the whole are very kind and open people, but the Brunos take it to another level. I have to say it seems rather miraculous to me that we have found such wonderful Sicilian friends. It will be hard to leave here in many ways, but I guess I have to face the real world sometime…Do I?

I'm enclosing some photos of the children in their *Carnevale* costumes. They all had classroom parties and wore their costumes to school. Hillary was a dashing Zorro, Drew a darling Charlie Chaplin, and Matt a super Superman. I have a photo of the party in Hillary's classroom showing the teacher slow dancing with a student with a cigarette in her hand! Now that is something you don't see every day in an American school. What ever they do that shocks me, they make up for with their *joie de vivre* and I am not complaining. I think the Italians are the original Erma Bombeck devotees; they don't sweat the small stuff.

We are all fine and our spirits are lifting with the war ending and spring beginning. Already the trees are full of blossoms and wildflowers are everywhere. It is so warm today we had the house (you must see this house!) all open and we were all in short sleeves. There is not much other news at the moment so I will close for now. I'll get better at writing again now that I can shake off these doldrums of war and winter. I owe about ten letters to people back home. I enjoy each one of yours like a best seller, so please keep writing.

Love you,
Susannah, *Baronessa di* Fool's Paradise

Hillary, Drew, and Matt in Carnevale costumes, February 1991

Drew's Italian school class celebrating Carnevale with Drew as Charlie Chaplin on the right

Sunday, March 4, 1991

Dear Sue,

I've been thinking about you and counting the days until June. It will be so wonderful having you back. Any more thoughts about extending? I have been unbelievably busy at work. Last week was wild! Beth and I are pretty much single-handedly putting together a school-within-a-school for the last two six-week sessions of the year for the very at-risk kids. It's been exciting, exhilarating, and rewarding with very positive responses from students and parents. It is just so much to organize, including hiring new teachers. This program runs from 1:00 to 6:00 p.m. It's been a good feeling doing something that will make a difference. Beth and I have a good time working together. She's positive, funny, compulsive, and we keep each other going. Thursday, we leave for Boston, Beth, the principal, and I. That should be fun, too. I have wished so many times you were here with me. Next year…

I am feeling less successful and optimistic on the home front. Charles is totally absorbed in work and yet, very unhappy with it. I am so tired of his complaining and moping and helplessness. He is the one who has to make the changes and yet, until he does, I suffer. On Saturdays, his usual pattern now is to either go back to work or mope around the house and complain. Meanwhile, I am handling all the kids' comings and goings, the laundry, housework, finances, shopping, cooking, etc. I am feeling so resentful. But if I bring it up, I'm nagging. I get so angry sometimes, I can hardly stand to stay in the same room with him. I sure wish you were here to listen to me. I know I've got to figure out myself what to do, but talking to you sure has helped in the past.

Sorry about this letter, but I can't think of anything else to report right now. I promise better next week. Take care.

Love, Anne

Viva la Donna

March 11, 1991

Dear Anne,

I am in such a better mood today than I have been in weeks. January and February were very hard months. The war was scary, but the situation on the home front has been even worse. This marriage is so strained. I have had to muster all my strength to keep things together. I've just decided that he is an ass, always was an ass, and always will be an ass, but I feel better about it. Ha! I am trying to be more understanding of the plain fact that he is always going to be a Maestro of Misery and I have to accept it. I am sorry that he is so unhappy and I really am doing all I can to make him happy, soothing all the rough edges, minimizing the chaos of the kids, and doing all I can to provide a happy environment. Nothing I do seems to make a dent, however, and it saddens me beyond words that I can't fix the situation. It sure is a drain on the human spirit and just when I am riding so high on all the wonder of Sicily. What is that saying that when one door closes another one opens? Anyway....

I really am in love with this place and find such joy in everyday life here; shopping in the markets, taking a coffee in the bars, just feasting on the visual beauty. There are so many times that I feel I have gone back in time which, by the way, has always been one of my flights of fancy. Many aspects of Sicilian life seem to be like turning the clock back to my small-town Southern childhood. I think that is one of the major appeals for me, as I have always wanted to travel back in time. The small individual shops, the meat markets, the greengrocers, the bakeries, all rule supreme here, not huge boring supermarkets. The people themselves seem much less jaded and more content than Americans. I think this is because of their tradition of graciousness and the fact that they are not all chasing the almighty greenback. They are living their daily lives open to people and experiences. On the other hand, most Americans are rushing around trying to make money, hold on to their jobs, get ahead and for them, the experience of real living is just a side gig. Many Americans find the slower paced, Italian, laissez-faire attitude frustrating, but I see it as a beautiful openness, a freedom to be more human. *Domani*, tomorrow, really is understood to mean that everything doesn't have to be immediate. Relax. Take your time. Rome wasn't built in a day.

I've heard them lament the lack job opportunities and I know their unemployment rate is sky-high. Many Sicilians say Americans are so lucky to have plenty of opportunities to earn money. I think if that day ever comes for them, they will have to sacrifice some of their *la dolce vita,* and they will then recognize it all comes at a price. But I do think that overall, Sicilians get up every day with the feeling that life should be enjoyed and they take the time to find the joy in their daily lives. They aren't looking to their jobs or the government or financial success to find happiness, but closer at hand, just daily living. I'm not so sure that this is true for Americans anymore.

Not to say that their lifestyle is perfect; basically, Sicily remains a feudalistic society and fear of the *Mafia* runs deep. There is a colloquial expression used here, "*Boop*", which means I don't know anything or at least, I am not saying I know anything. In many instances, it is better to not know anything or anyone. I have mentioned to many Sicilians living here in Motta that my landlords are the Brunos and, even though they are a family who has lived in this small town for generations and operate a t*abacchi* shop, no less, I haven't met anyone who admits to knowing them.

We just got back from another weekend in Palermo, complements of the Brunos, which always increases my joy in life. I am always in a better mood when we spend time with them. The occasion for the visit was March 8th, International Women's Day, which is celebrated throughout Italy in a big way. Parades are held and women are treated to gifts and flowers. The Bruno daughters, Grazia and Titti, had a party for their girlfriends and we had champagne and toasted *Viva La Donne,* meaning long live the women. We all had a great time. The yellow mimosa flower is the symbol of womanhood here and is given out and worn as corsages. The mimosa trees are in full bloom now and the tiny little yellow ball blooms are beautiful.

We also visited the Capuchin Catacombs, which are strange beyond belief. Dressed up dead bodies hanging on the walls which creeped me out. I was told that relatives come and visit occasionally and fluff up their outfits every now and then, etc. Can you imagine saying to the family, "Let's go freshen-up Grandma's corpse?" I just wanted to get out of there as I kept thinking of the air quality and how all the dead bodies were probably shedding cells of God only knows what! We also went to the Royal Place and the

Cathedral of Saint Rosalie, patron saint of Palermo. Salvatore is simply the best tour guide.

My other good news is Jackie is back! I've rarely been as happy to see anyone in my life. I really love her and she is basically my one and only American friend here. She is a great one, for sure, and I missed her terribly while she was gone. She is a riot, so now I have a pal here again to goof off with. Hillary was also happy to see Candice!

My other news is good and bad. The bad news is that if you are celebrating your 40th birthday in the States, I am going to miss it. We are not leaving here until mid-July; however, I am throwing you a big birthday party here and I am sure hoping my guest of honor will be showing up. Really, it will be perfect. I can meet you in Rome for a couple of days then we can take the train down to Sicily. You will be out of school by then and we could spend a couple of weeks touring around; me saying my goodbyes and you getting a feel for the place that I am probably going to be talking about for the rest of my life. Sicily is the perfect place to turn 40 and at that age, my God, don't put anything off! Ha. Ha. I hate to beg you but I don't think you can afford not to come at this point and, selfishly, I think having you here will help me adjust to the idea that I am leaving. I am having a hard time with that idea. I love this place so much; I don't think I am ever going to get it out of my system and having to give it all up is not going to be easy for me. Truthfully, I can't stand the idea of leaving and I can't stand the idea of you not ever seeing my Sicilian paradise. And otherwise, how are you going to get me through the withdrawal that I know is coming for sure when I hit reality back home? Ok, ok, I will stop begging and even stop asking if you absolutely write back and say it is completely out of the question. I won't ask again, I promise...well, maybe.

I have learned to make a few wonderful Italian dishes. Gaetano and Santina have taught me how to make *spaghetti carbonara* to perfection so I will make that for you when I get home. I doubt I will ever be able to make it as good as theirs so you should come and try theirs, but I will do my best if we have to settle for that. Besides, remember you are only 40-years-old once and I promise to spend my 40th with you anywhere in the world you choose. I know I am being a pest about this, but I just can't stand the fact that you will be missing out on all this. If I weren't so taken with the place, I don't think I would be so insistent, but this place is my heart now and I am pretty sure it is the love of my life, not to be replaced. I'll take you shopping for an expensive birthday present. Let me see, can I think of any more bribes? The food, the wine, the scenery, the people, the shopping and me... we are all calling your name...don't you hear us? Besides, I need your advice. I've been thinking about trying to open a ceramics and linen shop back home so that I might be able to come back a couple of times a year to buy stock. Anything to keep me connected to this place.

We are all fine, the kids are doing well in school. They all went skiing again last weekend and are becoming quite good at it and very taken with the fun of it. Hope you are all fine and all is well. Our spirits were so lifted when that nasty war was over that now I am ready to celebrate with you on one side of the Atlantic or the other.

Take care, much love.
Susannah, Besotted *Baronessa di Sicilia*

On the Rocks

March 12, 1991

Dear Anne,

Why is marriage so hard? Seriously, I can't figure it out. I have been committed from the beginning that this must work but no amount of my trying seems to improve the situation. Most days, I feel like I am running in place trying to keep everyone fed, bathed, clothed, and ready for each day. It is hard work and as you know, takes a lot of energy, foresight, planning, and constantly thinking of everyone else, and trying as hard as possible to keep all happy and healthy. I can take the daily grind, but the constant negativity of Mr. Discontent so wears me down. Always unhappy, always complaining, never a kind word. He's always walking around with a look on his face as if he is in pain or suffering from indigestion. It takes a huge toll. I am lonely and overworked and treated like a household slave. I am so tired of feeling like both the children and I are the cause of all his despair. He acts like he wishes we would just go away. I understand that keeping the family going does take so much of our focus, but to feel like I am doing all I can and dragging along an unwilling partner is more weight than I can bear. Most of the time I can bear it, but sometimes I cannot just take the crumbs and be satisfied. It doesn't help much that our scenery and surroundings are so romantic. The sea, the music, the people all seem to celebrate love, and I feel so lonely and unwanted. It is like twisting the knife. As much as I love this place, I think I will be glad to get back home where life is not dripping in beauty and romance. Maybe when we can go back, I can lose myself in the daily grind. Ha. At least, the rat race distracts from the flaws of everyday life. Boy, that is a sad statement.

Hopefully, I can get a job as soon as I get back and that will fill the void and give me some sense of reward. Being the family pack mule, doormat, and Fairy Godmother is a thankless job. I am not bellyaching about the role as mother or wife, per se. I am happy to do it all, and more, for the children and the family but to be faced daily with a partner who exhibits nothing but discontent is just too much for me. He acts like he is just so unhappy with his life and nothing cheers him up. One thing I know for sure, one partner can only do so much when the other one consistently sits on the sideline and pouts. At some point, one is just trying to survive it and that is not a good way to live.

I'm not sure we will make it, no matter how hard I try and hang on. Maybe I am asking for too much to want a pleasant relationship with the man I married. Maybe I have read too many romantic novels but I can say for sure that what we have now is nothing like what I thought it would be. At least friendship would be something, and we don't even seem to have that. I have put all my eggs in this basket and seem to spend all my time trying to keep it protected from the daily kicks and smashes. I don't think I am that much of a martyr but I'm afraid this sadness is making me crazy. I suppose I should do what women have done for centuries and just stuff it down, brush it off, deny the facts, drink heavily, or resort to the myriad of mother's little helpers that exist. Unfortunately, I am not good at pretending.

Sorry this letter is such a rant and I hope you understand but if I don't let some of it out, I think I'll erupt like Mt. Etna. I want better. I want more. I want to be happy. I want to laugh and appreciate all we have been given. Tell me if I am asking too much and please send me any ideas you have on how to fix it.

Hope things are okay with you. We got a low-ball offer on our lot back home, but we aren't going to take it unless they offer more. I got a nice letter from Gretchen. I just love her. Not much other news. I am planning a big Easter surprise that I will fill you in on in the next letter. It is a crazy idea that I am working on, something to distract me from this vexing wedlock. All for now.

Love you,
Susannah, *Baronessa di* Discord

PS I wish we would both just violently scream at each other and have a real knock-down-drag-out fight as some normal couples do. This sour silence is infinitely more painful. It is pure torture.

With All the Frills Upon It

March 21, 1991

Dear Anne,

Buona Pasqua! Happy Easter! It is a lovely time of year here. The bars have their display windows all dressed up with huge chocolate eggs elaborately decorated. Each one trying to outdo the others. The marzipan lambs and special candies and treats are a sight to behold. The Kinder Egg Company makes thousands of large chocolate eggs wrapped in colorful cellophane with a prize inside for the children. The bigger the egg, the bigger the prize. Large ones come with stuffed animals inside. The idea of the egg is big here, but not so much baskets and rabbits.

That is about to change for a small group of Motta Sant' Anastasia first graders. The grade mother in me has taken over and I had the grand idea to invite Drew's Italian school class to our home for an Easter egg hunt. I wrote a well-translated invitation to her teacher who promptly accepted it in a truly Italian fashion. There are 23 students in her class, but the teacher informed me that they would love to accept the invitation as it would be lovely for both first-grade classes to attend. How American of me to think that I could invite only Drew's class and so Italian of them to think that the invitation would be interpreted to extend to all the first-grade students. Of course! So, I have 46 students and three teachers coming here next week for an egg hunt extravaganza! I had purchased 23 small baskets and rushed out and got 23 more along with Easter grass. There were no plastic eggs to be found on the base or anywhere on this island, so I have resorted to boiling and dyeing real eggs. Two hundred and forty-four eggs to be exact. I have a few dozen plastic eggs from our personal stash to fill with candy. I made bunny-shaped nameplates for each student and tied them on each basket with ribbon. They are very charming, if I do say so myself. Luckily, there is an empty meadow that the Brunos own beside the house that I can use for the hunt. Right now the grass is perfect and is filled with wildflowers. I plan to serve cupcakes, brownies, candy, chips, and punch. All will be served outside on card tables. I understand that the concept of an egg hunt is foreign to Italian children so I have translated a passage for the teachers to read with instructions about finding the eggs. Once I saw it in print, the instructions really did sound rather nonsensical, to hide chicken eggs in the grass. I'm not sure it will make much sense to the children but, hopefully, it will be fun nevertheless. I'll let you know in the next letter how it goes over. I'm letting Hillary stay home from school that day to assist me and Jackie and Candice are also coming. I'm excited about it! My first big Italian garden party!

Everything else is good here. We are trying to plan our last few trips. We want to go to Venice, Malta, and Greece. I think we will go to Greece for two weeks during spring break. We can drive our car to Brindisi, which is a port city on the backside of Italy's boot, and take the overnight car ferry. We will get cabin rooms for the passage. The ferry disembarks in Corfu and then we will drive around and tour the main Greek islands. The weather should be nice. We have had a few 80-degree days here so we are hoping for perfect springlike weather. Also, Jackie has offered to keep the kids so the two of us can go to Venice alone. I think that will be a nice treat. I just wish I was going with someone who had one romantic bone in his body, but I am sure to enjoy the architecture. Ha!

Tuesday was a holiday for the kids...It was St. Giuseppe Day (St, Joseph's Day). They say of all the saint days, St. Joseph is the most important. It represents an end to famine and also the new harvest. There are street altars decorated with elaborate sculptures made of bread. We had fireworks in Motta and Santina sent over a traditional dessert eaten on this day made of rice and cinnamon. I just love her, she is such a funny, smart person. She reminds me of Lucille Ball with her sense of humor. She is willing to teach me everything about cooking and customs and if I can find the time, I want to learn some of her best recipes.

I really must find the time to knock out some of those video courses for renewal credit for my teaching certificate. My current certificate is good until next year, but I would really like to get it redone so I will be ahead of things when I get back. We are going to need the money as this family budget will be in for some big changes when Uncle Sam is no longer footing the bill for us. Yikes!

Hope things are good with you. I know that yesterday was Laura's birthday and I have a few little things for her but was hoping to buy something for her and Hailey together. Do they still play with dolls? Write and tell me soon because I want to send it by Hailey's birthday at least. If they aren't into dolls anymore, it is not a good choice.

Hope things are better with you and Charles; things seem somewhat better with me on the marriage front. Last Wednesday he came home to find a note on his dinner plate and dinner on the stove. I went with Jackie to the movies. We bought a bottle of wine and sat in the parking lot and drank it and then saw *Mermaids* with Cher. It was a good movie and lots of fun to be out on the town. I guess I just need to make my own fun from here on out and stop trying to make a silk purse out of a sow's ear. But I'll work on that *domani*. Take care, much love, hope Boston was fun for you.

Love,
Susannah *Baronessa di* Easter Parades

Let the Good Times and Easter Eggs Roll
March 25, 1991

Dear Anne,

Hope everyone there is well and happy. We are all fine. We had a great day last Friday at our egg hunt party. The children were so cute. They had never heard of an egg hunt and really loved it. Everyone found eggs, some had baskets full. The whole experience was a delight. The teachers were so nice and appreciative. These people are really wonderfully warm and loving. Each child and the teachers brought Drew a present, a hostess gift I guess, so she had more gifts than she could ever dream of. They ranged from stuffed animals, dolls, banks, diaries, candy, picture frames, to toys. The teachers brought flowers for me which provided a lovely centerpiece. They came on two school buses and lined up in the driveway and sang a song for me in appreciation for the party. It was the sweetest experience; I really had to fight back tears. It surely is one that I will never forget. One thing I have learned is that whatever you do, you will never out-do these people in the kindness department. It is quite remarkable.

The weather was lovely, sunny, and perfect. It was a splendid party and I only hope the children enjoyed it as much as I did. I can't remember when I had so much fun. The children were so polite and adorable. Some of the mothers told me later that their children came home wanting to color eggs and have their own hunts. Some children found 5 to 10 eggs and proceeded to eat them all on the spot! It was wild and I kept trying to explain that the eating was purely optional. I took lots of pictures so I will send you some. I am so glad I did this and, speaking strictly for myself, it may be my finest moment.

Today Jackie and I went to the Catania market. It was crowded and bewildering as usual, but always fun. The variety there is impressive. I will never get enough of just people watching. It is a feast for the eyes here everywhere you look. The Catania market is the ultimate yard sale.

I've sent letters to the Board of Education explaining my return to the county and that I would like to be considered for any job openings. We will see where that goes. Do you think two years is enough time for them to forget my last exit? Just think, I will be seeing you soon. I can't wait to see you, but I will admit that I am a little worried that I will miss being here. I think if I stayed any longer, I wouldn't be able to leave at all. I do love Sicily and hope I can adjust to giving it all up. I am carrying a sense of foreboding about leaving now everywhere I go, as if this may be the last time I see this or that.

We have so many places we want to visit before July. I am still crossing my fingers and hoping you will give in and come. Whatever you decide will be the right thing. I am sure I will try to come back sometime. I wouldn't hesitate to do this kind of thing again depending on how the children felt about it, of course. The experience has been wondrous. It has changed us all and I am especially glad the children have experienced it. Italy was a wonderful choice in so many ways. Best of all are the warm, kindhearted people. Even the kids have remarked about how unpretentious and loving they are. They are now used to seeing grown men walking arm-in-arm and kissing each other on the cheek, not to mention singing in public for the pure joy of it. I know we are bringing home some very precious memories. Well, have to close for now. Thanks for anything you can do to help me in the job category. I can't believe they would pass me up if there is an opening! Ha!

Love to you all.
Susannah, *Baronessa di* Italian Garden Parties

The egg hunt for the Italian school children, 1991

Sue and school children at the egg hunt, 1991

Friday, March 29, 1991

Dear Sue,

It's been so long since I've written you that I almost don't know where to begin. I have enjoyed your letters so much and have read and re-read them. I get a lot of mileage from them. I know I need to answer your wonderful invitation to come to Sicily. Two years ago, I was saying positively I would come. I've really thought about it and have been trying to think through all the possible scenarios to make it happen. I don't want to drag this out, but I'm afraid it is just not going to work out this year. I know, I know, I'll hate myself for this decision. It's just the wrong year for me to manage this. Please understand. I have struggled with trying to come up with a way to make it work. I think Stephen's age, work, and money make it impossible to plan such a big trip now. Don't be too mad.

You're probably also wondering about the camera. I just left a message for the repairman to call me. He's about three weeks late in having it ready. I just hope that he's able to fix it. I am sorry it has taken so long. I will send it as soon as he has it done.

My schedule has been incredibly busy at school. Beth and I have started a *school-within-a-school* with more than sixty students, all of whom were failing miserably, and I have been staying at school until 6:00 p.m. Charles has been wonderful about taking over with the kids. I have enjoyed the challenge and excitement of doing something innovative. We are in the third week and, so far, it's been very successful. Our $50,000 grant money was spent in a flash. Salaries accounted for $31,000 and Beth, the principal, and I went to Boston to visit a high school with an innovative drop-out prevention program. We left on Thursday and returned home on Sunday. We did have fun! We had all day Saturday to sightsee. We stayed in a very nice hotel in Boston and enjoyed margaritas and Irish coffee at the end of the day! The program was impressive and, hopefully, we can implement some of their ideas here.

April 1

My letters have a way of getting cut short. Can you imagine that?! I think I'm still expecting the same feeling of satisfaction from letters to you that I got from conversations with you, so I try to tell you everything. Maybe I will make it until June.

Here's a joke. Santa Claus, the Easter Bunny, a good man, and a good woman all drove up to an intersection at the same time. Who had the right-of-way? Answer: A good woman, because the other three are just figments of your imagination.

Your letter about married life could have been written by me. Charles and I had a big fight on Easter Sunday before church and I'm still so mad! Susan and Sarah are visiting, which always adds stress, and always results in Charles acting weird and needy. I'm not sure what happens to him... jealousy, resentment that she's here, or just plain intolerance.

He makes things harder, not easier, for me during the short time she's here...always! Now Susan and I are having a spat, mainly because I try to keep both of these self-absorbed, demanding individuals happy and it is impossible. I wish Charles could see things through my eyes, just once. I never get all pissy and pouty when we are dealing with his screwed-up family. You'd think he'd do the same for me during one brief visit. Good God, at least Susan and Sarah don't live in Morehead and just drop in unannounced and expect a visit, like his family.

I miss you so much, Sue! Susan has taken the girls to the Marine Resource Center. Stephen is with Charles' mother so I am home alone and mad at the world. I guess maybe it's me...no one can suit me, not even my kids.

On that subject, I am pretty sure it is getting harder as they get older. Stephen, of course, is at a very demanding age. Being a boy (heaven help him!), he does all kinds of reckless things, like climbing and jumping and running into the street and hitting people with hammers, at times, and carrying around nails, etc., etc., and I'm responsible for his safety! That is expecting too much! Then there's Hailey who delights in bossing the other two, lording her abilities over Laura, telling me, "No!" and being very unpredictable. After several hysterical Sunday evenings with Hailey sobbing that she couldn't go to school, I scheduled a conference with the principal, then with the Spanish teacher. It turns out Hailey hates Spanish. She can't be a perfectionist so she wants no part of it. Here I am paying tuition to send her to a school she hates. I could have done that for free at a public school. Then there's Laura who vacillates from being a real people-pleaser to having full-blown temper tantrums. She hits when she's mad and is now sitting in the back of the room in the first grade because she gets into other people's business. She seems to delight in using bad words and sharing shocking bits of news with her friends, which I find out from other mothers! To top it off, she also uses food like I do, something to turn to in times of stress. So, have I screwed up everything? Just hurry home and be my friend no matter what and I'll try to make it through this mess I have created. We will have *life-after-raising-kids*, won't we?

I talked to the video camera repairman. He hopes to have it ready by the end of the week. I hope he comes through!

I guess I need to close for now. Any minute, Susan and the girls will burst in the door and I want this letter sealed and in the mailbox before they do. I may call you before you get this. Where are you planning to enroll Drew and Matt next year? Registration for next year for St. Andrews is starting now and you know how they always make it sound so crowded with a waiting list only. If you want them there, send $75 per kid to the principal asap. Hailey's class, if that's where you want Matt, is big. There is probably no size problem with Drew's class.

Let me know about the job plans. Now is the time to apply. Send me copies of letters, or anything else, so I can follow up for you, if I need to. Carteret County Schools seems like a black hole sometimes with paperwork getting lost. Also, if you don't talk to the *right* person (first you have to figure out who that is), you don't get anywhere. What kind of job do you want? Teaching social studies? Do we dare dream that we could both be working at the same school next year? That would be heaven! Let's count on it!

Take care. Forgive me for not coming to Sicily. I know I have let you down. I'm letting myself down by not doing it, too. Here's to Summer '91!

Lots of love, Anne

PS The pictures were great! The children look beautiful and very happy. We sure miss them. I stuck some pictures in this letter. Terrible quality, I'm afraid. Yours are so good but thought you might enjoy these which are now three months old.

Happy Easter...Festum Festorum

April 6, 1991

Dear Anne,

Just a short note to say I hope your Easter celebration was enjoyable. Ours was the whole Italian enchilada. *Festum Festorum* means the grandest of festivals and the Brunos certainly made that a reality for us. They had us over to their house for the traditional family *Pasqua* meal. There were the five of us, the four Brunos from Palermo, the four Brunos from Motta, Maria's parents, Santina's parents, Grandma Bruno, and *Zia* Angela. That made nineteen people in all. It was a five-course meal that was awe-inspiring. I sometimes still have trouble perceiving the fact that we are so lovingly included in this tight-knit family, just like we belong. I must be the luckiest traveler alive. They have the unique ability to make you feel at home and like the guests of honor at the same time. Don't ask me how they do it. Gaetano bought huge Kinder Eggs for all the children. We ate and laughed and spent the entire afternoon surrounded by warm-hearted people. Needless to say, it was delightful. I made a coconut bunny cake and a congealed green jello salad, the one with pineapple and cottage cheese. The jello salad was a big hit.

Easter is a two-day event for Italians. On the Monday after Easter, all Italians go to the countryside and cook over an open fire and we were invited for that, too. It is called *Pasquetta*, "Little Easter." It's an outdoor picnic to celebrate the coming of spring and to rest and recuperate from the Easter Sunday meal! We roasted sausages and artichokes. Grandma Bruno scrounged around in the grass for mint and other herbs and stuffed the artichokes right on the spot. She then placed them right down in the coals of the fire for roasting. The food was delicious and it was such a pleasant day. The kids all ran around and we lounged on blankets and enjoyed the countryside. I know I am an outsider looking in, but Italians do seem to have their priorities correct…that of family and friends and companionship. Simple pleasures of life. It is days like this that make me want our time here to never end. But, end it will.

We are already beginning to think about leaving and all the hoops we have to jump through to pack out of here. It is coming up all too soon. We are trying to figure it all out; to get Leonardo the cat home and find homes for the chickens…what to buy before we leave, etc., etc. Sometimes it is overwhelming…thinking of leaving here…and not having a clue where we will live when we get back. Good thing I am a dogged pilgrim. I think I am happiest when I don't know the outcome. Guess that is why I like traveling so much. Does that make me the ultimate optimist or just a wandering fool? A bit of both, I think. Sicily is making it hard for me to imagine wanting to be anywhere else, and moving forward much harder. I know I am leaving stones unturned and I am not ready to say goodbye.

Right now, the poppies and wildflowers are gorgeous; the skies are mesmerizing. We have the most amazing sunsets every day. I think it must be the volcanic ash that makes them so brilliant orange and red. The view from our terrace is stunning. I sit there in the afternoons and gaze across the plains of Catania and the surrounding mountains as the sun is setting. The *Parco Zoo* is not too far away and sometimes I can hear a lion roar. Those are my *Out of Africa* moments and I know how hard it is going to be to leave. Like Isak Denison, I know I will always remember Sicily, but I wonder if Sicily will remember me. No doubt this place is imprinted on my heart in so many ways.

Much love,
Susannah, *Baronessa di* Sunsets

Tuesday, April 9, 1991

Dear Sue,

I can't tell you how much it meant to me to talk to you on Sunday. It gave me a new lease on life. Your letters have been a lifeline these past two years and our phone conversations have been wonderful. Am I going to be able to believe it when you are finally back? I will think that I have died and gone to heaven. It won't be soon enough.

I talked to Maryann Bertram yesterday and gave her your kids' registration money. She was so excited about having you back. She asked me to tell you that it made her week to know that the Hall children would be back next year. There are twenty students in Drew's class, so no problem there. Next year's fourth-grade class has twenty-six students registered and I think that is technically full, but she kept saying she would do what she could, couldn't promise, and didn't want to make anybody mad, etc. I think that she was referring to a possible waiting list. I got the feeling Matt is fine. I kept reminding her what a sweet, mild-mannered, well-behaved child he was (I was serious!) and she assured me she remembered Matthew as such. I told her to keep the registration fee and that you want Drew enrolled, even if there isn't room for Matt. She said the money would be refunded in August if it doesn't work out. But, Sue, I'm almost positive he's in.

Giving her the registration fee did the trick, I think. She knows you want them there. I'm enclosing the registration forms. Tell Matthew that Hailey was ecstatic when she found out he would be in her class. She already has plans that they will be doing their homework together; I think that she is counting on Matt's help. She is thrilled at the thought!

I stayed home today, after one day back at work. I'm a trooper, aren't I? Louise had to take her in-laws to Greenville so I didn't have a babysitter for Stephen. I felt like using that as an excuse to take some comp time. They owe me. I do enjoy work, though. It was nice to be back. Beth had not read your letter when I talked to her on Monday, but I think it was in her mail and she just hadn't gotten to it. I'll check with her and the principal on Wednesday. We (the teachers) are signing intent-to-return forms now. They are due on May 3, so it is a good time to start the process. Leave it to me.

Well, Stephen is stirring. It is almost 8:00 a.m. Charles took the girls to McDonald's for breakfast. I'll close for now, so I can mail this today. Take care.

Love, Anne

April 16, 1991

Dear Sue,

Your phone call has been the highlight of my week. I just kept smiling to myself all day but not saying a word to anyone. I loved having a private secret. Charles and the kids asked me what I was laughing about, but I just brushed them off...our memoirs need some surprises.

Do you remember right before you left that our backyard had been completely dug up? Well, the grass had finally filled in after two years and now we need a new septic tank. Two years ago, it was a new drain field. So here we go again with a backyard full of dirt. I'll tell you, remodeling is a never-ending job.

Friday night, Charles and I once again went to the Gapner's annual party at the Civic Center. The food is unbelievable. When I think about it, the whole thing is pretty unbelievable. It's hard to imaging hosting a shindig like that.

Saturday, we took the kids and went to the Cherry Point air show. I had never been. It is pretty nice, even with a two-year-old. Immediately after the show, about twelve Harrier jets arrived from Saudi Arabia via Spain. It has been exciting around here with the return of the troops. Who would have thought it would have been over so soon? We Americans will all now be celebrating while the Kurds are suffering and dying. I can hardly bear to think about it.

I guess you will receive this birthday card a month late. You will be thirty-nine and one month. Time marches on. Well. it's time to put the kids to bed...not my favorite thing to do. Happy Belated Birthday!

Love, Anne

Cutting Loose, Kick off the Sunday Shoes

May 2, 1991

Dear Anne,

Seems like forever since I have written. Got your birthday card and really appreciated it. My birthday was a real bust and I do mean explosion. Hubby took me out to dinner where we were joined, unexpectedly, by twelve American friends who had been invited unbeknownst to me. Not exactly my idea of a great surprise. Later, I was called a spoiled brat and made to feel less than human. So, about par for the fun times. Anyway, things are better now and I'm over it. No more wasting time thinking things are going to get much better.

We did take a ten-day trip to some interesting places. Jackie kept the kids and we took the train up to Naples, and then over to Capri for a few days, and then over to Venice for three days. Venice was wonderful, we rode in a gondola and it was a nice experience, enough said. From there we rented a car and drove over to Yugoslavia along the coast for a few days. It was very interesting and very gray...quite communist-looking, no capitalistic franchises there but the food was cheap. Then we drove back to Verona for a day. I stood on Juliet's balcony and wondered how life could be so full and so empty at the same time. Verona is a beautiful, medieval city that is so perfect that you feel as if you are walking the streets of Shakespeare's plays. If you want to experience a medieval city, Verona is it. Charming and reminiscent of every feudal stereotype there is. I wish we had had more time there. We took the overnight train back to Catania in first class with a private sleeping car. Very classy...I kept thinking of a James Bond movie. All in all, it was a nice trip, as nice as can be expected for a sour puss and a spoiled brat. At least, it was educational!

The children survived our absence but it took a real toll on Jackie. I convinced her that we were now flat broke, couldn't afford to take any more trips, and would never ask her to do that again. God bless her, she did not know what she was getting herself into. She is the mother of only one thirteen-year-old girl. She had equated my life, even before the trip, as living in a work camp but she really didn't know half of it. Today she is a wiser woman.

Now we must face the huge job of shipping us out of here. Don't know yet what day the pack-out will be. We have to sell the Fiat, ship the Volvo, decide what to put in the express shipment, and sell some transformers, etc. I'm ready or as ready as I am ever going to be. To tell the truth, I am never going to be ready. Even the thought of leaving is breaking my heart. Pray that I have the strength to do it gracefully.

My application and all the necessary paperwork have been mailed to apply for any positions with the Board of Education, and I have sent the registration forms to St. Andrews for the kids to enroll in school. Thanks again for the forms. Back to reality for better or worse. I have to have a job, something for next year. It is the top priority on my list. I will take anything as long as it is outside the home. All

I can think about is that I am busting loose! A job will be my ticket out of this work camp I call home and, hopefully, will soothe the despair I am feeling about leaving Sicily

All I can concentrate on now is counting the days until I see you. I keep telling myself that it won't be long now. Please do everything you can to help me find a job. Seriously, I know I'm asking a lot, but I think having a job is now crucial to my sanity, maybe even my existence. I really need a life apart from just being a wife and mother. My self-esteem is somewhere between rock bottom and the Continental Shelf. I am hoping that my full-time wife and mother status is about to be replaced with some personal confirmation of individual status and reward. At least they pay you for what you accomplish as an employee, don't they? Just to write those words makes me feel powerful. There were plenty of interesting things to do in Sicily without working but I know that back home I won't survive without something to give me self-gratification. I am hoping that work will be the antidote I need to mend my broken heart and my Sicilian withdrawal symptoms. Not sure I can detox cold turkey without substituting something in its place and work is the best idea I have. I might need clinical help. I wish I were joking about this, but I'm not.

Saying goodbye to the world as my oyster is not going to be easy and my emotional attachment to Sicily may be stronger than a drug. I hope I can get over the craving. I know that withdrawal is an uncomfortable process and I am not looking forward to it. Is there methadone for this sort of thing? Hopefully, work will be the cure. I know you will do all you can to help me find something. Thanks. Must close for now.

Love,
Susannah, *Baronessa di* Busting Loose

A Pox Upon Us

May 8, 1991

Dear Anne,

The children were ecstatic about the checks you sent! Hillary couldn't believe the $25.00! The only problem was that you forgot to sign it. I took the liberty to sign it for you knowing that you just forgot. Hillary's face was a mile long when I said it was no good unless signed, so I fixed it in short order. I thought it was a bit telling, but it made me want to tell you to slow down. That was not like you at all, however, I know what your life is like and I am worried about you. Take it easy.

Hillary came home from school today with spots that look suspiciously like chickenpox. I will have to take her to medical tomorrow and have that checked. If it's chickenpox, we are in for it, none of the three have had them, so we will be quarantined for a while. I guess it is as good a time as any to go through it. Our other bad news also concerns chickens, which seems to be a theme lately. A fox or dog or something killed our chickens. Poor Drew cried and cried and has been in deep mourning ever since. Her prized hen, Penny, was a great loss. Jackie had purchased her for Drew at the Motta market months ago. When she bought her, the hen's legs were tied together. After we brought her home, I got really concerned that her legs may have been broken since most likely she would have been purchased for the dinner table. Thankfully, she was fine and the tamest chicken I have ever seen. She immediately jumped into Drew's arms and snuggled right under her sweatshirt and had been riding on Drew's hip pretty much every day since then. Losing her was devastating for Drew and sad for us all. But on the bright side, that is one chore, finding homes for all the chickens, I can mark off the list for moving. Not the best outcome, but I have promised more chickens in the future, so I guess we are moving to the country when we get back to the States. I really can't even think that far ahead yet.

There is so much to do here. The Volvo goes out on Tuesday for shipment which leaves us with just one car. That means I will be pretty much stranded until we move into the hotel in two weeks, scheduled for June 3rd. School ends here on June 13th, so after that we can just swim in the pool and eat our fill of pizza before D-Day (departure day). Honestly, I know we will never get enough of the pizza, among other joys, and I'm trying hard to adjust to the idea that we are leaving. Can't quite take in the fact that it is almost here. I am trying to be positive about it and the one thing that helps is that I really will see you soon.

Much love,
Susannah, *Baronessa di* Embarkations

May 12, 1991

Dear Sue,

There's not a day that goes by that I don't have a real need to write you and a hundred things to tell you. I will be so glad when you are back. As you know, I don't write every day, not even every week, but just talking to you in my head helps. I can't even remember now exactly when I wrote you last or what was going on here, so if I repeat myself, I apologize.

Charles was in Durham all last week because his father was critically ill. He got sick at 2:00 in the morning on Friday and by 2:00 that afternoon was being airlifted to Duke Hospital. Charles drove up on Friday. His father is better. He had a heart attack complicated by a systemic infection, the latter being the reason for moving him so quickly. I thought of your father, the symptoms seemed similar. The doctors at Duke weren't sure what the infection was and just treated Charles' dad with massive doses of antibiotics. The infection is gone now, but they still have to deal with the heart problems. They have scheduled tests and possibly surgery this week. Charles will be going back up later this week. I am glad that his father is doing better, but I am realistic enough to know that this is the beginning of a new phase of involvement.

I got your letter about wanting a job next year. You're right, it does add a balance to the other overwhelming parts of our lives. It has become clear to me that the picture in my head of my ideal role as a wife and mother is not realistic and my continuing to spend 24-hours a day trying to make reality fit that mental image will lead to certain insanity. My job has been my salvation, despite the stress and pitfalls inherent to being an at-risk counselor. At least, I am getting paid, being treating like an adult not a mother, and at quitting time, can walk out without guilt.

I must admit, however, that things are getting weird in Carteret county. The assistant superintendent and the financial officer have been fired! The superintendent has gone on a rampage. No one knows yet whether our principal will be back next year. So far, his contract has not been renewed and he is still being evaluated. He has mellowed out a bit in these two years. I have gotten used to him, but still have mixed feelings about his ability to handle the job.

It is Mother's Day here, May 12. I've had a pretty good day. Everyone in the family is asleep. It's 8:30 p.m. I had to threaten the girls, with some guilt thrown in, to get them to bed. Charles had a headache and went to bed early and Stephen is just continuing a late nap that he started earlier.

I can't believe that you will be back here in a couple of months. I know it is going to go by fast for you. Your trip through Italy and then to Yugoslavia sounded great! I am so glad the Middle East conflict ended when it did. Where do you think you will go before you come home? England? I was thinking I'd be through with summer school when you got home, but now it looks like summer school won't start until after the first of July, so I am not sure now what my schedule will be.

I can hardly wait! I have so much to tell you. The first thing on the list will be a job, then a house. I wish the house next to us, not the Chapmans, the other side, wasn't such a poor prospect. I think that it is being foreclosed. I just can't imagine there is any way it would do for your family unless you razed it and started over, and I doubt the price is that low. Oh well, I have to believe something will turn up. We have to refinance our house by November 1st. Hopefully, we will end up with a lower house payment since the interest rates are still going down.

I will close for now. Don't worry, you will have a job. See you soon.

Love, Anne

All's Well That Ends Well

May 31, 1991

Dear Anne,

Got your letter about the firing of two assistant superintendents in one blow! Wow, what prompted that? Maybe clean slate will be better in my case, ha. Remember that I will take anything…. Also, thanks for all you have done to help enroll the kids back in St. Andrews. That school is right where I want them to be when we get back.

Speaking of school, things are pretty crazy here right now. The kids are back in DoDDs school on base. Long story, but I woke up in a cold sweat thinking about enrolling them in St. Andrews in the fall and needing a report card that says promoted to the next grade. I had their father contact the school principal, Dr. Anthrobus, who had assured me he would write a letter to that effect when I transferred them to the Italian schools. Well, when he was contacted, Dr. Anthrobus said he did not remember saying that! So, I immediately re-enrolled them in school on base. This will give them the last six weeks of school there and should get us a report card stating promotion. Whew! The kids would murder me if I had cost them a year of school and they had to repeat a grade. Luckily, they are all smart and can pass with flying colors and their teachers have been very understanding. The kids are delighted to be back in "American school." So, mission accomplished, everyone is happy, no harm, no foul on that caper. All in all, I think it was a positive all the way around. It was a great experience for them and they left on a good note, so we will finish where we started on that front.

The car is now shipped, the furniture goes Monday and I am fine with it all. It has been a great two years, but I suppose it is time to go home. Can't even conceptualize where that is right now? Mr. Indecision keeps talking about Harkers Island! Leo the cat is flying out on Monday and will be picked up at the New Bern airport by Ray, who is keeping him for us until we get there.

We will be moving into the Sigonella Inn for thirty days next week. Right back where we started from there, too. We will fly to London and have a week there to tour around before we fly home. I hope to take the kids to see *Cats* and I want to see *Les Misérables*, visit Hampton Court and Windsor Castle, then homeward bound. I think the trip to London is diverting my attention from the fact that we are leaving. At least, I feel like we are finishing up with a bang or a hurrah or a "cheerio" ...

Hillary did have a bang-up case of chickenpox and fourteen days to the day, the other two came down with them. Matt still has a face full of pox. Whew, what a horrible disease. Luckily, you only have to endure it once. I've been shut in with two sick children, no car, and piles of household goods sorted and stacked up all over the place for the movers. So, disorganization has been my life for a while and I don't do very well with that. Mostly, I am in a fog of transition. I did get the belated presents mailed for Hailey and Laura.

I am sorry to hear about Charles' father. I am glad he is in Duke and hope he improves. At least, he is getting the best care available. I hope he recovers soon.

We are invited for our last weekend in Palermo with the Brunos. Spending time with them now is bittersweet as I know the more time we spend together with them, the harder it will be to say goodbye. It really will be tough for me. I am trying not to think about it. I have fallen in love with this family. I do love yours, too, and that is a comfort to me.

I've waited until last to comment on your last letter. Trust me it went straight in the burn pile as soon as I read it. I will have to see you face to face to discuss it. My only advice is don't be like me and do anything rash. Think it through and don't work too hard! Ha! Speaking of which, it is 7:30 PM and our breadwinner hasn't come home from work yet. It really riles me, but now I am looking at it as money in the bank. For the next thirteen years, I should be able to work as late as I want without a word. Won't it be great if we are working together...do you think we will ever be able to tear ourselves away and go home? Ha, Ha! I hope we get that chance.

Take care and much love,
Susannah, *Baronessa di* Happy Endings

Sunday, June 2, 1991

Dear Sue,

Charles saw Ray yesterday so I know you've moved to the Sigg Inn and that you may be home by late June. What a wonderful birthday present that would be for me! I know these last weeks must have been terribly busy for you. I can't believe you'll be home so soon. Are you rushing around buying things? I guess you had to do that before everything was shipped.

The package for the kids arrived safe and sound and didn't even make it into the house. They were so excited that they opened it right on the porch with paper flying and squeals of delight! Such a wonderful assortment of gifts, the clay, the holy cards, the little cross and beads (like one decade of the rosary, right?), Hailey's pen, Laura's books and pencils, the backpacks, and, the most appreciated of all, the make-up. Thank you so much! Stephen takes his soccer ball everywhere. He loves it. He's quite a sports enthusiast. Where he got that, we don't know. We're going to miss receiving all these beautiful things from Italy, but having you all back home will be the best gift of all. I really can't believe I have survived two years without you.

School will be ending next week. The girls have half-days on Monday and Tuesday and then the entire school will attend the fifth-grade graduation ceremony on Wednesday. I have found a very mature 17-year-old who has agreed to watch the girls for me this summer. Stephen will continue to go to Miss Louise. Of course, I'm doing the Parallel High School in summer school. I am somewhat dreading getting that going because I have been so busy with other things, like the grant, that I haven't even thought about what I am going to do. I am so tired of school and my house is a wreck, to name a few of my stressors, but I can't turn the money down. Three thousand dollars a month on top of my 12-month pay is too good to refuse. There are still so many other things I want to do to this house. You won't believe (yes, you will) how little we have accomplished since you left as far as the remodeling goes.

Kay and Chuck Jones had a pig-pickin' at their house. I can't believe they're leaving. She's very disappointed she will miss seeing you. It was a nice get-together last night. I think that I have a bit of a hangover.

Things at school are pretty much the same. Nothing to add concerning the behind-the-scenes drama; it still adds a new dimension to things. Have I told you that the principal's contract was renewed for only one more year? That doesn't seem like a big vote of confidence. He hasn't sold his house or found another job so being extended for another year is something.

Monday evening

Got your letter today. I am glad you are looking forward to coming home. I'm afraid that when you get here it is going to be such a letdown. I'm sure you'll think time has stood still in Carteret county. There are still a lot of homes for sale so I think you will have quite a few choices. I can understand why you want plenty of room. Charles will be so envious if you guys raise chickens. He's always talked about wanting to do that. I sure hope you don't live too far away. There's a doctor in town who has ten acres of land for sale across from the Oglesby farm. It's back in the woods, about a half a mile east of the entrance to East Shore Estates. Of course, there is no house there. I know how you feel about building and I have no idea what it is listed for. I'll keep trying to find something close, especially closer than Harkers Island. Well, I've got to get everyone to bed. Hope all goes well with your trip. See you soon!

Love, Anne

Ciao Bella

June 13, 1991

Dear Anne,

This will be my last letter as I will be home before any other would arrive. The thought of seeing you makes me happy, but saying goodbye to Sicily is just too much for me. It has all been too much. We read before we came here two years ago that "Sicily is Italy, only more so." I think that is true. The food, the wine, the charm, the beauty, not to mention the friendships we have developed with the Bruno family are all overwhelming. I don't know if I can give it all up. I am not sure I can go home to our one-horse town and ever be satisfied.

Sicily has captured my heart. I will sorely miss the blooming bougainvillea creeping up a wall, the cobblestone streets, the markets, the church bells, the smoke rings of Etna, and a million other little things. Most of all, I will miss the kindness of the people who are happy and who really do live *la dolce vita*. They live as if they expect every day to be filled with joy. Perhaps it is this expectation of pleasure that guides them and produces such vitality out of ordinary life. Sicilians make their world beautiful. This beauty draws you in and once immersed in it, you are changed. I know Sicily has changed me.

We went to Motta to say goodbye to the Brunos and to thank them for all they have done for us. I could barely speak; my heart was so heavy. I couldn't tell them how much I loved them and how their overwhelming kindness had been a wonder and a treasure to me. I didn't have the words to describe how deeply they had touched my heart and soul, how strangers could feel like family, and how they drenched us, without measure, in their generosity and graciousness.

How do you describe the mystery of love? When we drove away in the dark of night, we left Grandma Bruno and *Zia* Angela standing in the middle of the street shrieking loud cries for us like paid mourners. How can I explain how much love I received sitting with Grandma Bruno in her small, bare kitchen while she sat by the window sewing? How can I explain to you all I am leaving behind?

Happiness, I know, is elusive but I have found much of it here. I wish I could capture all the pleasures of Sicily and take them home with me or better yet, stay here forever. But, of course, there's always tomorrow and the next episode and new horizons. We have sold the Fiat and all our worldly belongings are on their way home so I guess it's time to say good-by and journey on.

Love to you all, and I really will see you soon.
Susannah, *Baronessa di* Glory Days

P.S.

During the pandemic of 2020, best friends Anne and Sue decided to revisit the letters they had written to each other more than thirty years ago. Remarkably, their letters and cards still existed as Sue, the nomad, had moved many times since her first trip to Sicily in 1989; to Cuba and back to Sicily twice before settling down in Harkers Island, North Carolina. Anne, the homebody, residing in the same house in Morehead City from which she had written to Sue, also had safeguarded her cache of old letters from her best friend. The original letters became *Between the Lines*, the unabridged account of how two women's bond of friendship sustained them through the challenges of marriage, parenting, careers and self-identity. As they worked to compile the letters into a book, Anne and Sue shared laughter, tears, and even some vexation, along with an abundance of gratitude for their friendship and their experiences as young wives and mothers. They both realized having a kindred spirit has been a lifeline for them all these years and they both agreed that their story in these letters was truly one for the books.

And they are both living happily ever after...

Anne and Sue in Taormina, 1996

CPSIA information can be obtained
at www.ICGtesting.com
Printed in the USA
LVHW040638030822
725063LV00004B/52